HIERARCHY AND VALUE

Studies in Social Analysis
General Editor: Martin Holbraad
University College London

Focusing on analysis as a meeting ground of the empirical and the conceptual, this series provides a platform for exploring anthropological approaches to social analysis while seeking to open new avenues of communication between anthropology and the humanities, as well as other social sciences.

HIERARCHY AND VALUE
Comparative Perspectives on Moral Order

Edited by

Jason Hickel and Naomi Haynes

berghahn
NEW YORK · OXFORD
www.berghahnbooks.com

First published in 2018 by

Berghahn Books

www.berghahnbooks.com

© 2018 Berghahn Books

Originally published as a special issue of *Social Analysis*, volume 60, issue 4.

Library of Congress Cataloging-in-Publication Data

Names: Hickel, Jason, 1982– editor. | Haynes, Naomi, editor.
Title: Hierarchy and value : comparative perspectives on moral order /
   edited by Jason Hickel and Naomi Haynes.
Description: New York : Berghahn Books, 2018. | Series: Studies in social
   analysis | Includes bibliographical references and index.
Identifiers: LCCN 2018014223 (print) | LCCN 2018026056 (ebook) |
   ISBN 9781785339981 (ebook) | ISBN 9781785339967 (hardback : alk.
   paper) | ISBN 9781785339974 (paperback : alk. paper)
Subjects: LCSH: Social structure—Case studies. | Hierarchies—Case studies.
   | Globalization—Social aspects—Case studies.
Classification: LCC HM706 (ebook) | LCC HM706 .H54 2018 (print) |
   DDC 302.3/5—dc23
LC record available at https://lccn.loc.gov/2018014223

British Library Cataloguing in Publication Data

A catalogue record for this book is available from the British Library.

CONTENTS

ACKNOWLEDGMENTS

This volume has had a long journey. It got its start as a series of thought-provoking papers for a panel at the 2012 meeting of the American Anthropological Association in San Francisco, and four years later became a special issue of *Social Analysis*. Now we are fortunate enough to have Berghahn publish it as a book. We wish to thank all of the original panel participants and the present contributors for their support, Knut Rio and the anonymous reviewers for their helpful comments on earlier drafts, and Vivian Berghahn, Kristyn Sanito, and the rest of the team at Berghahn for carrying the project through to completion. We are grateful to have had the chance to work with so many talented people.

Jason Hickel and Naomi Haynes

PREFACE

Toward a Political Anthropology of Hierarchy

This book comes at a crucial juncture in political history. In the fall of 2016, Donald Trump won the presidential election in the United States after a campaign to "Make America Great Again," which poured disdain on liberal multiculturalism and brought explicitly racist and sexist narratives into mainstream political discourse. The previous summer, British voters opted by a slim margin to withdraw the United Kingdom from the European Union, stirred by a "Leave" campaign rooted in nationalist nostalgia and anti-immigrant sentiment. In 2014, Narendra Modi—a Hindu nationalist and member of the right-wing RSS—won the presidential elections in India. The Islamist Recep Tayyip Erdoğan became the president of Turkey that same year. Xi Jinping, who ascended to the presidency of China in 2013, has become popular for his cultural counter-revolution to restore Confucianism as a guiding ideology, along with a renewed focus on 'traditional' Chinese values. And strongman Vladimir Putin has forged ties to the Russian Orthodox Church and is emerging as a figurehead for conservatives around the world.

Whether it be restoring the lost glory of the Ottoman Empire, recreating the India of Vedic times, or returning to the family values and racial order of 1950s America, these political forces succeed by combining a moral vision of the past with the promise of economic and political revitalization, growth, and expansion. This temporal orientation is what Charles Piot (2010) has aptly called a 'nostalgia for the future'. And this nostalgia is often organized according to clearly structural parameters (Silverstein 2004)—a moral order imagined in terms of 'natural' hierarchies between children and parents, women and men, lower castes and upper castes, disciples and church leaders, minorities and majorities, the people and the state. In these movements, hierarchy is conceived as the wellspring for political and economic prosperity and the basis for restoring lost dignity. To the extent that they seek to enforce their visions of moral hierarchy through the power of the modern state, they veer increasingly toward authoritarianism.

This book does not speak directly to these political events, but it does grapple with questions that are crucial to understanding them. How do we, as anthropologists, think about social forms that place hierarchy at the center of their moral vision? How do we analyze non-liberal or even anti-liberal conceptions of human well-being? And how do we make sense of the curious fact that even those who are rendered subordinate within hierarchical systems quite often embrace them, or even regard them as necessary to the realization of their own moral aspirations (see Mahmood 2005)? The temptation is to draw on the tools of critical theory—to see it all as a cynical veneer for political power, bolstered by supporters steeped in false consciousness and ignorant of their own interests. Such a move is not necessarily incorrect, but it does run the risk of making analytical mistakes. What we need is to find ways of understanding these movements on their own terms—ways of recognizing the moral and affective forces that shape them and drive them—although without of course losing sight of the violence that they can and often do engender. Without ethnography, without thick description, we may in the end gravely underestimate their power.

The great contribution of political anthropology is its firm insistence that politics and political economy can never be separated from the apparently unrelated domains of kinship, domesticity, religion, and ritual (McKinnon and Cannell 2013). There is no distinct realm of human behavior where 'interests' can be found floating about in the ether, organized according to the pure, sanitized models of Machiavelli or *homo economicus*. There is no political movement that is not culturally and historically contingent, that is not intimately informed by particular cosmologies of personhood and relatedness (Hickel 2015). It falls to ethnography to do the difficult work of identifying and rendering intelligible the pillars that frame political consciousness.

The contributions here explore a variety of ethnographic contexts from around the world where people seem to support and value illiberal—and specifically hierarchical—social formations. It examines how notions of hierarchy have come to anchor normative conceptions of justice and well-being, provide powerful moral orientations for desire and action, and shape social, political, and economic processes and events. Crucially, what emerges from this investigation is a clear sense that not all hierarchies are the same—that there is a diversity among various kinds of hierarchy and that people think about hierarchy in significantly different ways. This book provides a comparative framework for studying the value of hierarchy in diverse social formations.

The work of Louis Dumont (1977, 1980) is an important touchstone for this comparative project, but it is also critical that we move beyond some of Dumont's limitations. In *Homo Hierarchicus* (1980), Dumont argues that the Hindu caste system is organized around the principle of purity and that this structures a hierarchical and holistic worldview that can be categorically contrasted with the egalitarianism and individualism of Western thought. Although Dumont (1977) takes a historical approach to the development of Western egalitarianism, he approaches the Hindu caste system in largely ahistorical terms. Western egalitarianism is understood as a unique historical development, but hierarchy is cast as somehow 'natural'—a prior state or some kind of Platonic form. While these aspects of his work have long been challenged (see Das 1997), Dumont also makes an important methodological intervention that too often we miss. He shows that from the vantage point of Western thought, hierarchy cannot be understood as anything but the exercise of power, a kind of chain of command in which powerful people subordinate those below them. This perspective makes it impossible to conceive of hierarchy as a shared value (Iteanu 2009), and impossible to understand people's affections for it. This book articulates an approach to hierarchy that builds on this key insight but makes room for the messy variety of culturally distinct configurations of hierarchy.

This is exactly the kind of social analysis that we need in the era of Trump and Brexit, Hindutva and Islamism, Confucianism and Orthodox Christian revivalism. Liberal pundits have a penchant for lumping these movements together under the banner of the same reactionary religious or cultural tendencies with little regard for the differences between them. Such differences are irrelevant when one starts from the assumption that hierarchy is intrinsically and exclusively bad and violent (Khan 2018). By contrast, on the Left one finds a tendency toward economic reductionism, whereby these forces can all be explained as an effect of neo-liberalism. In the wake of Trump and Brexit, bitter spats ensued between liberals and leftists over what drove these shocking political events—whether it was a deep-seated culture of racism and sexism, on the one hand, or class anxieties and neo-liberalism, on the other. Not surprisingly, the world is more complicated than this debate allows. Neither of these perspectives adequately accounts for the particular moral concerns and aspirations that drive these movements. The ethnographic chapters of this book attest to the fact that there is something more afoot.

It is tempting to regard all of these political forces as proceeding from the same general logic. It may be politically useful to draw equivalences between Trump and Brexit, Modi and Putin—but, again, analytical risks abound. We need to be careful about letting categories like 'right-wing populism' overdetermine our analysis, or else we cannot think clearly about the important differences between, say, neo-Nazis in Charlottesville and Confucians in Chengdu. The task of ethnography is to do the difficult work of understanding what is particular about these various political movements, how they make sense within their own cultural and political milieu, and how they have created popular support by drawing on the value of hierarchy. This requires a more robust concept of culture than is conceived in dominant strands of liberal or left discourse. To paraphrase Daniel Rosenblatt (2004: 467), without some idea of culture, we can only understand the political lives of others in terms of our own projects. In an era of rising authoritarianism, the specter of capitalist crises, and the all-pervasive threat of climate change, we no longer have the luxury of avoiding the difficult conversation about the value of hierarchy in social life.

This approach comes with its own risks, of course. It can be politically inconvenient. "Radical politics," Marilyn Strathern (1988: 27) points out, "has to be conceptually conservative. That is, its job is to operationalize already understood concepts or categories." By the same token, "academic radicalism often appears to result in otherwise conservative action or nonaction." Strathern is surely correct about this. But perhaps we can recoup the possibility of radical politics here. Perhaps a truly radical politics—one capable of moving us beyond the impasse that blights contemporary capitalism and democracy—can emerge from truly radical analysis. What such politics might look like is yet to be seen.

Jason Hickel and Arsalan Khan

References

Das, Veena. 1997. *Critical Events: An Anthropological Perspective on Contemporary India*. Delhi: Oxford University Press.

Dumont, Louis. 1977. *From Mandeville to Marx: The Genesis and Triumph of Economic Ideology*. Chicago: University of Chicago Press.

Dumont, Louis. 1980. *Homo Hierarchicus: The Caste System and Its Implications*. Rev. ed. Chicago: University of Chicago Press.

Hickel, Jason. 2015. *Democracy as Death: The Moral Order of Anti-Liberal Politics in South Africa*. Berkeley: University of California Press.

Iteanu, André. 2009. "Hierarchy and Power: A Comparative Attempt under Asymmetrical Lines." In *Hierarchy: Persistence and Transformation in Social Formations*, ed. Knut M. Rio and Olaf H. Smedal, 331–348. New York: Berghahn Books.

Khan, Arsalan. 2018. "Pious Masculinity, Ethical Reflexivity, and Moral Order in an Islamic Piety Movement in Pakistan." *Anthropological Quarterly* 91 (1): 53–78.

Mahmood, Saba. 2005. *Politics of Piety: The Islamic Revival and the Feminist Subject*. Princeton, NJ: Princeton University Press.

McKinnon, Susan, and Fannella Cannell, eds. 2013. *Vital Relations: Modernity and the Persistent Life of Kinship*. Santa Fe: SAR Press.

Piot, Charles. 2010. *Nostalgia for the Future: West Africa after the Cold War*. Chicago: University of Chicago Press

Rosenblatt, Daniel. 2004. "An Anthropology Made Safe for Culture: Patterns of Practice and the Politics of Difference in Ruth Benedict." *American Anthropologist* 106 (3): 459–472.

Silverstein, Paul A. 2004. "Of Rooting and Uprooting: Kabyle Habitus, Domesticity, and Structural Nostalgia." *Ethnography* 5 (4): 553–578.

Strathern, Marilyn. 1988. *The Gender of the Gift: Problems with Women and Problems with Society in Melanesia*. Berkeley: University of California Press.

INTRODUCTION
Hierarchy and Value

Naomi Haynes and Jason Hickel

> Modern man is virtually incapable of fully recognizing [hierarchy]. For a start, he simply fails to notice it. If it does force itself on his attention he tends to eliminate it as an epiphenomenon. Should he finally accept it, as I did, he must still take pains to see it as it really is, without attributing imaginary properties to it. By contrast, all the difficulties vanish if we keep it firmly before our eyes, accustom ourselves to following its outlines and implications, and rediscover the universe in which it operates. (Dumont ([1970] 1980: xlvii)

Hierarchy is not the sort of thing one typically hears Western academics describe in positive terms. There are both political and intellectual reasons why this is so. With regard to the former, it is not difficult to see that the notion of hierarchy runs straight against the grain of the liberal sensibilities that most scholars share, and placing hierarchy in a favorable light therefore seems to fly in the face of these core political commitments. In terms of the latter, in the current intellectual

Notes for this section begin on page 18.

climate, perhaps particularly in anthropology, we are still struggling to get past the preoccupation with power that has been central to disciplinary thought over the past two decades. As Marshall Sahlins (2004: 138–154) has pointed out, this orientation has produced a reductive overemphasis on the subject, which in turn has made it difficult to take cultural systems, including those characterized by hierarchy, seriously (also see Rio and Smedal 2009b: 2–3). As Sahlins (2004: 149) puts it, under these intellectual circumstances such systems "appear as the political cum intellectual enemy," monuments to structures of power that, when compared to "the experience-near, embodied world of excluded subjects, demanding their own identities and contesting the authoritative narratives of the larger society," seem like inflexible anachronisms.

Despite these barriers to treating hierarchy as a serious object of study, much less as a positive social phenomenon, we believe that as anthropologists we cannot ignore this topic. This is true first and foremost because many of the communities in which we work are organized hierarchically, and people in these communities often represent hierarchy in positive terms (see, e.g., Ansell 2010; Ferguson 2013; Haynes 2012; Hickel 2015; Iteanu 2013; King 2014; Scherz 2014; Smith 2007). While individualism and egalitarianism are central to Western conceptions of justice and the good, many people in hierarchical societies see them as immoral and destructive, as eroding the relationships that make meaningful personhood possible. Our primary aims in this book are therefore to explore a variety of ethnographic contexts in which hierarchy is portrayed as desirable and to examine the role of hierarchy in people's efforts to produce a social world that reflects their understanding of a good society (Robbins 2013a). Situating hierarchy in local conceptions of the good life in turn opens the way for us to speak not only of hierarchical social organization but also of values. This connection is most immediately evident in the fact that when people speak positively of hierarchy, they are speaking about what they value. Even more fundamentally, hierarchy draws our attention to the way that values are organized with respect to each other, since values are hierarchically ranked, with some being more important than others. Hierarchy is therefore a central component of any theory of value (Dumont [1970] 1980: 20).

In light of these observations, our goal in this book is twofold. First, as an ethnographic project, this book foregrounds hierarchy as a mode of social organization, building on a solid foundation of important work (Mosko and Jolly 1994; Peacock 2015; Rio and Smedal 2009a) in an effort to expand our understanding of the sorts of relational worlds that, for reasons we describe in more detail below, anthropologists have found difficult to engage in empathetic terms. Second, we seek to explore the central position of hierarchy in the process and production of value. Here again we build on previous discussions in the discipline, where the topic of value is enjoying something of a revival (see, e.g., Eriksen 2012; Graeber 2001; Otto and Willerslev 2013; Pedersen 2008; Robbins 1994, 2004, 2015). In what follows, then, we address hierarchy both as a mode of social organization and as a model for social theory, while also seeking out connections between these two approaches. Our goal is to cultivate a conversation around the issue of hierarchy animated by difficult questions. Why, for instance, should anthropologists—and especially young scholars interested in the neo-liberal moment—be concerned with hierarchy? What is the place of hierarchy in contemporary social theory? How are we to think about reassertions of hierarchy in the era of globalization? How have people leveraged ideas about hierarchy in order to challenge liberal models of the social good? More specifically, how have societies reimagined and reconfigured the ideas and institutions of Christianity, democracy, and development—which have figured so often in social theory as forces for egalitarianism and individualism—to suit their own hierarchical values and goals? And how has hierarchy itself been retooled, reinvigorated, and restructured, especially in contexts of social change and conjuncture?

In this introduction, we offer a theoretical framework for these questions, which are variously engaged by the authors featured in this book. We begin by specifying what we mean by hierarchy and then go on to consider why this topic is especially difficult for contemporary Western scholars, in particular, to think with. We follow this discussion with some short ethnographic examples from our own work in southern Africa that illustrate the importance of hierarchy in the specific contexts of Christian practice and political democratization. These examples then open the way for a brief treatment of the topic of value. We conclude by providing an overview of the various contributions to this volume.

Dealing with Dumont

As we turn our attention to developing a definition of hierarchy, we begin by positioning ourselves in relationship to the theorist whose work has unquestionably had the greatest impact on anthropological engagement with this topic. We have already invoked Louis Dumont in the epigraph above, and his influence is evident throughout this book.[1] Beyond the fact that most of the chapters engage with Dumont directly, this introduction is also indebted to his work. That said, we want to make clear from the outset an important distinction between our analysis and that offered by Dumont. While we recognize the merit of Dumont's holism, not least as an analytic device that brings many of the unquestioned assumptions of Western individualism to the fore, in the discussion that follows we hope to avoid the confusion that the tight coupling of holism and hierarchy in Dumont's anthropology sometimes creates by drawing a distinction between what we mean by hierarchy as a model of value and hierarchy as a social form.

In Dumont's work, hierarchy and holism are inextricably linked. This is because hierarchy for Dumont is defined by what he terms 'encompassment' and more specifically encompassment "of the contrary" (Dumont 1986: 252; see also Dumont [1970] 1980: 240). By this he is referring to the relationship between a whole and its parts; the latter are at once constitutive of and, as such, identical to the whole, and yet they are different from and, as such, contrary to it.[2] Hierarchy therefore presupposes a whole. In a detailed discussion of Dumont's holism, Bruce Kapferer (2010) notes that for Dumont the whole is not social or territorial.

It does not, in other words, connote the boundaries of a society or community but is instead ideological: it is a system of ranked and competing values. Kapferer thus views Dumont's holism as a methodology aimed at the comparative study of ideology across a large swath of human existence—a method "that assumes that values in relations are never balanced or equivalent … but hierarchical when conceived through and defined in relation to the whole" (ibid.: 198–199).

Given Kapferer's clarifications, so far we find little to disagree with in Dumont. The notion of hierarchy more generally is fundamental to any theory of value, and toward the development of such a theory hierarchical encompassment is a compelling idea. Nevertheless, we are cautious about taking up Dumont's work for several reasons. First, at least some readers will feel that Dumont has found in non-Western societies not only a point of contrast to the modern West, but also, and more problematically, a perennial past in the present (Appadurai 1988; Fabian 1983). Faced with such critiques, one employs Dumont's theory only at the risk of being thought guilty by association of a neo-colonialist conceit. So too, while we find it helpful to explore values in terms of hierarchical encompassment, we want to keep our distance from a reading of Dumont that cites his occasional references to a 'paramount value' (Dumont 1986) as evidence that all values can ultimately be reduced to one.[3] Finally, and most importantly for the purposes of this book, we must make clear that the definition of hierarchy that Dumont puts forward for values—hierarchy as encompassment—is not the same as the definition of hierarchy that we will be using when we speak of it as a social form. This requires a bit of explanation.

For Dumont, social hierarchy comes from a kind of holism that is very different from the ideological holism we have just described. In this second usage, the whole is not "an analyst's construction" but rather "a conception in the indigenous culture" (Robbins 1994: 31). Here, the integrity of the whole is the central concern behind much, if not all, of social life, and the latter is therefore organized in such a way as to reproduce and reorient the whole on terms that are ideologically salient, such as the religious notion of purity. Drawing on this socio-cultural definition of holism, it is no surprise that for Dumont social hierarchy is also marked by encompassment: in the case of India, lower castes are encompassed by higher castes so as to preserve the purity of the whole. It is in this interpretation of holism and hierarchy as social forms that we diverge from Dumont. Laying aside the vexed question of whether holism is indeed an indigenous conception in South Asia (we leave that to the regional specialists), we nevertheless want to make clear that while there may be cultural settings in which social hierarchy does take the form of encompassment, it is by no means necessary to define social hierarchy in these terms.[4] Indeed, in this introduction we have chosen not to do so. Rather, our definition of hierarchy as a social form refers not to encompassment but rather to difference and asymmetry, and often also to rank. Examples from the ethnographic record of social hierarchy as we define it include the rich literature on 'clientistic' relationships (e.g., Eisenstadt and Roniger 1980), seniority (e.g., Pritchett 2001; Richards 1982), and what James Ferguson (2013) has recently called ties of 'dependence' (see also Barnes 1967; Bolt 2014; Scherz 2014).[5] In addition, we would note that based on this definition it is possible for hierarchy to co-exist with a certain kind of ontological egalitarianism. While in some cases hierarchical sociality presupposes basic ontological difference—that is, the people who inhabit different ranks in the system are considered to be fundamentally different types of beings, as in the caste system as Dumont describes it—in other cases people are regarded as ontologically equivalent, and the various ranks of the system are theoretically and often actually open to anyone. In such instances, 'egalitarian hierarchy' is not a contradiction in terms, but rather an important analytical descriptor.

In keeping with our reading of Dumont as we have outlined it here, it should be clear that what is most interesting to us about hierarchical social arrangements is the way that they reveal particular ideological arrangements, that is, topographies of value. Put differently, we might say that we are not simply interested in hierarchy as such, but rather in why hierarchy has emerged as so important in so many ethnographic contexts. Addressing this issue means engaging with value and, more specifically, with the values that hierarchical relationships express. In this way, while there are certainly parts of Dumont's complicated apparatus that we leave behind or do not take up, our discussion in this introduction is offered very much in the spirit of Dumont, both in the connections we draw between social forms and values and in our insistence on the structuring influence and hierarchical arrangement of the latter. It is in a similar spirit that we now turn our attention to a more detailed discussion of the problems that attention to hierarchy—and particularly attention to hierarchy as a moral good—raises in contemporary anthropology.

The Problem of Hierarchy

We are by no means the first anthropologists to observe that hierarchy represents an uncomfortable topic for the discipline. As Dumont's words have already reminded us, hierarchy has for decades presented a problem to modern, Western anthropologists. One of the reasons for this is that anthropology—and particularly American cultural anthropology—is very firmly rooted in the classic liberal tradition that underpins Western academia. Kant's enlightenment mantra ("Dare to be wise!") called for individuals to exercise their own capacity for critical thought without relying on the guidance of establishment authority figures and to question the conventional wisdom that such figures hand down. "For true enlightenment," Kant said, "all that is needed is *freedom*." Anthropology has taken up this enlightenment project and added its own spin, drawing on the perspectives of other cultures to gain distance from the entrenched assumptions and taken-for-granted values of our own. Indeed, many of the Boasians believed that this cross-cultural relativist stance provided the anthropologist with a sort of transcendence from the cognitive limitations of any single culture and therefore a special degree of freedom.

Yet it is not only their own freedom that anthropologists have been concerned to achieve, but also that of others. We can see this even in the early stages of the discipline's history. The Boasian tradition began in large part as an anti-racist project—an ambitious attempt to upend the dominant social hierarchies that characterized early-twentieth-century America. More recently, anthropologists have been at the forefront of challenging gender hierarchies and other social inequalities, both at home and abroad. It is for these reasons that anthropology departments across the world have developed a reputation for being bastions of progressive thought and action. At the heart of this movement is a concern, once again, for human freedom, conceived as the emancipation of the suffering subject (cf. Robbins 2013a) from the constraints of oppressive social norms, of which hierarchies of race and gender seem to be the most troubling. On a more abstract theoretical level, we can see this concern for freedom reflected in the long-standing debates that anthropologists have engaged in over the tension between structure and agency (cf. Obeyesekere 1992; Sahlins 1995), with the contemporary consensus leaning heavily toward the latter—a stance that is as much political as analytical. As we pointed out above, the analytical project of recognizing and describing the agency of the subject against the material and symbolic structures that 'constrain' or overdetermine agency runs parallel to the political project of emancipating the subject by challenging hierarchies.

In other words, a deep tension exists in liberal thought between the value of individual freedom, on the one hand, and the social hierarchies that are thought to constrain freedom, on the other. In light of this tension, we need to ask ourselves, why are freedom and hierarchy regarded as incompatible? We argue that it has to do with the particularly Western conception of freedom that this formulation assumes. Webb Keane's work offers insights into how this plays out. Demonstrating that the dominant Western conception of freedom—that which underpins narratives of modernity and progress—focuses on human emancipation as a project of progressive self-mastery, Keane (2007: 6) states: "If in the past humans were in thrall to illegitimate rulers, rigid traditions, and unreal fetishes, as they become modern they realize the true character of human agency. Conversely, those who seem to persist in displacing their own agency onto such rulers, traditions, or fetishes are out of step with the times, anachronistic premoderns or antimoderns." Liberation, in other words, is conceived as the emancipation of the individual from the arbitrary authority of others.

This conception of freedom presupposes a fundamental dichotomy between the individual and society. The individual is regarded as the proper locus of reason and the source of 'authentic' desire. The individual exists *prior* to society, which is imagined as a series of external constraints. Social norms, rules, values, and beliefs are thought to overdetermine the desires of individuals and appear as a form of bondage. The process of liberation, then, involves excavating and asserting the inner autonomous agency of the individual. It is, above all, a process of self-realization. These assumptions about the tension between the individual and society appear repeatedly in Western social science (Sahlins 2008) and, in various iterations, inform the work of Hegel, Freud, and much of the structural functionalist tradition. Indeed, they even seem to inform Marx's theory of ideology: the 'false consciousness' handed down by society—which reflects the interests of a ruling class—precludes objective knowledge of the external world and therefore stifles the expression of true political agency and desire.

In view of all this, it becomes clear why hierarchy poses a problem for the liberal conception of freedom: it represents an arrangement wherein persons are embedded in relations of interdependence that appear to hamper their prospects for self-mastery. The subject entangled in hierarchies appears as the antithesis of the modern political subject—the disembedded, free-thinking, rights-bearing individual.

We know, of course, that these assumptions are incorrect. The subject does not precede society or social norms but is in fact formed through those norms. Michel Foucault and Judith Butler are often credited with pointing this out, but it is an observation that is nearly as old as anthropology itself. Persons do not exist outside of social relationships—or, as the Boasians would have it, persons do not exist outside of culture. If this is the case, then the idea of agency—and of freedom—needs to be rethought. The subject's capacity for agency does not inhere in some authentic inner self or a prior substratum of personhood. Rather, it is a product of the processes—the norms and the relationships, including hierarchical ones—that produce the subject in the first place. As Charles Taylor (1989: 33) has argued, human agency is what is possible within some given moral orientation rather than an absolute freedom from all orientations. Based on this viewpoint, we need to relativize our conception of agency to take into account choices that people make and desires that they hold which may not accord with our assumptions about what counts as liberation or resistance (see, e.g., Frank 2006, Meyer and Jepperson 2000; Peacock 2013).

As some of the chapters to this book demonstrate, hierarchy often provides a very powerful moral orientation for human action and desire. Indeed, in many cases it appears that people seek to re-establish the conditions for what they consider to be justice, well-being, and full human flourishing by constituting or reconstituting hierarchies rather than by seeking to abolish them. This seems to be increasingly true when people are confronted with alternative models of society and personhood. Christianity, democracy, and development, for example, often seek to challenge pre-existing social structures and values, many of which are hierarchical. It is at these conjunctures, when hierarchy is called into question, that it is often most vehemently defended and, as a result, most clearly articulated. This presents a challenge to the standard narrative of globalization. Rather than creating communities of liberal cosmopolitans, globalizing forces such as democracy and development often produce what Meyer and Geschiere (1999) have called 'cultural closure'—new longings for forms of social order that often pivot on the value of hierarchy, whether as a social form, as an ideology, or as nostalgia for an idealized past.

But cultural closure along these lines happens not only 'out there'; it also takes place in the West itself, often giving way to social movements that provoke scholars' own political reactions. In the United States, for instance, we see this sort of cultural closure among conservatives who express longing to return to the putative 'Golden Age' of the American family with its stable gender hierarchies (Ginsburg 1989). In Europe, it appears in the form of right-wing nationalist groups that seek to reassert racial hierarchies as a supposed solution to economic crisis. It may be that these more familiar, experience-near expressions of hierarchy are driving the renewed interest in the subject among Western scholars today. Or perhaps it is being driven by the recognition that Western society is marked by inequality to an unprecedented degree, yielding a highly stratified social order, reminiscent of feudalism, that some pundits have sought to portray as a 'natural' hierarchy (e.g., Clark 2014).

How are we to think about ideologies or social movements that reject liberal values in this manner and instead express a preference for hierarchies? Confronted with such situations where class struggle is at stake, progressives and leftists tend to resort to explanations that rely on theories of false consciousness. Even when class struggle is not a factor, it can be tempting to say that when people represent hierarchy favorably, they are merely reproducing an ideology promoted by those on the 'senior' end of the scale—men, elders, and patrons—to perpetuate the subservience of those on the 'junior' end of the scale—women, minors, and clients (e.g., Crehan 1997). These explications are not entirely without merit, but they often assume that there is something intrinsic to humans that *should* predispose them to reject hierarchy—an assumption that we would argue does not always bear out ethnographically. Such explanations ignore the possibility that in some contexts people might actually regard hierarchy as central to their conceptions of the good and to their ideas about human flourishing. To paraphrase the words of Saba Mahmood (2005: xi), we cannot arrogantly assume that liberal forms of life exhaust ways of living meaningfully and richly in this world. We have to be able to parochialize our own political certitude.

On Wanting Hierarchy (Back): Two Examples from Southern Africa

Southern Africa—where the two of us have conducted fieldwork for many years, and where our interest in hierarchy first emerged—provides a productive context in which to consider some of these issues. The two case studies we discuss here, from South Africa and Zambia, admittedly represent a narrow geographical and cultural focus. However, our observations can be read back on the chapters in this book that engage other regions as a means of expanding—and doubtless challenging—the framework presented in the introduction.

During the decade leading up to South Africa's first democratic elections in 1994, it became clear that not all black South Africans necessarily wanted to sign on to the vision of a liberal democratic future as promoted by the African National Congress (ANC). In rural Zululand, large numbers of people were so disturbed by the prospect that they mobilized vigilante militias under the banner of the Inkatha Freedom Party in an attempt to sabotage the ANC-led revolution. While they embraced the principles of racial equality and universal franchise, many questioned the underlying idea that all individuals are autonomous and ontologically equal—especially in relation to gender and kinship hierarchies.

This skepticism persists today. As Hickel (2012, 2015) has argued, many people who retain deep ties to rural areas in KwaZulu-Natal perceive liberalism as a threat to the hierarchical social order that remains crucial to their conceptions of fruition and collective well-being. By equalizing individuals across boundaries of gender and generation, liberalism dismantles kinship hierarchies and reduces the world to a state of sterile sameness that opens the door to serious misfortunes. Dismantle hierarchies, they say, and the very foundations of social reproduction fall apart. Many in rural KwaZulu-Natal believe that the increasing poverty and unemployment rates that characterize contemporary South Africa—which we might regard as the consequence of the government's embrace of neo-liberal economic policies—are due rather to the liberal social policies that the ANC promotes under the banner of development and progress. People who hold this view seek to restore their good fortune by ritually re-establishing or reasserting hierarchies in the home, specifically through the sacrifice of cattle and the distribution of meat.

It is tempting to regard this position—this valorization of hierarchy—as flowing from a sort of primordial location, a holdover from a premodern past. In fact, it is a wholly modern phenomenon. Hickel (2015) shows that the hierarchical order cherished by rural Zulus proceeds in part from the Native Administration policies of late colonialism, which governed rural areas by imposing a set of so-called customary laws that ossified hierarchies as a way of extending control into the minutiae of domestic life. Today, the rules of hierarchy are often naturalized as 'traditional', even though evidence suggests that social order in pre-colonial Natal was a good deal more flexible. This point serves as a cautionary tale in our present discussion. Contrary to the developmentalist trajectory presupposed by thinkers like Maine and de Tocqueville, and to some extent Dumont, hierarchy can be just as modern as individualism or egalitarianism.

Turning our attention to another ethnographic case from southern Africa, we are given a further example in which hierarchy is reasserted in the face of individualized egalitarianism. Christianity, particularly in its Protestant guises, has historically been associated with egalitarianism and individualism. Weber, Mauss, Dumont, and Foucault have been the most important thinkers behind this idea, and recent work in the anthropology of Christianity has often—although not always—emphasized the individualist and egalitarian thrust of this religion (see, e.g., Robbins 2004; cf. Daswani 2011). Pentecostalism, a form of Protestantism that has witnessed exponential growth across the globe in recent decades, takes Christian egalitarianism still further through its emphasis on spiritual gifts such as prophecy and glossolalia. Because Pentecostals take seriously the biblical promise that the Holy Spirit will be poured out on "all flesh" (Joel 2: 28), regardless of age or sex, from a theological perspective theirs is among the most egalitarian forms of Christianity. Indeed, in at least some instances, Pentecostal adherence has meant the breaking down of pre-existing social hierarchies, especially those of seniority (van Dijk 1992).

Despite the egalitarian impulse of Pentecostalism, however, in many parts of the world the most important social ties developed in Pentecostal groups are structured by hierarchies of charismatic authority. This is certainly the case on the Zambian Copperbelt, where the key relationship in Pentecostal congregations is that between leaders and laypeople. As Haynes has argued in greater detail elsewhere (Haynes 2012, forthcoming), these ties are hierarchical and

are often framed in terms of one of the most salient hierarchies in Zambia—
that of generation—as on the Copperbelt pastors are regularly referred to as
'parents' (*bafyashi*). What this very brief ethnographic outline suggests is that
in Copperbelt Pentecostalism hierarchy emerges as a clear choice in the face
of other models of social organization. Yet we must also bear in mind that the
Pentecostal preference for hierarchy does not mean that there is no place for
egalitarian relationships. While much of Pentecostal life is devoted to creating
and maintaining hierarchical ties between leaders and laypeople, the egalitarian 'charismatic space' of Pentecostal ritual (Eriksen 2014) allows existing
hierarchies to be broken down or replaced when necessary, for instance, if they
become corrupted by unwelcome economic interests (Haynes 2015). In this
case, egalitarianism is made to serve hierarchical ends, but it has not for that
reason ceased to be an important part of Pentecostal social life.

The foregoing examples, along with the various contributions to this book,
provide a clear illustration of the sort of social movements we invoked above.
Having had direct encounters with liberalism or individualism, and having been
presented with spaces in which they could legitimately organize their social lives
according to these principles, the groups and communities we have just described
have chosen another way. In these cases, hierarchy is regarded as socially desirable, and a social world where at least some key relationships are hierarchical is
considered a good to be pursued. Expressed in this way, we can begin to think of
hierarchy in relation to value, and it is to this topic that we now turn.

Hierarchy, Value, and Values

Anthropological discussions of value often begin by outlining the various ways
in which this term has been used in the discipline (see, e.g., Graeber 2001:
1–22; Miller 2008: 1122–1123; Otto and Willerslev 2013: 1–2). These differences
are most simply described by the distinction between 'value' (use, exchange,
economic) and 'values' (family, cultural, religious, aesthetic). Following David
Graeber (2013: 224), who suggests that there is more commonality than difference between value and values so defined, we would like to reframe this
distinction as one between 'value' as a verb and 'value' as a noun.[6] The notion
of value as a verb refers to the process of valuing and encompasses not only
structuralist theories of value—what Graeber (2001: 2), drawing on Saussure,
calls "'value' ... as 'meaningful difference'"—but also economic theories of
value, which are about equivalence, exchange, and so forth. In contrast, value
as a noun refers to notions of the good. While this concept certainly may have
moral implications, the most important feature of the good as an ethnographic
object (as opposed to a philosophical one) is its connection to a certain model
of sociality: values are ideas about a good social and relational world.

Understood in these terms, values as nouns can be defined as those parts
of culture that transform the constellation of relationships, actions, and objects
that we find in any society from a neutral field of open-ended potential to a
field that is differentiated, a field with topography. Simply put, values value.

Stated yet another way, the good structures the move from 'is' to 'ought', from difference to value, and therefore serves as the metric that animates the process of valuation—values as verbs. Without some notion of the good, it is hard to understand why someone would choose to exchange taro with a person in a neighboring village, or to build a table to sell to someone else, or to buy that same table. Nor can we see why people would prefer to marry their cross-cousins, or to regard men as more important than women, or to pursue hierarchical forms of social organization in the face of other options. These actions are rendered sensible in a framework of values that exists beyond the purely material or structural—a point that Sahlins (1976) has made very well.

Joel Robbins (2004, 2009) has provided a detailed description of what this process of valuation looks like in his work on the Urapmin of Papua New Guinea. For the Urapmin, a good social world is one that is characterized by the formation and maintenance of egalitarian social relationships, which are in turn fundamental to Melanesian models of the person (Strathern 1988). Following Dumont, Robbins therefore argues that the value that he calls 'relationalism' determines the position of all other elements of Urapmin society.[7] This means that those ideas, institutions, or practices that most effectively produce relationships are more prominent, "more elaborately worked out" (Robbins 2009: 66), than those that do not. Here again, the particular hierarchical ordering of values as nouns—that is, the particular model of the good—found in a given community is responsible for the arrangement of all sorts of other things: the kinds of relationships people pursue, the objects they choose to display, the rituals they perform. The arrangement of values in a particular society thus reverberates through it in numerous visible ways, which means that values are observable in social life, as values "find their existence in people" (Rio and Smedal 2009b: 20).

A final thing to bear in mind when examining how values are organized is the possibility that this order can change. One can infer this not only from Dumont's (1986) work on the emergence of individualism in the West (see also Robbins 2013b), but also from Weber's (1946: 323–359) notion of value 'spheres', in which various domains of value—religious, political, aesthetic—compete for superior positions of influence. In the cases provided above, we have seen how this competition can involve the position of hierarchy in the constellation of elements that make up a particular society. Similarly, it is important to pay attention to when and where hierarchy is elaborated. In most cases, hierarchy does not define all social contexts. In the examples from southern Africa discussed earlier, people might demonstrate a strong preference for hierarchy within the family or the church but reject it in other social spaces. To value hierarchy in some scenarios does not preclude an egalitarian ethic in others.

It should be clear in these southern African examples that hierarchy is central to local models of a good society. This does not mean, however, that hierarchy is a good in and of itself, but rather that hierarchy is a good because it is part of a larger ideological framework of value. In the case of rural KwaZulu-Natal, for instance, hierarchy is valued as a means to fruition—to the achievement of health and good fortune and the conditions for social reproduction (Hickel 2015). Indeed, in many cases people neglect kinship hierarchies until their fortunes take a turn for the worse, at which point they seek to police them with singular rigor. In the case of the Copperbelt, the importance of hierarchy follows from its connection to what Haynes (forthcoming) calls 'moving'. On the Copperbelt, moving refers to measurable advancement, whether progress through the life-course in the form of marriage and children or upward mobility indexed by consumer goods, from a new suit to a second-hand Toyota sedan. For Pentecostals, it also carries spiritual components. Importantly, moving does not refer to progress as such, but to a larger social process in which personal advancement is achieved through social relationships. Put differently, moving is not so much a matter of getting ahead as it is of being pulled up. There are multiple relational forms through which moving can be realized, but the most important of these are ties of patronage or hierarchical 'dependence' (Ferguson 2013), which facilitate moving especially well. Hierarchy is therefore important to people on the Copperbelt as a means of realizing local models of a good social world—in this case, a world in which everyone is moving.

The foregoing discussion has provided a framework through which to approach the remaining contributions to this book. While different chapters address different aspects of the model we have developed here, and while they vary in their theoretical orientation, one nevertheless sees the thread of value running through these discussions of hierarchy.

Overview of Chapters

Signe Howell's chapter provides an excellent illustration of the sort of contest of values that we have already seen in the Copperbelt and Zulu cases. In the Lio example that Howell describes, the conflict between hierarchical and egalitarian social systems reveals that egalitarianism has been incorporated into Lio society without being allowed to transform it in any significant way. Traditional Lio social organization is hierarchical, and the authority of priest-leaders structures a political-religious system that Howell, using Dumont's terms, refers to as 'holist'. With the arrival of Catholicism, Lio hierarchy has been challenged by an egalitarianism that emphasizes individual relationships with God (Dumont 1986). Identification with the Catholic Church has become important to the Lio primarily as a means of interacting with the state, as national identity cards require Indonesian citizens to indicate their affiliation with one of five world religions. Lio also participate in a circumscribed set of Catholic rituals, narrowly defined according to the category of 'religion'. Nevertheless, Howell argues that hierarchy remains the encompassing value, as Catholic egalitarianism is allowed to order only less important domains of Lio life—in this case, the small, discrete category of 'religion' or occasional interactions with the state. Howell suggests that, ironically, the subordinate role given to religion, which clearly falls short of the Catholic ideal of conversion, presents a striking parallel to the way that post–Vatican II efforts toward 'inculturation' have treated culture. To wit, culture here is largely reduced to a set of constructed (mostly aesthetic) particles and objects, a few rituals, songs, and pieces of clothing—what Carneiro da

Cunha calls "culture in quote marks" (cited in Vilaça 2014: S323). Just as Catholic practice has made culture into a reified and modular category, something to be encompassed by religion, Lio culture, as a totalizing system, has done the same with religion. For the Lio, then, a hierarchy that originated with their ancestors through the authority of priest-leaders remains the central mode of social organization, as well as, Howell adds, a model for the structure of values.

Christianity also figures in the Ethiopian Orthodox case presented by Diego Maria Malara and Tom Boylston, although to very different effect. Here, Christianity serves as part of a larger relational framework that Malara and Boylston argue structures Amhara social life. This framework is fundamentally asymmetrical and undergirds not only hierarchical patronage ties, which are familiar from the ethnographic literature on Ethiopia, but also intimate ties of love and care. Included here is the bond between a mother and child, as well as that between the Virgin Mary and Orthodox Christians. In both of these cases, love is asymmetrical because it is unconditional and can never be repaid. Love also enters into other asymmetrical ties through the work of mediators—often, again, mothers or the Virgin—who are willing and able to intercede on behalf of those they care for. It is in light of this model of 'vertical love' that Malara and Boylston are able to address the difficult question of whether we can think of hierarchy as an Amhara 'value' in the sense of a positive moral good. On the one hand, there is no question that hierarchy can lead to coercion and even exploitation. On the other, it is clear in Malara and Boylston's analysis that hierarchy is linked to some of the most intimate and important relationships in Ethiopian Orthodox society, and this is the key to understanding the place of asymmetry in Amhara relational life. As the authors put it: "Without an account of vertical love and the daily practicalities of care and affection, it is difficult to see how a system based on naked domination, as Amhara is supposed to be, could ever be livable, or how claims about the values and virtues of hierarchy could ever be convincing." In other words, if hierarchy is a value in Ethiopia, it is not because people are blind to its potentially negative effects or even simply because they enjoy the benefits of patronage. Rather, hierarchy is part of local models of the good because it is central to the politics of care, to the most important sites of intimacy and protection.

Frederick Damon's chapter takes a bold shot across time and space—drawing on a number of classic anthropological texts and a variety of ethnographic contexts—to examine the role that destruction and sacrifice play in the production of human hierarchies. Destruction, he states, seems necessary for the creation of difference, which allows for the elaboration of rank. He begins with the example of the Kula ring, the site of his own original research. In the Kula system, when one man sends a valuable to another, he destroys part of himself: the giver's name 'goes down' (his body thereby depleted), while the receiver's name 'goes up'. In other words, exchange requires a kind of destruction, and destruction produces hierarchical difference. A similar logic operated in the past in Polynesia, Damon argues, where literal human sacrifice served as the basis for hierarchy, and we can also see it at play in the lynching that became so common in the United States, especially the American South during the years following the Civil

War, as a method of differentiating white from black. In each of these systems, continuity needs to be replaced by tangible discontinuity or differentiation in order for some kind of hierarchized semantic field to exist. Destruction produces hierarchies, which are regarded as essential to a well-ordered social totality. Damon takes this one step further, arguing that we can understand the capitalist world system through this same lens. Why does the United States devote so much of its wealth to overdeveloping its military capacity? One might think of this as 'waste', but Damon suggests it is necessary to the continuity of the world system in two ways: it mops up overaccumulated capital in order to avoid widespread devaluation, and it maintains the relative ranking of hegemonic positions. Mass destruction—be it wasting wealth on non-productive assets such as fighter planes or laying waste to entire cities—figures as a structural component of the modern world system.

Stephan Feuchtwang's chapter is equally ambitious in its scope. He mounts a fresh critique of the ahistorical and structuralist dimensions of Dumont's approach to hierarchy with a corrective from another great French thinker, Dumont's teacher Marcel Mauss. While Dumont asserts a type-anti-type dualism between hierarchical and egalitarian societies, Feuchtwang derives from Mauss's theory of 'civilization'—and from Dumont's concepts of encompassment and ideology—an argument that all societies, including avowedly egalitarian ones, "hang together" on hierarchies of valuation, distinction, and aspiration. Indeed, Feuchtwang suggests that inasmuch as ideals of order, etiquette, civility, and so on are hierarchically organized and distinguished from the values of 'others' outside, hierarchy may even be intrinsic to the very concept of civilization—except in the case of specific hunter-gatherer civilizations. So much for Dumont's dualism. As a corrective to Dumont's tendency toward ahistorical analysis, Feuchtwang insists that anthropology should not shy away from exploring and analyzing the long processes by which hierarchies are formed and transformed through the history of specific civilizations. By way of example, he takes us on a dizzying tour through some 6,000 years of China's history, moving from early forms of social hierarchy in the archaeological record to the rise of the imperial dynasties, illustrating how hierarchies have changed in that context, as has the idea of civilization itself.

Arsalan Khan offers a thoughtful ethnography of the Tablighi Jamaat in Pakistan, a local instantiation of what has become the fastest growing Islamic movement in the world. Tablighis are interesting in that they maintain a strong stance against the Islamist movement that has become so powerful in Pakistan. While Islamism seeks to use state power to legislate adherence to Islamic values, Tablighis believe that such efforts are in vain. For them, the only way to draw Muslims back to Islamic piety is through proper praxis, specifically a distinct form of face-to-face preaching known as *dawat*, which involves extensive traveling with groups of men going house-to-house across the country. Even if these missionary efforts fail to refresh the religious commitments of others, they are important to the development of piety among the travelers themselves. *Dawat* is efficacious toward this end, not only through the discipline and sacrifice that it requires, but also through the relationships that it produces. These relationships are hierarchical, modeled on kin relations between brothers and fathers with rankings laid out along a gradient of closeness to God. As Khan puts it: "Becoming a proper Islamic subject requires that a Tablighi must learn how to live in a hierarchically structured social world as both giver and recipient of Islamic knowledge." Tablighis regard Islamist praxis, by contrast, as inefficacious because it stresses the agency and autonomy of the individual, and therefore produces persons who disregard their place in the hierarchical order. Because of this, Tablighis blame Islamism for disrupting the harmonious order of the family, causing moral chaos (*fitna*) in communities, and ultimately contributing to the general sense of violence and crisis that pervades Karachi today.

Olaf Smedal's discussion of hierarchy among the Ngadha of Flores, Indonesia, provides a helpful counter-example to many of the other cases treated here. Smedal describes the slow erosion of Ngadha hierarchy through the increasingly common practice of noble women marrying lower-ranking men. When this happens, a woman loses her rank and, more importantly, is not able to pass that rank along to her children. Although she can be ritually reincorporated into her family, as Smedal describes, a noble woman who has married a commoner erases aristocratic distinction in the next generation. As more and more women find themselves in this position, the long-term dissolution of Ngadha hierarchy is not difficult to imagine. Instead of defending hierarchy as socially necessary, then, the Ngadha are slowly and painfully watching it slip away. Smedal is clear that this is not a rejection of hierarchy as such—at least, not on the part of the nobility, although commoners are generally happy enough with its passing. Rather, aristocratic hierarchy seems in this example to be a victim of its own inflexibility, particularly in view of Ngadha women's increased access to education in other parts of the country, where they are unlikely to find marriage partners from the Ngadha nobility. Smedal suggests that the reason this shift is possible is that nobility was never necessary to the Ngadha social world in the first place—that while Ngadha sociality was structured by purity in a manner similar to Dumont's description of India, the social classes that exemplified purity never encompassed the whole of Ngadha society. In this way, Smedal's example provides a helpful complement to the definition of hierarchy that we have offered above by separating it from encompassment.

Finally, David Graeber has graciously contributed an afterword for this volume. We reached out to him knowing that he would have interesting things to say on the topic, and he did not disappoint. He shares our interest in how anthropologists, in their eagerness to celebrate popular resistance to 'power' and 'hegemony' and 'global capitalism', tend to avoid grappling with the alternative political visions that those engaged in such resistance actually mobilize, possibly because those visions are quite often unpalatable to prevailing liberal sensibilities. What do we do with what Graeber calls "conservative anticapitalist movements," which reject the values of bourgeois modernity but do so in the name of hierarchical (and often authoritarian) holism rather than in the name of egalitarian universalism? This question is particularly pressing in a world where, as Graeber puts it, "opposition to the American empire is now being spearheaded above all by Putin's patriarchal authoritarianism, a Chinese government increasingly shedding Marxism for Confucianism, and a ragtag collection of would-be Islamist theocracies."

Graeber also uses his piece to offer a broad critique of Dumont and Dumontian scholarship and—more interestingly for us—of the rise of 'hierarchy' as an analytical term in anthropology. He argues that—unlike terms such as inequality, rank, and domination—the term 'hierarchy' ends up naturalizing social stratification and presents it as always already ideologically legitimated. It is a strong point, and we agree: no one should go about assuming that hierarchy is somehow natural or naturally good. But words like 'inequality' and 'domination', which carry ideological baggage of their own (to the opposite effect), are hardly ideal alternatives (indeed, Graeber himself has developed a critique of the word 'inequality').[8] While these terms offer useful leverage for political critique, they may end up obscuring more than they reveal about how people experience the social formations in question.

There is an interesting empirical question at stake here. Graeber notes that anthropologists' use of the word 'hierarchy' has exploded over the past century: it featured in less than 1 percent of English-language articles in JSTOR's anthropology collection in the 1910s, but rose steadily to nearly 20 percent by the 1990s. He reads this as a conservative shift in how anthropologists handle the question of rank and stratification, suggesting that they are too quick to accept the rationalizations of their interlocutors. If so, this would run against our claim that anthropological analysis is increasingly concerned with *critiques* of power and domination—a conclusion that is shared by Robbins (2013a) in his reflections on the centrality of the suffering subject in contemporary anthropology, and by Sherry Ortner (2016) in her essay on 'dark anthropology'. Indeed, given that the use of the word 'inequality' in anthropological writing also increased on a dramatic trajectory during the twentieth century (nearly matching the rise of 'hierarchy' according to the same JSTOR data set), one might just as easily make the argument opposite to Graeber's.

What is the political disposition with which anthropologists approach hierarchy, and how has this changed over time? This will require further empirical research, beyond just word counts. Indeed, such research would constitute an important intervention in the historiography of the discipline. In the meantime, what has become clear is that none of the terms we have at our disposal are adequate to the analytical task at hand, and—as Graeber warns—we need to think carefully about how we deploy them. But regardless of the words we use, when it comes to ethnography, the point should be neither to justify nor to denounce hierarchy (or rank or inequality), but rather to show how it works and to explain why people might find it either repulsive or attractive. This is the burden that ethnography needs to bear.

Conclusion

While social scientists would agree that hierarchy operates in all places, there are few who place it at the center of their analysis, and fewer still who seek to understand it on its own terms, as part of a model of a good society. In this book, our aim is to do precisely that—to explore people's insistence that hierarchy is good for them and for their communities, and to do so in a framework that takes these ideas seriously. What we have found is that hierarchy is remarkably assertive and that in many places it is central to local understandings of the good. This is not to say that hierarchy is not implicated in power relations; indeed, nearly all of the chapters show that it is. However, hierarchy is much more than power and certainly much more than inequality.

As we seek to move beyond, or at least to break new ground within, the concerns that have dominated the discipline for the past two decades— namely, those of power and resistance, especially in light of the global spread of neo-liberalism—the message of this book is that anthropologists will do well to keep hierarchy in view. This is not to say that it is not our business to expose and denounce injustice where we find it. On the contrary, what we are suggesting is that, at least in some instances, hierarchy may in fact be a key way of resisting the atomizing effects of liberalization in particular. And even in those instances where this is not specifically the case, the critical examination of liberalism that has made such an impact on anthropology in the recent past should highlight the importance of taking seriously seemingly illiberal, hierarchical ways of organizing social life and being in the world. As our discussion in this introduction and the contributions to this book make clear, what emerges from a whole range of social conjunctures is the fact that people seem to want hierarchy or, in some cases, to want their hierarchy back. Anthropology must do the difficult and politically contentious work of understanding why.

Naomi Haynes is a Lecturer in Social Anthropology at the University of Edinburgh. Her research interests include the anthropology of Christianity, political economy, exchange, gender, hierarchy, and value. Her publications include *Moving by the Spirit* (2017) and a special issue of *Current Anthropology*, "The Anthropology of Christianity: Unity, Diversity, and New Directions" (2014, co-edited with Joel Robbins). She is a co-curator for the Anthropology of Christianity Bibliographic Blog and has recently begun an ESRC-funded research project that explores Zambia's constitutional declaration that it is a "Christian nation."

Jason Hickel is an anthropologist at Goldsmiths, University of London. His research spans several related themes, including political conflict, inequality, post-development, and ecological economics. He is the author of *Democracy as Death: The Moral Order of Anti-Liberal Politics in South Africa* (2015) and *The Divide: A Brief Guide to Global Inequality and Its Solutions* (2017). He writes a column on political economy for the *Guardian* and *Al Jazeera*, sits on the executive board of Academics Stand Against Poverty, and serves as Policy Director for /The Rules collective. He is a fellow of the Royal Society of Arts.

Notes

1. What we do not offer here is a close reading and summary of Dumont's corpus, which would require another book in itself.
2. One of Dumont's favorite examples is that of 'goods and services'. On the one hand, services are encompassed by goods as the dominant category, included with them as essentially part of the whole. On the other, services and goods are quite different from one another and, in that difference, contrary to each other (see Dumont 1986: 252).
3. See Robbins (2013b) for an alternative reading of Dumont's apparent 'value monism'.
4. Indeed, Greg Acciaioli (2009) has argued that the definition of hierarchy as encompassment in the revised 1980 edition of Dumont's *Homo Hierarchicus* does not fit well with the ethnographic material presented in the same volume, which instead suggests a model of hierarchy more similar to the one we propose here.
5. In light of these examples, it may be that this definition works especially well with the material from southern Africa that we draw on in this introduction. Whether or not this is the case, we think that this definition of hierarchy is best suited to addressing those situations in which a preference for hierarchy is actively asserted, as people appear to be choosing hierarchical modes of social organization despite being confronted with other relational possibilities.
6. Although he does not use this terminology, Graeber (2001) makes a similar argument in *Toward an Anthropological Theory of Value* in his sustained analysis of what he calls 'action' and 'reflection' that in many ways correspond to the notion of value as a verb and as a noun, respectively. Similarly, Michael Lambek's (2013: 155) brief discussion of Marx's labor theory of value and Karl Polanyi's notion of fictitious commodities points to this distinction. Naomi Haynes also makes this point in the introduction to her forthcoming book.
7. Making good use of Dumont's ideological holism in this analysis, Robbins (2009) refers to relationalism as the 'paramount value' of the Urapmin.
8. See Graeber and Wengrow (2018) for reflections on the political assumptions embedded in the word 'inequality'.

References

Acciaioli, Greg. 2009. "Distinguishing Hierarchy and Precedence: Comparing Status Distinctions in South Asia and the Austronesian World, with Special Reference to South Sulawesi." In *Precedence: Social Differentiation in the Austronesia World*, ed. Michael P. Vischer, 51–90. Canberra: ANU E Press.

Ansell, Aaron. 2010. "Auctioning Patronage in Northeast Brazil: The Political Value of Money in a Ritual Market." *American Anthropologist* 112 (2): 283–294.

Appadurai, Arjun. 1988. "Putting Hierarchy in Its Place." *Cultural Anthropology* 3 (1): 36–49.

Barnes, John A. 1967. *Politics in a Changing Society: A Political History of the Fort Jameson Ngoni*. 2nd ed. Manchester: Manchester University Press.

Bolt, Maxim. 2014. "The Sociality of the Wage: Money Rhythms, Wealth Circulation, and the Problem with Cash on the Zimbabwean-South African Border." *Journal of the Royal Anthropological Institute* 20 (1): 113–130.

Clark, Gregory. 2014. *The Son Also Rises: Surnames and the History of Social Mobility*. Princeton, NJ: Princeton University Press.

Crehan, Kate. 1997. *The Fractured Community: Landscapes of Power and Gender in Rural Zambia*. Berkeley: University of California Press.

Daswani, Girish. 2011. "(In-)Dividual Pentecostals in Ghana." *Journal of Religion in Africa* 41 (3): 256–279.

Dumont, Louis. (1970) 1980. *Homo Hierarchicus: The Caste System and Its Implications*. Rev. ed. Chicago: University of Chicago Press.

Dumont, Louis. 1986. *Essays on Individualism: Modern Ideology in Anthropological Perspective*. Chicago: University of Chicago Press.

Eisenstadt, S. N., and Louis Roniger. 1980. "Patron-Client Relations as a Model of Structuring Social Exchange." *Comparative Studies in Society and History* 22 (1): 42–77.

Eriksen, Annelin. 2012. "The Pastor and the Prophetess: An Analysis of Gender and Christianity in Vanuatu." *Journal of the Royal Anthropological Institute* 18 (1): 103–122.

Eriksen, Annelin. 2014. "Sarah's Sinfulness: Egalitarianism, Denied Difference, and Gender in Pentecostal Christianity." *Current Anthropology* 55 (S10): S262–S270.

Fabian, Johannes. 1983. *Time and the Other: How Anthropology Makes Its Object*. New York: Columbia University Press.

Ferguson, James. 2013. "Declarations of Dependence: Labour, Personhood, and Welfare in Southern Africa." *Journal of the Royal Anthropological Institute* 19 (2): 223–242.

Frank, Katherine. 2006. "Agency." *Anthropological Theory* 6 (3): 281–302.

Ginsburg, Faye D. 1989. *Contested Lives: The Abortion Debate in an American Community*. Berkeley: University of California Press.

Graeber, David. 2001. *Toward an Anthropological Theory of Value: The False Coin of Our Own Dreams*. New York: Palgrave.

Graeber, David. 2013. "It Is Value That Brings Universes into Being." *HAU: Journal of Ethnographic Theory* 3 (2): 219–243.

Graeber, David, and David Wengrow. 2018. "How to Change the Course of Human History (at Least, the Part That's Already Happened)." Eurozine, 2 March. https://www.eurozine.com/change-course-human-history/.

Haynes, Naomi. 2012. "Pentecostalism and the Morality of Money: Prosperity, Inequality, and Religious Sociality on the Zambian Copperbelt." *Journal of the Royal Anthropological Institute* 18 (1): 123–139.

Haynes, Naomi. 2015. "Egalitarianism and Hierarchy in Copperbelt Religious Practice: On the Social Work of Pentecostal Ritual." *Religion* 45 (2): 273–292.

Haynes, Naomi. Forthcoming. *Moving by the Spirit: Pentecostal Social Life on the Zambian Copperbelt*. Berkeley: University of California Press.

Hickel, Jason. 2012. "Subaltern Consciousness in South Africa's Labour Movement: 'Workerism' in the KwaZulu-Natal Sugar Industry." *South African Historical Journal* 64 (3): 664–684.

Hickel, Jason. 2015. *Democracy as Death: The Moral Order of Anti-Liberal Politics in South Africa*. Berkeley: University of California Press.

Iteanu, André. 2013. "The Two Conceptions of Value." *HAU: Journal of Ethnographic Theory* 3 (1): 155–171.

Kapferer, Bruce 2010. "Louis Dumont and a Holist Anthropology." In *Experiments in Holism: Theory and Practice in Contemporary Anthropology*, ed. Ton Otto and Nils Bubandt, 187–208. Malden, MA: Wiley-Blackwell.

Keane, Webb. 2007. *Christian Moderns: Freedom and Fetish in the Mission Encounter*. Berkeley: University of California Press.

King, Diane E. 2014. *Kurdistan on the Global Stage: Kinship, Land, and Community in Iraq*. New Brunswick, NJ: Rutgers University Press.

Lambek, Michael. 2013. "The Value of (Performative) Acts." *HAU: Journal of Ethnographic Theory* 3 (2): 141–160.

Mahmood, Saba. 2005. *Politics of Piety: The Islamic Revival and the Feminist Subject.* Princeton, NJ: Princeton University Press.

Meyer, Birgit, and Peter Geschiere, eds. 1999. *Globalization and Identity: Dialectics of Flow and Closure.* Oxford: Blackwell.

Meyer, John W., and Ronald L. Jepperson. 2000. "The 'Actors' of Modern Society: The Cultural Construction of Social Agency." *Sociological Theory* 18 (1): 100–120.

Miller, Daniel. 2008. "The Uses of Value." *Geoforum* 39 (3): 1122–1132.

Mosko, Mark, and Margaret Jolly, eds. 1994. *Transformations of Hierarchy: Structure, History and Horizon in the Austronesian World.* London: Routledge. Special issue of *History and Anthropology* 7 (1–4).

Obeyesekere, Gannanath. 1992. *The Apotheosis of Captain Cook: European Mythmaking in the Pacific.* Princeton, NJ: Princeton University Press.

Ortner, Sherry B. 2016. "Dark Anthropology and Its Others: Theory since the Eighties." *HAU: Journal of Ethnographic Theory* 6 (1): 47–73.

Otto, Ton, and Rane Willerslev. 2013. "Introduction: "Value *as* Theory": Comparison, Cultural Critique, and Guerilla Ethnographic Theory." *HAU: Journal of Ethnographic Theory* 3 (1): 1–20.

Peacock, Vita. 2013. "Agency and the Anstoß: Max Planck Directors as Fichtean Subjects." *Anthropology in Action* 20 (2): 6–16. Special issue on "The Study of Organisations."

Peacock, Vita. 2015. "The Negation of Hierarchy and Its Consequences." *Anthropological Theory* 15 (1): 3–21.

Pedersen, David. 2008. "Introduction: Toward a Value Theory of Anthropology." *Anthropological Theory* 8 (1): 5–8.

Pritchett, James A. 2001. *The Lunda-Ndembu: Style, Change, and Social Transformation in South Central Africa.* Madison: University of Wisconsin Press.

Richards, Audrey I. 1982. *Chisungu: A Girl's Initiation Ceremony among the Bemba of Zambia.* Pbk ed. New York: Tavistock.

Rio, Knut M., and Olaf H. Smedal, eds. 2009a. *Hierarchy: Persistence and Transformation in Social Formations.* New York: Berghahn Books.

Rio, Knut M., and Olaf H. Smedal. 2009b. "Hierarchy and Its Alternatives: An Introduction to Movements of Totalization and Detotalization." In Rio and Smedal 2009a, 1–63.

Robbins, Joel. 1994. "Equality as a Value: Ideology in Dumont, Melanesia, and the West." *Social Analysis* 36: 21–70.

Robbins, Joel. 2004. *Becoming Sinners: Christianity and Moral Torment in a Papua New Guinea Society.* Berkeley: University of California Press.

Robbins, Joel. 2009. "Conversion, Hierarchy, and Cultural Change: Value and Syncretism in the Globalization of Pentecostal and Charismatic Christianity." In Rio and Smedal 2009a, 65–88.

Robbins, Joel. 2013a. "Beyond the Suffering Subject: Toward an Anthropology of the Good." *Journal of the Royal Anthropological Institute* 19 (3): 447–462.

Robbins, Joel. 2013b. "Monism, Pluralism and the Structure of Value Relations: A Dumontian Contribution to the Contemporary Study of Value." *HAU: Journal of Ethnographic Theory* 3 (1): 99–115.

Robbins, Joel. 2015. "Ritual, Value, and Example: On the Perfection of Cultural Representations." *Journal of the Royal Anthropological Institute* 21 (S1): 18–29.

Sahlins, Marshall. 1976. *Culture and Practical Reason.* Chicago: University of Chicago Press.

Sahlins, Marshall. 1995. *How "Natives" Think: About Captain Cook, for Example*. Chicago: University of Press.

Sahlins, Marshall. 2004. *Apologies to Thucydides: Understanding History as Culture and Vice Versa*. Chicago: University of Chicago Press.

Sahlins, Marshall. 2008. *The Western Illusion of Human Nature*. Chicago: Prickly Paradigm Press.

Scherz, China. 2014. *Having People, Having Heart: Charity, Sustainable Development, and Problems of Dependence in Central Uganda*. Chicago: University of Chicago Press.

Smith, Daniel J. 2007. *A Culture of Corruption: Everyday Deception and Popular Discontent in Nigeria*. Princeton, NJ: Princeton University Press.

Strathern, Marilyn. 1988. *The Gender of the Gift: Problems with Women and Problems with Society in Melanesia*. Berkeley: University of California Press.

Taylor, Charles. 1989. *Sources of the Self: The Making of the Modern Identity*. Cambridge, MA: Harvard University Press.

van Dijk, Richard A. 1992. "Young Puritan Preachers in Post-Independence Malawi." *Africa* 62 (2): 159–181.

Vilaça, Aparecida. 2014. "Culture and Self: The Different 'Gifts' Amerindians Receive from Catholics and Evangelicals." *Current Anthropology* 55 (S10): S322–S332.

Weber, Max. 1946. *From Max Weber: Essays in Sociology*. Trans. and ed. H. H. Gerth and C. Wright Mills. New York: Oxford University Press.

Chapter 1

BATTLE OF COSMOLOGIES
The Catholic Church, *Adat*, and 'Inculturation'
among Northern Lio, Indonesia

Signe Howell

Western ideas, values, objects, and practices may, or may not, find resonance in a community whose ontological reference points are very different. Where old and new metaphysical and moral systems confront one another, local reactions and resulting effects upon values, categories, and practices are not predictable. For example, when Christianity is introduced into regions where other forms of religious values and practices are well established, this may result in immediate acceptance and the abandonment of existing metaphysics (e.g., Knauft 2002; Robbins 2004, 2009), or, as in the case of the Indonesian Lio,[1] it may meet resistance. Catholicism was introduced to the Lio in the late 1920s, and today most Lio individuals will say that they are Catholic. In this chapter I will explore to what extent it can be argued that Catholicism has replaced their previous cosmology (*adat*) as a point of existential orientation. I shall show that the

Notes for this chapter begin on page 38.

Catholic priests and the Lio 'priest-leaders' are competing for overall supremacy in the religious field, and I argue that, so far, Lio cosmology retains an overall paramount position. This is so, I suggest, because Lio *adat*, unlike the Catholic religion, is holistic—that is, it "valorizes the social whole and neglects or subordinates the human individual" (Dumont 1986: 279). Within holistic ideologies, the parts are organized according to a hierarchical system of value in which the whole encompasses the parts (cf. Dumont 1979, 1986). Lio *adat* encompasses its opposite, Catholicism, except in a few isolated contexts when Catholic dogma and practice are superior (as discussed below). Following Dumont, I suggest that on such occasions this can be understood as a reversal of values that occurs at a lower level in the overall system, a Lio metaphysics in which *adat* and Catholicism both play a part. If their relationship is symmetrical, then a reversal signifies nothing. If, on the other hand, it is asymmetrical, then a reversal indicates a change in level (Dumont 1986: 230). Hierarchy in the Lio case may be understood as a model of value expressed relationally in wholes and parts.

Lio is a highly stratified society, made up of aristocrats, commoners, and, in earlier times, slaves, whose council of 'priest-leaders' (*mosa laki*) wields political, religious, and ritual authority. The priest-leaders' authority is grounded in the cosmogenic past, manifested and perpetuated through aristocratic patrilineal descent and the prescriptive alliance system, as well as by demonstrably superior esoteric knowledge and personal fierceness, all of which are enacted through ritual. Rites of what I call 'cosmic kinship' are critical in the hierarchical structures at all points in the dynamics of reproduction of Lio social order. An example of this is the fact that all land is under the priest-leaders' authority: it is handed out to individual families to cultivate in return for an annual tribute to be made during a special ceremony. It is a statement of the unequal relationship between them and must be viewed together with the annual pre-planting ceremony, performed by the superior priest-leader and his wife, and the first harvest ceremony, similarly performed by them. The fecundity of the soil is dependent upon the power of the priest-leader couple (the quality of their relationship with the ancestors and spirits world), and the tribute from the farmers acknowledges their dependency upon this power.[2] The priest-leaders' personhood is qualitatively different from (superior to) that of the rest of the population. It is also (so far) superior to that of Catholic priests. I shall argue that while Catholicism and *adat* (traditional religious system) may engage people according to different contexts, Catholicism and the Catholic priests' attempts to merge the two, through the ideology and practices of inculturation, fail to capture the people's imagination and emotions.

Value and Hierarchy

I find it useful that, to follow Robbins (2009: 66), values be understood as parts of culture that structure other parts, and that "radical cultural change should be understood to have taken place only when values have changed—either because new ones have been introduced or because the relations between traditional values have shifted." It is by this yardstick that I shall interpret the relationship between the values of the Catholic Church and Lio *adat*. Values are by definition hierarchical, and "[w]e cannot define the meaning, or 'value', of any one element without understanding its place in a total system … it must be viewed in contrast to other elements within the same system" (Graeber 2001: 13, 14). The anthropologist's task is to understand what motivates people to act the way they do, rather than act in any other way.

According to Dumont, hierarchy must not be confused with social stratification, but treated as a way of organizing a system, or schema, of relative values in which the dominant value is superior to all others and constitutes the particularity—the whole—of each schema. Hierarchy, in such cases, is fundamental to the whole society. This, he argues, is characteristic of many non-Western societies. By contrast, according to contemporary Western ideology,[3] egalitarianism (which is coupled to the idea-value of the individual) is the dominant value (Dumont 1982, 1986; Rio and Smedal 2009). This opposition between holistic and individualistic (hierarchal and egalitarian) ideologies is useful for my analysis of Lio reactions to the challenges presented by the Catholic missionaries. I shall suggest that Lio *adat* is an example of a hierarchically ordered holistic schema. By contrast, Catholicism, despite the hierarchical nature of the Church's organization, preaches an egalitarian ideology in which the dominant value is the individual and the individual soul.

I shall explore the notion of hierarchy at two levels. Drawing upon Dumont (1979, 1982, 1986), I shall argue that Lio hierarchical relations constitute social and ritual organization and practice in which the whole is superior to the individual, but that the Catholic religion is founded upon an ideology of egalitarianism in which, arguably, the value of the individual is superior to that of the whole. Unlike Lio *adat*, which results in a holistic understanding that permeates all aspects of life, the Catholic religion (in Lioland) occupies only a demarcated niche of religion alone. This, I suggest may account for the failure of Catholic proselytizing to emerge triumphant in the silent battle for religious and moral supremacy between Catholic priests and Lio priest-leaders. I say this despite the recent Catholic policy of 'inculturation'—the so-called two-way incorporation of concepts and practices between Catholic and 'pagan' dogma in Indonesia. Notwithstanding avowals to the contrary, inculturation as practiced by Catholic priests on Flores seeks to replace the hierarchically organized cosmology (*adat*) that constitutes Lio hierarchical and holistic symbolic order and social practice with an egalitarian and individualistic Catholic dogma and practice. The call for dialogue is turning out to be little more than a matter of folklorizing Lio *adat* beliefs and practices rather than taking them seriously as contributions to religious life in general. However, on a day-to-day basis, Catholicism and *adat* engage people's imaginations according to different contexts and, as such, are not in direct conflict. Nevertheless, attempts by the Catholic priests to merge the two through the rhetoric of the Vatican policy of inculturation can be interpreted as a takeover bid. Although most Lio individuals today will say that they are Catholic, *adat* continues to constitute values, concepts of personhood, and sociality for the majority of the population.

Although, as the editors point out in the introduction, social stratification is not to be confused with the hierarchical ordering of values, I will suggest, contra Dumont, that a hierarchical conceptual schema in holistic societies may be expected to parallel a hierarchical (socially stratified) socio-political order and that the two should be examined together as part of the whole value system. This, I argue, is the case of the Lio—the conflation of the cosmological and socio-political may account for Lio resistance to abandoning *adat*. It may also explain why the much more 'loosely structured' egalitarian New Guinea societies more easily embrace Christianity at the expense of their *kastom*, or traditional culture (see Knauft 2002; Robbins 2004), for the 'Big Men' of those societies are not the product of descent lines that are legitimized in the cosmogenic past and confirmed through asymmetric alliances across generations.

Adat and Church: Two Opposed Value Systems

The Lio *adat* schema is fundamentally hierarchical and holistic, or, as Dumont would put it, the dominant value of the whole, with certain key elements, encompasses the inferior value of the individual. The dominant value of Catholic dogma is the individual. The value of the individual and individual choice is emphasized in Catholic teaching to the Lio, perhaps as a means toward undermining the authority of *adat* and the *adat* leaders. However, in doing so, the significance of sociality and of belonging is reduced. The claimed universal nature of the Church does not have the same impact on Lio imaginaries as does the lived experience of ancestors and spirits. The Trinity is a rather remote concept. One key to understanding the persistence of Lio *adat* is precisely the way in which the cosmogenic past constitutes their metaphysics as a hierarchical classification of elements, symbolic as well as social. According to this order, some categories of people (the aristocrats) are by definition superior. They are the legitimate guardians of *adat*. *Adat* is manifest in their person as well as in time, space, and place—all of which they control, or try to (Howell 2001).

This authority reveals itself most clearly at key ritual moments when the cosmogenic past collapses into the present, thereby paving the way for a future that reproduces the past and the present for the benefit of all. Such moments are enacted in the sacred spaces of the core village that embody and manifest the cosmology: the temple (*keda*), the ceremonial space in front of the temple (*kangga*), and the wooden sculptures inside the temple of the original ancestral pair, as well as a number of mythological animals and skulls of sacrificed water buffaloes. Ideologically, the core village is of ancient origin and has occupied the same site since the beginning of time. Graves of dead priest-leaders are within and on top of the *kangga*, and this is where people dance on ceremonial occasions and where they perform sacrifices. The space denotes cosmogenic times and the origin of sociality constituted through kin categories and the MBD-FZS marriage system.[4] It does not just remind them of their origins; it makes them re-enact them through words and action in complex ritual cycles. In all these respects, Catholicism fails to provide a real overall alternative. In emphasizing the dominant value of the individual and individual choice and by promoting an egalitarian ethos within the congregation, Catholic priests try to undermine the authority of the *adat* priest-leaders—and *adat* values. Even though it is decreasingly adhered to in practice, Lio prescriptive matrilateral cross-cousin marriage ideology permeates people's sense of identity and constitutes political and ritual practice. By contrast, the Church advocates free choice of marriage partners and insists on a wedding ceremony that takes place in church. While this egalitarian ethos appeals to some ambitious commoners who through descent are excluded from entering the group of priest-leaders, the Catholic religion does not emerge to most Lio as a "total social phenomenon" (Howell 2001: 149; see also Mauss [1925] 1966) and therefore, I suggest, fails to supersede *adat*.

The Indonesian policy of maintaining three separate domains of public life, that is, religion (*agama*), the state (*pemerintah*), and tradition (*adat*),[5] allows for a parallel co-existence of the domains rather than a competition between them. In principle, none is superior to any other, as each fulfills different functions (Howell 2001). Religion is intended to refer to the five monotheistic world religions—Islam, Protestantism, Catholicism, Bali Hinduism, and Buddhism—which are not hierarchically ordered. In order to obtain an identity card and derive the benefits of the modern nation-state, such as education, health services, freedom of movement, and participation in official events, every Indonesian citizen must belong to one of them, and his or her religious adherence is included on the identity card. This separates religion from the many *adat* traditions that are found throughout the nation. It also removes from religion the seemingly more mundane activities of daily life, such as earning a living or reproducing family and collective life, thus relegating religion into a separate niche. However, such a division is not in line with *adat* perceptions of many of the social groups in Indonesia. Certainly, Lio *adat* does not operate based on distinctions between the different aspects of life, and this, I suggest, is a major reason why its hold on people's existential orientation and emotions continues, and why Catholicism in the region, despite efforts by the priests, largely remains within a rather narrow niche of religion. Being Catholic is for many people a necessary requirement of modern life, but it is not constitutive of their sense of personal and social identity.

The physical layout of Lio villages further demonstrates an important difference between *adat* and the Catholic religion. While the Church and the priest's residence and offices are built of white-painted brick outside the village compound, manifesting to the village population an alien modernity that marks a distance—spatial and conceptual—between the Catholic religion and themselves, the *keda* is right in the center of the compound, surrounded by ceremonial clan houses. Built according to traditional designs and methods, and made of wood and thatched straw roofs, each clan house is headed by a priest-leader and his priest-leader wife.[6] Lio hierarchical order is expressed and realized through ancestry and the ancestral past. Everyone in the village domain belongs to one of the clans. Each priest-leader couple is responsible to the members of a clan, but for clan ritual performances, they are not of equal significance: there is a hierarchical ordering of the seven priest-leaders based on descent and marriage over time. The proven lineage through mother and father back to the inhabitants of the original village on the sacred mountain renders clan priest-leaders superior to descendants of migrants or slaves in the hierarchical ordering of relationships. Together, the clans become a category that stands for the whole society, yet there are also levels of hierarchical relations within the Lio clan order. The council of priest-leaders is headed by the 'trunk' priest-leader, whose status and role encompass the clan priest-leaders. He is the part that stands for the whole, the equivalent to the right hand that stands for the whole body (Dumont 1986: 227–233; Hertz [1907] 1960), encompassing not only the other priest-leaders, but also the rest of the community. Hierarchy becomes manifest as a model of value (as per Dumont). The 'trunk' priest-leader guards the *keda*, the ultimate living symbol of the cosmogenic past's relationship to the present, and he orchestrates the life-giving rituals that affect every Lio regardless of clan affiliation. He has final say in matters both political and religious.

This is not to suggest that the Catholic religion on Flores is not very influential. It clearly is, as today the vast majority of Lio individuals are Catholic. The question is whether Catholicism is as meaningful to its adherents as is *adat*. Here one must distinguish between those who have a vested interest in the superiority of their own domains—Catholic priests and Lio priest-leaders—and the rest of the population. Lio commoners have less to lose. They move with apparent ease between the domains according to context. What is certain is that, for the time being, most Lio manage to practice the official separation between the Catholic religion and *adat* without allocating absolute superiority to either regardless of context. Context promotes different values and activates different modes of sociality. What must be determined is whether the contexts are of equal value or if, following Dumont, a reversal of values must indicate a lower level within the whole. Bringing Dumont's ideas to bear on the philosophical question of how values relate to one another, Robbins (2013) suggests a typology of four configurations: monism, monism with stable levels, (relatively) stable pluralism, and unsettled pluralism (see also Smedal, this book). While Lio might be said to practice a version of Robbins's (relatively) stable pluralism—whereby the two ideological domains take a dominant position in particular contexts and thereby temporarily encompass their opposite at the same time, as there is no absolute hierarchical relationship between them—I nevertheless wish to suggest that *adat* ideology maintains an overall superiority. It falls more easily into the category of monism as characterized by Robbins (2013: 106), since it "does not fail to recognize values other than its paramount one, nor to assign them levels of their own, but … appears wholly to subordinate all these other values and their levels under a single paramount one." Whenever Catholicism emerges as the paramount value schema, it does so as a reversal, and its dominance is at a lower level in the overall schema (cf. Dumont [1970] 1980; 1982; 1986: 230). Sunday service, prayer meetings, and religious activities are constituted through the dominant value of the Catholic religion. During those times, its opposite, *adat*, is encompassed and relegated to an inferior position in the totality of the event, only to resume its superior position once the event is concluded. At all other times—in rituals as well as in daily practice—*adat* ontology and its associated values, being an expression of the whole, constitute a meaningful life for most Lio individuals.

Inculturation and the Catholic Church

The island of Flores is the citadel of Catholicism in Indonesia. Today, the second-largest training college of priests in the world is located on the island. Missionary activity on Flores began during the early years of the twentieth century, and the first church was built in the northern Lio region in 1926. From an early focus on the formal conversion of pagans to Catholic Christianity, foreign priests allowed people to continue those *adat* practices that were not anathema to them.[7] As a result of Vatican II (1962–1965), a new approach called inculturation has been pursued in Indonesia during the past three decades.[8] Inculturation was coined as the new term by which local ideas and practices could be integrated into the preaching and practice of Catholicism in areas still in the process of 'being converted'. Whereas previously the Church sought to teach orthodox Catholicism at the expense of *adat* values, now missionaries seek to integrate selected *adat* ideas and practices into the Catholic liturgy. This is explained as a more tolerant approach, one that shows respect for pre-Catholic beliefs and practices. Lio seminary students are encouraged to write about the concept "from the perspective of their own local cultures" (Barnes 1992: 170).

According to the document *Fourth Instruction on the Right Application of the Conciliar Constitution on the Liturgy (Nos. 37–40)*, published by the Society for the Renewal of the Sacred Liturgy (see Congregation for Divine Worship 1995: 16), "by order of his Holiness Pope John Paul II, who approved it and ordered it published," inculturation is defined as a 'double movement' whereby "[t]he Church assimilates these [non-Catholic] values, when they are compatible with the Gospel, [in order to] deepen understanding of Christ's message and give it more effective expression in the liturgy and in the many different aspects of life of the community of believers" (ibid.: 2). According to Aylward Shorter (n.d.), an advocate of inculturation: "In a true inculturation, therefore, there are no winners or losers. Inculturation means the presentation and re-expression of the Gospel in forms and terms proper to a culture. This process results in the reinterpretation of both, without being unfaithful to either. Anything less … would be a syncretism and not a synthesis."

On the face of it, inculturation could be taken to mean an open invitation for heathen cultural traditions to collaborate on equal terms. However, a close reading of relevant documents, as well as my observation of practices in Lioland, has led me to conclude that, despite the many avowals to the contrary, inculturation on Flores and elsewhere in eastern Indonesia (Barnes 1992) is largely a one-way relationship, not a dialogic one as claimed by its ideologues. Apart from some colorful but rather superficial introductions of local practices into the Church service, mainly in the form of music, songs, dances, and traditional cloths, Catholic dogma largely ignores, redefines, or replaces *adat* beliefs and practices. A hierarchical ordering of the two belief systems is undoubtedly being enacted in which the Catholic Church and its dogma are presented as superior to *adat*. Little, if anything, is being changed through the Church's relationship with Lio *adat*. A tactic employed by the Church on Flores is to folklorize the *adat* of all the ethnic groups on the island. Presenting life-giving ritual acts as charming expressions of folklore, which can be performed by schoolchildren as theatrical events, removes all profound significance from them. The message is clear: *adat* can in no way be thought of as equivalent to the Catholic Church.

To select a few palatable *adat* ideas and practices at the expense of the rest shows how Catholic priests fail to appreciate the holistic nature of Lio *adat*. Without taking into account the intellectual, moral and emotional meaning of the *keda*, as well as the sculptures and the *kangga*, none of the other Lio beliefs and practices makes any sense. Or perhaps the priests' very selection process is a tactic to disintegrate *adat* as a holistic ontology. At the same time, attempts are being increasingly made to introduce Catholic references during Lio ritual activities. I next present one such event performed by a Catholic priest in connection with an important *adat* ritual: the rebuilding of an ancient and highly venerated *keda*. I argue that the priests' action demonstrates a more aggressive missionary approach that threatens the previous tolerance shown toward *adat*. Described by the Catholic priest in question as an act of inculturation that was requested by the community (Prior, pers. comm.), it represents, I suggest, a deliberate move toward the attempted superimposition of Catholic values at the expense of *adat*. However, the reaction of most of those present demonstrates that this attempt was met with rejection.

The Rebuilding of a *Keda*

During my fieldwork in 1996, I was told by the priest-leaders of a village domain that they were planning to rebuild their *keda* the following autumn. I had to return home before that, so on my way to the airport I told an English Catholic missionary who worked at the seminary, a man with a PhD in the sociology of religion, about the plans. Since he was a researcher into Lio social and cultural life, I thought he would be interested in observing the ceremony. At the time I had not come across the ideology of inculturation. The rebuilding of a *keda* does not take place very often, but as stated above, the *keda* is the physical manifestation of Lio chief deities: Ana Kalo, the main culture hero, and the original ancestor couple. The *keda* is of central constituting importance (Howell 1986, 1996). In fact, when I first started my fieldwork among Lio in the mid-1980s, I was informed by various foreign missionaries that I should not expect to witness such a ceremony, as the *keda* had ceased to be important to the people. This turned out not to be the case. In 1986, I was able to participate in the protracted and elaborate ceremony, performed in connection with the rebuilding of a *keda* in another village domain, and I know of several more having being performed subsequently, the most recent one in 2008 (Harr 2013). Each time I return to the Lio, I become further confirmed in my belief that the *keda* and the ancestors are fundamental to the way Lio perceive themselves and that it is the associated objects and personages that render their world meaningful.

The various ritual activities that are enacted throughout the year in connection with the agricultural cycle (hunting, births, deaths, weddings) and with the rebuilding of clan houses more than demonstrate that Lio understandings about life crises and reproduction are firmly focused upon their cosmogenic past and their deities, culture heroes, ancestors, and spirits. The *keda*, as a building, as a category, and as a value (Howell 1995), epitomizes them all, being the material manifestation of Lio core values. Hence, I suggest that the Lio *keda* may be described as a total social phenomenon in a Maussian sense, by which "social phenomena are not discrete; each phenomenon contains all the threads of which the social fabric is composed. In these *total* social phenomena ... all kinds of institutions find simultaneous expression: religious, legal, moral, and economic" (Mauss [1925] 1966: 1). In other words, the *keda* and everything related to it constitute a metaphysical pivotal point, hierarchically encompassing both church and state.

Upon my return to Lioland in 2001, I found that the *keda* in question had indeed been rebuilt. It was done with all the accompanying prescribed ritualized activities that confirmed its constituting position in Lio ontology. Each punctuated event was followed by an animal sacrifice and a communal meal.[9] Such meals are eaten in a large circle on the sacred space (*kangga*) in front of the *keda*, with the priest-leaders in full regalia sitting at the end closest to the *keda* itself. Each night everyone joins in the prescribed ring dance on the *kangga* to the accompaniment of the insistent gongs and a lead singer who knows the ancient songs that describe the beginning of life on earth and the growth and spread of humankind. During this 'sacred work' of *keda* rebuilding, the whole central village area becomes taboo and may not be entered by outsiders. The climax of the proceedings is the final ceremony during which the roof is closed and the two wooden figures of the original ancestral pair are placed in their new home.

Imagine, then, my surprise when I was told that the Catholic priest whom I had informed about the event not only had attended the ceremonial activity (or at least the last part of it), but, immediately following the final sacred act of closing the roof and returning the figures of the deities, had also performed a Catholic Mass in front of the new *keda* on the *kangga*. I was shown some photographs of the temporary alter that he had constructed. Many of those present—priest-leaders and commoners alike—had reacted strongly to what they described as gross interference. Yet no one had dared to oppose it. I was told that in his sermon the Catholic priest likened the Lio chief deities (Earth and Sky) to God and the ancestors to the saints. The original couple, he said, were the same as Adam and Eve, and life on the sacred mountain Lepembusu was like the Garden of Eden. The mythic act of self-sacrifice for the benefit of humanity by the Rice Maiden (Howell 1996) was characterized as an act in the spirit of Christianity.[10] The Catholic priest seemed to have stressed features of Lio *adat* that he suggested represented overlapping notions in Lio mythology and the Bible.[11] These Lio personages, places, and events are the most sacred in Lio ontological understanding. They symbolize both the pre-social ideal existence—no illness or death, no hunger, no marriage rules, no priest-leader, in effect, a non-hierarchical state of being—and the rupture that led to the socio-symbolic hierarchical conditions of the present day. According to Lio historical discourse, after the critical event that marked the transformation, Lio people had to work hard to keep hunger at bay; illness and death became part of the order of things. From that time on, they organized themselves in lineages and houses. Marriage became governed by rules, and priest-leaders emerged as the mediators between the ancestors and deities and humans. That relationship became pivotal for survival and well-being, and it is enacted in numerous rituals. From what may be called a 'flat' ontology, that is, one with no hierarchy of values (see Howell 1985), Lio symbolic and social life turned into one that was constituted upon a coherent system of values.

Whereas most priest-leaders today have converted to Catholicism and perform its requirements in the appropriate contexts, the 'trunk' priest-leader (*mosa laki pu'u*) of the village domain and his second-in-command, the priest-leader of sacrifice (*mosa laki wela wawi*), have resisted every attempt to convert them. The transgression of boundaries between religion and *adat* performed by the Catholic priest when he sanctified the *keda* was felt to be extremely provoking. Up to this point, the *keda* and everything connected to it had, by some tacit agreement, remained outside the bounds of the Church. On this occasion, something new had taken place—namely, a clear and undisguised attempt to practice inculturation in a context that had until then been out of bounds. Moreover, it was undertaken with the Church's explicit interest and point of view in mind, not as a dialogue between equals. Interestingly, the Mass performed on this occasion did not have any repercussions with regard to *adat* practice: it was totally irrelevant.

Adat versus Church

Lio ancestors are in a very real sense part of Lio contemporary life; the people's relationship with them is integral to their moral order (Harr 2013; Howell 1986, 1992, 1995, 1996). It is my suggestion that the Lio have managed to reconcile the contradictions of modern life by successfully maintaining a clear demarcation between 'religion' (*agama*), that is, the Catholic Church, and *adat*. Each relative value is manifested in different contexts when one or the other emerges as superior. The Lio have thus accommodated the powerful outside force of the Catholic Church in appropriate contexts while at the same time maintaining the encompassing superiority of practices predicated upon the pre-Catholic ontology (Howell 2001). Interestingly, the priest who performed the Mass at the end of the inauguration of the *keda* has written about inculturation among the Lio. I did not discover this until after my return in 2001 when I tried to understand the reasoning for his action. In one of his writings, after a presentation and discussion of inculturation as a Catholic approach, he concludes that despite efforts, "[t]he incoming Church has not been instrumental in bringing about radical change in the socio-cultural values of the people despite their efforts, and that they had failed to address ... issues which have proven to be not essentially tied up with root paradigms and dominant symbolic patterning" (Prior 1988: 219). This confirms my own impression and may help explain his motive for performing the Mass.

According to the document published with the approval of the Vatican cited above, inculturation signifies "the incarnation of the Gospel in autonomous cultures and at the same time the introduction of these cultures into the life of the Church" (Congregation for Divine Worship 1995: 2). It is the second part of this intention that I wish to question. Inculturation, again according to the same document, has a long tradition in the spread of Christianity. Perhaps in order to provide legitimacy to the current policy, there is an interesting discussion of the inculturation that took place in the meeting between Judaism and Christianity and between early Christianity and Greek thought, as well as a discussion of how early Christianity borrowed and transformed beliefs and practices among the people it encountered throughout Europe (ibid.: 3). But on a closer reading of the examples provided, we find that the influence described seems to be one that moves from Christianity into other religions and cultures, with only a few concrete examples of the opposite flow. We are told that "from the beginning, the Church did not demand of converts who were uncircumcised 'anything beyond what was necessary'" (ibid.: 4), which seems to indicate a tolerance for, rather than an incorporation of, other practices not deemed necessary for the pursuit of Christianity. However, one example provided in the text demonstrates a conceptual flow in the opposite direction—from Judaism to Christianity, as the following statement shows: "[T]hey spontaneously took the forms and texts of Jewish worship and adapted them to express the radical newness of Christian worship. Under the guidance of the Holy Spirit, discernment was exercised between what could be kept and what was to be discarded of the Jewish heritage of worship" (ibid.: 5). This all took place a long time ago, when Christianity was in its infancy and in no position to lay down the law. Yet on Flores, where the Church occupies a powerful position, it is difficult to find examples of the Church having incorporated pre-Christian elements into the liturgy or the sacraments—except for some superficial elements as mentioned above. Certainly, from my observations of the relationship between the Catholic priests and the Lio people on Flores, the communication appears to be more of a monologue than a dialogue (cf. Barnes 1992).

Regardless of the emotional depth of Catholicism experienced, or not, by the individual Lio, Catholic religious activities have increased in the whole region. For example, the enactment of the Stations of the Cross at Easter, the regular confirmation of schoolchildren (a major public event), and Bible reading groups organized during the month of September—all these demonstrate how Catholic concerns are infiltrating social life. Most villages have built small praying halls (*kapella*) where (mainly) women gather on Sundays under the auspices of a schoolteacher or lay religion teacher (*guru agama*). Focused Catholic spaces, such as local shrines with statues of the Virgin, are being built and competing for attention with sacred Lio spaces. All of these activities take place within the discursive thrust of Catholicism. The *adat* discourse is not in evidence on such occasions beyond the more superficial manifestations already mentioned.

However, Catholic practices are sometimes challenged. This became clear during a performance of the Stations of the Cross at Easter. Schoolchildren and active Christian adults—teachers from the local primary school—dressed up in homemade costumes representing the disciples, Christ, the two Marys, Roman soldiers, and Pontius Pilate. The young man chosen to represent Christ experienced some kind of seizure when the cross that he was tied to was raised in front of the chapel. His parents became very upset and insisted on him being untied and taken to a senior priest-leader for an *adat* blessing. The whole event collapsed in chaos. The following morning, the boy and his parents brought a pig to the priest-leader who performed a sacrifice on the family's behalf to the ancestors, asking for their forgiveness. The event caused much concern among the rest of the villagers. Although not expressed in open critical terms, several opined that Lio people should not impersonate Christian deities and historical figures. Lio ancestors become offended and angry, I was told, and who knows how widespread the repercussions of their anger would be. The local Catholic priests chose to ignore the event.

Catholic priests introduce values derived from a Western human rights discourse that affect issues of both class and gender. In Lio value schema, women and children rank lower than men, male priest-leaders rank higher than male commoners, and children rank lower than adults. The priests are fully aware of this when they encourage commoners, girls, and women to participate publicly in Church affairs and thus challenge the *adat* hierarchy of values. On such occasions, Lio ritual practices are decontextualized and introduced into Church events as sideshows. When schoolchildren are dressed in the regalia of priest-leaders and perform traditional *adat* dances inside the church, this can only be interpreted as a direct attempt to undermine Lio cosmology and the priest-leaders' authority. Powerless to prevent this, the priest-leaders grumble among themselves.

Many individual Lio are able to navigate the two separate categories of religion and *adat*. One old and senior priest-leader I know well is also a schoolteacher and a Catholic. Early missionary Catholic policy was to remove young sons of important priest-leaders from their families and bring them up at missionary boarding schools in the colonial centers on the island. Here they were raised as Christians, and no reference was made to the cultural values and practices that they had left behind before they had time to learn them. The idea was that when they returned home as young converted and educated adults, they would abhor the pagan practices that they would observe and would persuade their parents and family to convert. Once influential individuals had converted, the population would follow suit, it was assumed. This policy, which was only partially successful, is what this priest-leader and schoolteacher has experienced. He handles the two traditions with seeming ease. He is very knowledgeable about Lio precepts and practices—their *adat*—and he takes his various *adat* duties very seriously. He is also a practicing Catholic. As a teacher, he has to go to church every Sunday, and his household is central in the observation of various Catholic calendric feast days, as well as those where Christianity constitutes the meaning of the occasion. He also participates actively in the forums where *adat* matters are in focus, when *adat* forms the mode of sociality. Having lived in his household for long periods of time and having observed his actions, I am in no doubt about where his prime allegiance lies. As a practicing senior priest-leader, his respect for his ancestors and for the metaphysical significance of cosmogenic times and the values and practices that spring out of this inform his personal value mode.

Undoubtedly, the Church has been successful in spreading Christianity among the population. The Church's power base on Flores was established during colonial times and was perceived by the local populations as indistinguishable from Dutch political and economic suzerainty. This aura of authority persists. The Church's success is also attributable, I suggest, to a policy of tolerating and defusing, rather than outright forbidding, pre-Catholic values and practices. By dislocating several *adat* customs and ideas from their usual contexts and putting them into a new context of Church and Christianity, *adat* was subsumed into the Church in an attempt to reorient values. However, this was done under the guise of mutuality and dialogue. "The liturgy, like the Gospel, must respect cultures," the Vatican document admonishes, "but at the same time invite them to purify and sanctify themselves" (Congregation for Divine Worship 1995: 24). This, I suggest, does not leave much room for an equal 'double movement'. Rather, in the process, Lio values are shed of their original ontological, moral, and epistemological significance and rendered harmless as objects or practices of folklore. An example of this is *wogé*, a spirited dance performed in front of the *keda* by the 'trunk' priest-leader on occasions of war (in pre-colonial times) or of life-threatening or life-enhancing events. Through this vigorous dance, the priest-leader demonstrates his personal power, which is derived from the ancestors. It is a highly charged moment when he leaps onto the *kangga* brandishing his sacred spear. To encourage schoolchildren to perform *wogé*, which is done on folklore occasions when outside dignitaries arrive, is to deny its sacred significance and potentially to render priest-leaders' religious-political power impotent. The Catholic Mass performed on the occasion of the inauguration of the new *keda* came in the immediate wake of the 'trunk' priest-leader's performance of *wogé*. I can only guess at the reactions to this in the Lio audience. Some commoners were probably rather pleased at this blatant bid for final superiority of Christianity in the face of *adat*, whereas the aristocrats and many others reacted negatively to this attempt to subsume *adat* and, in terms of Dumont, place it at a lower level in the overall Catholic value schema.

Despite efforts to emasculate *adat*, much *adat* practice retains its vitality. The continued rebuilding of *keda* and clan houses bears witness to this, as do the complex ritual activities performed in connection with planting and harvesting. Attempts at instigating thanksgiving festivals in churches following harvesting have met with minimal success. So far, at any rate, most Lio farmers do not attribute a good (or bad) harvest to God or Christ or the Virgin Mary, but rather to the quality of their relationship with the ancestral spirits. Goodwill is achieved by the ministering of the priest-leaders during the year and especially at the planting and harvesting rituals. Not surprisingly, there is little enthusiasm for bringing samples of the harvest into the church in order to participate in a thanksgiving service.

Some Thoughts about the Future

There is little to indicate any genuine desire among Catholic priests to learn something profoundly new from Lio traditions. As more and more Indonesian men become ordained, and as Church policy continues to send priests to areas far away from their own localities of birth and family, several important consequences follow. Indonesian priests have no reason to take an interest in the religious beliefs and practices (*adat*) of the unknown communities among whom they live and work. They do not speak the local language and have no connection with the local people except that which pertains to the relationship of priest and parishioners. In my experience, Indonesian priests in Lioland know very little about Lio *adat* and are even less interested in it. The folkloristic manifestations of *adat* on Church occasions are usually as far as it goes. It is possible that, with the demise of foreign missionaries, future attempts at a relatively tolerant inculturation will decline, and we will instead witness a move toward acculturation, encouraged by efforts to ensure the final superiority of Catholic dogma.

Catholic priests in the Keo region on the south coast of Flores are seemingly willing to engage more dynamically with local *adat*. According to Philipus Tule (2001: 260), a Keo Catholic priest with a PhD in social anthropology, during the so-called inculturative Mass, Catholic priests wear vestments inspired by the dress of the Keo priest-leaders and tie the traditional headcloth (*desu*) around their heads. Tule further describes how the priests will place a crucifix on the sacrificial pole and old graves of priest-leaders in order to "show respect to ancestors who were not yet Catholic" (ibid.: 265). The apparent validation of *adat* as seen in Keo ritual practices is at best, I suggest, nothing but a temporary reversal of levels of value (cf. Dumont 1979): *adat* is being given prominence for a moment or so before being relegated once again to an inferior position compared to the superiority of the Church. It is difficult not to interpret this as a more deliberate strategy compared to that observed in Lioland—that is, not to collapse *adat* and Catholicism into one, but ultimately to ensure the superiority of the latter. This is especially manifest in the placing of the crucifix on the two paramount symbolic spaces of *adat*: the sacrificial pole and the graves.

Sensitive to challenges arising out of criticism of single-mindedly imposing its creed and values upon non-believers in non-Christian parts of the world, the Catholic Church developed its policy of inculturation. However, it seems that this policy is difficult to implement in parts of Indonesia. When Pope Paul II spoke to a delegation of Indonesian bishops in Rome in March 2003, he demonstrated his, to my mind, failure to appreciate how Catholicism has emerged as superior in his definition of inculturation, supposedly intended as a program for mutuality. He said: "[E]vangelization goes hand in hand with the profound, gradual and exacting work of inculturation. The truth of the Gospel should always be proclaimed in a way that is persuasive and relevant."[12] How can one interpret such a statement in any other way than a command to use whatever means are available to bring the Catholic truth home? There is little that indicates any genuine desire to learn something new from other religious traditions. That the Church has used, and continues to use, any and all means to enhance the proselytizing imperative is not, in the nature of that activity, surprising. Whether inculturation as a strategy may be characterized as qualitatively different from earlier proselytizing, however, remains an open question. So far, the indications are that Catholic priests are seeking to override *adat* in all important contexts.

At the same time, as Catholic practices appear to be on the increase, a revival of many Lio rituals have been observed following the devolution policy in Indonesia since the year 2000 (Harr, pers. comm.). This is especially noticeable in local politics. Candidates for election to public office legitimize their claims to authority within a discourse of *adat*, stressing an (often fictive) aristocratic descent, and perform *adat* rituals at important political gatherings, indicating a felt need to merge in some way the demands of state and *adat*.

In Conclusion

In this chapter I have treated hierarchy both as a value schema expressed through relations of asymmetry and as a mode of social organization. Although I use Dumont as a springboard for my analysis, I am not indiscriminately following all his propositions. I have chosen to extend the notion of hierarchy from an abstract ordering of elements of value into the social-political realm of stratification and to use it as a conceptual tool to interpret the relationship between *adat* and the Catholic Church. Having said that, Lio social life may usefully be analyzed in terms of Dumont's concepts of holism, by which the Lio social whole is predicated upon its pre-Catholic ideology and practices— *adat*. I contrast this to Catholicism, which has become the main global religion in the area and which may be analyzed as an example of individualistic ideology in which the value of the individual subordinates that of the social whole (Dumont 1986: 279).[13] In my analysis of the Lio, I have argued that hierarchical relations must be understood to order both abstract and social relations, and that one without the other would not add up to hierarchy as either a relational form or as a model of value. As far as the Lio are concerned, it is this (i.e., *adat*) that promotes the 'social good' (see the introduction to this volume). This may be contrasted to those socio-symbolic modes where equality is the dominant value and constitutes the ordering principle of elements, such as the Catholic Church's stress on the superior value of the individual.[14]

Priest-leaders' authority is framed within a discourse of cosmic kinship: the patrilineal descent groups, the asymmetric marriage system, the named clan houses associated with them, the *keda*, and the *kangga* sacred central space.

As a category, priest-leaders encompass those who can make no such claims. They stand for the whole society. At moments of communication with ancestors and spirits, the priest-leaders themselves become infused with the ancestral spirit, manifesting a temporal collapse between past and present. From my observations, I can find no evidence that suggests that the Catholic Church and Catholic priests are understood in a similar manner. Catholicism has not, so far at any rate, got under the skin, as it were, of the majority of the Lio population. Despite the many efforts of inculturation to incorporate Lio concepts and practices into Catholic ones, people do not draw their cosmological, ontological, or ethical references from Christianity, but from the hierarchal classification of their own world.

Acknowledgments

I am grateful to the editors for including me in this project and for the pertinent comments made to an earlier version of the chapter. I also want to take this opportunity to thank those at ERASME (Equipe de Recherche d'Anthropologie Sociale: Morphologie, Echanges) of the Ecole des Hautes Etudes en Sciences Sociale, Paris. Under the leadership of the late Daniel de Coppet, they included me in their intense discussions about hierarchy and the analysis of empirical findings. As a newly qualified DPhil, I was overwhelmed by their engagement and grateful for the opportunity to enter their theoretical world. My current chapter may not satisfy them, but it could not have been written without the time I spent with them.

Signe Howell is Professor Emeritus of Social Anthropology at the University of Oslo. Her fieldwork with the northern Lio on the island of Flores, Indonesia, began in 1984. Her focus has been on the significance of the cosmogenic past in the constitution of social, political, and religious life. Her many articles on the Lio include "Of Persons and Things: Exchange and Valuables among the Lio of Eastern Indonesia" (*Man*, 1986) and "Nesting, Eclipsing, and Hierarchy: Processes of Gendered Values among Lio" (*Social Anthropology*, 2002). She is the editor of *For the Sake of Our Future: Sacrificing in Eastern Indonesia* (1996). Other publications include *The Kinning of Foreigners: Transnational Adoption in a Global Perspective* (2006) and *Society and Cosmos: Chewong of Peninsular Malaysia* (1989). She has edited *Returns to the Field: Multitemporal Research and Contemporary Anthropology* (2013, with Aud Talle).

Notes

1. My fieldwork with the northern Lio, who live in the highlands of central Flores in eastern Indonesia, began in 1984. Subsequent field research was undertaken in 1986, 1989, 1993, 1996, and 2001.
2. The tribute consists of one bottle of palm arak, one chicken, and one small basket of millet. It does not represent wealth to the receiver or any hardship to the giver.
3. My use of 'ideology' follows Dumont (1986) to mean a set of ideas and values that are common in a society.
4. This MBD (mother's brother's daughter) and FZS (father's sister's son) system constitutes a matrilateral cross-cousin marriage alliance.
5. Present-day Indonesia is a country made up of several hundred islands whose inhabitants speak more than 600 languages. The independent Indonesian state continued a colonial policy of enforcing conformity under the slogan "Unity in Diversity." One of its demands was that all citizens must adhere to one of the five monotheistic world religions: Islam, Catholicism, Protestantism, Bali Hinduism, or Buddhism. A tripartite division of socio-political life was adopted whose intention was to introduce new institutions based on a modern, globally applicable understanding of the categories of 'religion' and 'government' at the same time that a continuation of a previous lifestyle, officially entitled 'tradition' (i.e., *adat*), was allowed to continue.
6. Ideally, there are seven houses and seven clans, but often there are fewer. The council of priest-leaders is always made up of seven men, each with his own name and role. Each has a wife, and if she is of the correct kin status (MBD from the same lineage over generations), she will also have the status of priest-leader and will perform the female priest-leaders' tasks during ritual occasions.
7. Those practices that were forbidden early on included so-called cousin marriages, arranged marriages, bride wealth (*belis*), and polygamy. It was thought important to perform marriage ceremonies in the church. In fact, controlling marriage seems to have been regarded, even up to the present, as more important than performing baptism and funeral service (Pater Smeets, pers. comm.). Human sacrifice, exposing the dead body of a priest-leader inside the clan house, and other 'primitive' ritual practices were also forbidden.
8. The first seminar on inculturation in Indonesia took place in Yogyakarta, Java, in 1983 (Shorter 1988: 10).
9. On the occasion of the rebuilding of a *keda*, all who descend from one of the village clans must attend. Culturally speaking, it is the most important of all events. Participants must contribute with sacrificial animals, rice, and palm wine for offerings and for communal meals. Today, many junior priest-leaders or senior clan members have migrated to the regional capital or farther afield. Nevertheless, they return for such an occasion.
10. On other occasions, the Rice Maiden may be conceptually collapsed with the Virgin Mary.
11. These are common Catholic representations.
12. See the English transcript of this address at http://www.ewtn.com/library/papaldoc/jp2indon.htm.
13. It is not controversial to say that by introducing the notion of value, hierarchy is automatically invoked. The contention that hierarchy itself—in the sense of an ordering principle of elements according to a set of asymmetrical oppositions—is conceptually linked to the whole of a social order has provoked debate. This is especially so when Dumont (1982: 221) denies "the modern tendency to confuse hierarchy with power."

14. An even more stark example is the Chewong of Peninsular Malaysia. I have argued that there, contra Dumont, equality and recognition, or symmetrically ordered pairs, constitute Chewong cosmology as well as Chewong social order (Howell 1995).

References

Barnes, R. H. 1992. "A Catholic Mission and the Purification of Culture: Experiences in an Indonesian Community." *Journal of the Anthropological Society of Oxford* 23 (2): 169–180.

Congregation for Divine Worship and the Discipline of the Sacraments. 1995. "Inculturation and the Toman Liturgy." *Adoremus Bulletin*, 29 March.

Dumont, Louis. (1970) 1980. *Homo Hierarchicus: The Caste System and Its Implications.* Rev. ed. Chicago: University of Chicago Press.

Dumont, Louis. 1979. "The Anthropological Community and Ideology." *Social Science Information* 18 (6): 785–817.

Dumont, Louis. 1982. "On Value." *Proceedings of the British Academy* 66: 207–241.

Dumont, Louis. 1986. *Essays on Individualism: Modern Ideology in Anthropological Perspective.* Chicago: University of Chicago Press.

Graeber, David. 2001. *Toward an Anthropological Theory of Value: The False Coin of Our Own Dreams.* New York: Palgrave.

Harr, David. 2013. "Suspicious Minds: Problems of Cooperation in a Lio Ceremonial Council." *Language & Communication* 33 (3): 317–325.

Hertz, Robert. (1907) 1960. *Death and the Right Hand.* Trans. Rodney Needham and Claudia Needham. London: Cohen & West.

Howell, Signe. 1985. "Equality and Hierarchy in Chewong Classification." In *Contexts and Levels: Anthropological Essays on Hierarchy,* JASO Occasional Papers No. 4, ed. R. H. Barnes, Daniel de Coppet, and R. J. Parkin, 167–180. Oxford: JASO.

Howell, Signe. 1986. "Of Persons and Things: Exchange and Valuables among the Lio of Eastern Indonesia" *Man* (n.s.) 24: 419–438.

Howell, Signe. 1992. "Access to the Ancestors: Reconstructions of the Past in Non-literate Society." In *The Ecology of Choice and Symbol: Essays in Honour of Fredrik Barth,* ed. Reidar Grønhaug, Gunnar Haaland, and Georg Henriksen, 225–243. Bergen: Alma Mater.

Howell, Signe. 1995. "The Lio House: Building, Category, Idea, Value." In *About the House: Lévi-Strauss and Beyond,* ed. Janet Carsten and Stephen Hugh-Jones, 149–169. Cambridge: Cambridge University Press.

Howell, Signe. 1996. "A Life for 'Life'? Blood and Other Life-Promoting Substances in Lio Moral System." In *For the Sake of Our Future: Sacrificing in Eastern Indonesia,* ed. Signe Howell, 92–109. Leiden: Research School CNWS.

Howell, Signe. 2001. "Creative Responses to Alien Forces: 'Religion', 'Government', and 'Tradition' as Co-existing Modes of Sociality among the Northern Lio of Indonesia." In *Locating Cultural Creativity,* ed. John Liep, 144–158. London: Pluto Press.

Knauft, Bruce M. 2002. *Exchanging the Past: A Rainforest World of Before and After.* Chicago: University of Chicago Press.

Mauss, Marcel. (1925) 1966. *The Gift.* London: Routledge & Kegan Paul.

Prior, John M. 1988. *Church and Marriage in an Indonesian Village: A Study of Customary and Church Marriage among the Ata Lio of Central Flores, Indonesia as a*

Paradigm of the Ecclesiastical Interrelationship between Village and Institutional Catholicism. Frankfurt am Main: Peter Lang.

Rio, Knut, and Olaf H. Smedal, eds. 2009. *Hierarchy: Persistence and Transformation in Social Formations*. New York: Berghahn Books.

Robbins, Joel. 2004. *Becoming Sinners: Christianity and Moral Torment in a Papua New Guinea Society*. Berkeley: California University Press.

Robbins, Joel. 2009. "Conversion, Hierarchy, and Cultural Change: Value and Syncretism in the Globalization of Pentecostal and Charismatic Christianity." In Rio and Smedal 2009, 65–88.

Robbins, Joel. 2013. "Monism, Pluralism and the Structure of Value Relations: A Dumontian Contribution to the Contemporary Study of Value." *HAU: Journal of Ethnographic Theory* 3 (1): 99–115.

Shorter, Aylward. 1988. *Toward a Theology of Inculturation*. Maryknoll, NY: Orbis Books.

Shorter, Aylward. n.d. "Inculturation of African Traditional Religious Values in Christianity—How Far?" http://www.afrikaworld.net/afrel/shorter.htm (accessed 12 May 2005).

Tule, Philipus. 2001. "Longing for the House of God, Dwelling in the House of the Ancestors: Local Belief, Christianity, and Islam among the Kéo of Central Flores." PhD diss., Australian National University.

Chapter 2

VERTICAL LOVE
Forms of Submission and Top-Down Power in Orthodox Ethiopia

Diego Maria Malara and Tom Boylston

Ethiopian Orthodox Christians consider top-down power a fact of life. In religious, political, and domestic spheres (and in the articulations and overlaps between them), showing proper deference to power is a critical social skill, alongside learning to manipulate one's connections and social resources in order, if not to become powerful oneself, at least to obtain the protections and benefits that power properly executed can offer. Whether this asymmetrical, top-down model of the workings of power is best described as a 'value', however, is a more complex question. This chapter looks to trace ambiguities between understandings of top-down power as a moral good and as a coercive force in contemporary Ethiopian Orthodox society. Is top-down power understood as a value in the sense of being a good and proper way to organize society, or is it simply seen as something that people desire, whether it is moral or not to do so? Sometimes it seems that top-down power is treated as a virtue, while at other times people describe the overwhelmingly vertical nature of their social relationships as an injustice and an imposition. This is because

Notes for this chapter begin on page 56.

relations of love and exploitation alike are understood as basically unequal. We will suggest that the exercise of top-down power in Ethiopia co-exists with and depends upon asymmetrical or hierarchical understandings of love and mediation, exemplified by relationships between saints and people, between parents and children, and ultimately between God and humanity.

In Ethiopia as elsewhere, moral authority and coercive power often feed into one another so as to become indistinct. This apparent contradiction is to be found at the root of Ethiopian Orthodox Christian popular theology. Archetypally, the power of God is that of both ultimate coercion and ultimate moral recognition. The proper attitude of humans toward God is loving fear: to love God in spite of or because of His total power over them. God's choices cannot and should not be questioned by human subjects, nor are they appropriate objects of individual or public moral scrutiny. Divine will is ultimately placed beyond the possibility of human comprehension. The negative value attributed to excessive speculation about the divine based on its immanent manifestation—an attitude that "verges on blasphemy" (Levine 1965: 67)—reinforces the hierarchical distance between the Creator and His creations. The marker of hierarchy is not just that you must obey your superiors, but that you must not question them: hierarchical relations are defined by silence. Loving God beyond understanding and questioning in spite of—or because of—His power over humanity may describe the core paradox of power in Orthodox Ethiopia. This paradox is central to forms of submission and attitudes toward legitimate power in different social arenas.

We have found that the play of power and legitimate authority that is typical of hierarchy cannot be described solely in terms of the organizing values understood per Dumont ([1980] 2013: 290) as culturally specific notions of the good. Instead, we have to pay attention to how people actually live with those principles. This may involve competing values (Robbins 2007; Weber 1949) or simply pragmatic ways in which people negotiate with the power of others. It is one thing to describe the values on which a society supposes itself to be based, and quite another to ask whether and how those values hold up in practice and who, exactly, considers them as values rather than impositions. In other words, it is not enough to describe the logic, or even competing logics, of hierarchy. It may well be possible and correct to describe Ethiopian Orthodox society, like Dumont's India, in terms of 'encompassing values' such as submission to divine will and 'consequent values' such as patriarchal authority. But such a description is incomplete unless it can also convey the paradoxes of living in asymmetric relations, where power and legitimacy are constantly morphing into one another. By shifting attention to the ethnographic practicalities of how people live with, manage, build, sustain, and change asymmetric relationships in their religious and family lives and in negotiation with a dominant value system, we hope to produce a fuller picture of the power-value relationship. Most significantly, this is the scale at which requirements of love and care come to the fore.

This chapter is based on ethnographic research by Malara in Addis Ababa and Bahir Dar and by Boylston on the Zege peninsula in semi-rural Amhara region and later in Addis Ababa. We have both worked on Orthodox Christianity, a deeply hierarchical religion, and its place in everyday life. This chapter comes out of our conversations about the contemporary relevance of the classic sociological literature on Amhara hierarchy (e.g., Hoben 1970, 1973; Messay 1999; Levine 1965; Molvaer 1995). Amhara social relations in the imperial era tended to be described in terms of hierarchical dominance, both internally and with regard to other groups in Ethiopia (Donham 1986; Weissleder 1965), and we perceived important continuities of these patterns in the contemporary Federal Democratic Republic of Ethiopia. But we also felt that the classical image of Amhara Christian hierarchy, dominance, and individualism needed to be updated and qualified. While we show that unequal relationships remain central to Ethiopian Orthodox understandings of how social life works, we argue that these relations include strong idioms of protection and care that cannot be reduced to power or wholly separated from it.

Hierarchy and Love

We begin by suggesting that the best perspective from which to understand hierarchy and love is neither holism nor methodological individualism but somewhere in between: in the making of relationships and in the exemplary models and social resources that are available to people in building relationships. The scholarly consensus on Amhara society suggests that most models of social relationships are vertical—that is, involving asymmetries of power and/or status (Teferi 2012; Messay 1999; Levine 1965). In kinship and in religion, it is at this level of relationship formation that the dynamics of normative asymmetric sociality are most apparent. Chief among these dynamics is a profound ambiguity between relations of love, care, and protection and those of power and domination. Most scholars of Ethiopia have overlooked dimensions of sociality and relatedness marked by practices and idioms of care, which are in fact regarded as expressions of socio-religious moral injunctions of the utmost importance (but see Hannig 2014). In focusing only on power, and particularly on its patently coercive aspects, much of the scholarly literature on northern Ethiopia misses a key component of the workings of asymmetry and hierarchy.

The classical position is presented by Messay Kebede (1999: 203) as follows:

[T]he modern meaning of equality before the law is not what Ethiopians have in mind when they speak of justice. In fact, the high respect for social hierarchy empties justice of the notion of equality. Nonetheless, the ranking of justice above all the other virtues may mean that it contains them all ... The riddle is solved if the whole thinking is referred to clientelism. God is expected to be just in the sense of rewarding those who obey and worship Him ... Rewards should be bestowed on them, not for their merits, but for their submission, for their acceptance of the role of God's servants. Divine justice does not therefore implicate equal treatment; rather, it leans toward favoritism, especially for those chosen by God Himself.

Messay locates the moral justification for inequality in the Ethiopian social theology of clientelism—a sort of contingent delegation of divine authority. This produces what he calls the 'fluctuating hierarchy', whereby individuals constantly rise and fall in status depending on achievement and imperial or divine whim, but the principle of social asymmetry endures. In contrast to Dumont's (1970) painstaking, contested efforts to show that power and value are separate in the traditional Indian case, here coercive power is presented as proceeding directly from the source of moral value. Submission to power would therefore be the same thing as submission to legitimate authority.

This is a useful picture, so far as it goes. It captures dynamic, competitive elements of hierarchy that have survived the collapse of the Orthodox Ethiopian Empire and still inform a great deal of social action today—as our ethnographic examples will demonstrate. However, the resulting portrayal of an entirely atomized society based on favor-grubbing and ambition is far more individualistic than the reality on the ground, in which a recognition of human selfishness and the realities of power co-exists with a deep-seated ethic of mutual care and neighborliness.

We do not wish to oppose a vertical notion of power to one of horizontal or egalitarian love. On the contrary, we argue that the forms of love and care that are emphasized in Orthodox Ethiopia are themselves largely asymmetrical, and that the local character of coercive power is therefore hard to separate from relations of love and care. Nor is such separation necessarily something that people want.

Anthropologists and historians have paid some attention to the politics of love, usually but not always choosing to focus on romantic love and its relation to prescriptive models of kinship (Abu-Lughod 1986: 208; Gell 2011) or on the Western-capitalist-Christian cultural development of the romantic love complex (Macfarlane 1987; Reddy 2012). The project of recognizing love's politics involves recognizing that love and care are not confined to private or domestic life but rather have broad legal, political, and religious ramifications. In contemporary Euro-American discourse, this becomes clearest in debates over gay marriage and adoption, in which apparently personal and private relations are made the concern of the whole society. It is in this context that Borneman (1997) has shown the degree of continuity between romantic-sexual relations and those of 'caring and being cared for', which, he argues, should be considered a basic premise of sociality. Borneman calls for "a shift in the object of anthropological research … away from either the institution of marriage or categories of kinship, sexual identities, gender inequality, or of power differentials generally, to a concern for the actual situations in which people experience the need to care and be cared for and to the political economies of their distribution" (ibid.: 583). Note that this introduces an element of benign asymmetry as constitutive of the politics of love.

This asymmetry is present in the Western Christian tradition and its universalization of *agape* as the love of God for all humankind. As Mayblin (2012: 249) writes, *agape* is for Catholics not just a way of relating, but the foundation of the possibility of relationships. It is also fundamentally asymmetric because it can never be reciprocated. The same is true of the love of mothers for their children, which is freely and unconditionally given. In Ethiopian Orthodoxy, as in Catholicism, Mary is the key figure of this love: her absence is unimaginable within this cosmology. Ethiopian Orthodox discourse refers to Mary as *yefik'ir innat* (the Mother of Love).[1] This is a love that equates to the giving of life, which is construed as the ultimate in disinterested, non-reciprocal giving. This love, Mayblin argues, is ontological in its scope (as a theory of existence) and roots a fundamental, nurturing asymmetry at the heart of Catholic tradition (ibid.).

Meanwhile, many have also found in Christianity the roots of the contemporary elevation of sexual love, perhaps precisely because of its distinction from *agape* (Reddy 2012; but see Macfarlane 1987). It quickly becomes apparent that Christian love is polymorphous and malleable in a great variety of political-economic contexts—from the imperial liberal individualism of the globalizing Euro-American mainstream (Povinelli 2006) to a paternalistic Catholic charity that, while quite different in its form and inspiration, is equally compatible with neo-liberalism (Muehlebach 2013). Schneider (1990) finds in Christian history the destruction of pre-existing 'equity consciousness'. While she also acknowledges the egalitarian potential of Christian love, she argues that Christianity's hierarchical charter has been the dominant factor in practice.

This literature makes it clear that love—especially in the Christian tradition, which has made love more of an obsession than in any other faith—is not necessarily an egalitarian force. Nor is it necessarily a relation that creates unity out of difference, as Hardt (2011: 678) argues:

> [A] political concept of love … would have to extend across social scales and create bonds that are at once intimate and social, destroying conventional divisions between public and private. Second, it would have to operate in a field of multiplicity and function through not unification but the encounter and interaction of differences. Finally, a political love must transform us, that is, it must designate a becoming such that in love, in our encounter with others we constantly become different.

This is distinct, Hardt says, from the Hollywood love story in which we are all searching for the person who will complete us and make us whole. Equally, it differs from the love of nation or race. These are loves of sameness and contribute to reactionary parochialism or xenophobia. In Ethiopian Orthodox Christianity, we can find some forms of the love of sameness as a unifying force, such as a fierce allegiance to one's church. But there is also, and inseparably, a constant reproduction of relations of difference between God, saints, and humans, that is, between protectors and faithful followers. This is not the non-hierarchical difference-in-love that Hardt envisages, but it needs to be acknowledged.

Cole and Thomas's (2009) volume *Love in Africa* aims for a similar politicization and deprivatization of the love concept. It maintains that the province of love is not just 'intimacy' and that intimacy and love are deeply implicated in a field of wider politico-economic forces, colonial legacies, and media representations. Megan Vaughan (2011) argues that the political nature of love in Africa is probably not so much a colonial phenomenon or a European import but rather a fairly universal aspect of the human condition. It is the notion of a love that transcends politics or personal interest that looks like a specific and unusual invention of the European Christian tradition.

The Euro-American romantic love tradition may portray love as basically a dyadic relationship between individuals (Gell 2011; Reddy 2012), but it is just as likely to describe an attachment between people and the collectivities they belong to—their church, their nation, or all of humanity (Muehlebach 2013). The love of a group or institution in which the individual is subsumed can create its own often highly asymmetrical collectives. This in turn raises the question of how love relates to power. In Orthodox Christian parts of Ethiopia, where the emotional and political attachment of Christians to the hierarchy of their church and its saints has only intensified since the secularization of the state (Bonacci 2000; Clapham 1988; Donham 1999), and where many are questioning the applicability of Euro-American egalitarian individualistic models (Girma 2012), these questions have particular political urgency.

Love, Power, and Religion

According to Messay (1999: 184), Ethiopian Orthodox theories of the morality of power derive from a sort of transcendental clientelism:

> [T]he conception of the Ethiopians derived the glory of power from its metaphysical stature. Power is not a mere phenomenon of the world; it binds the created world to the Creator and determines its fate. It is therefore the most visible manifestation of the will of God, its favored language. Accordingly, those who have power in this world appear as those to whom God lends power. So conceived, power in this world denotes divine favoritism; it is a distinction from the common people, a sign of election. This belief tied every Ethiopian more to God than to his/her superior."

In this account, not only does divine hierarchy legitimize worldly political power, but worldly power is a manifestation and an index of divine power. Equally important, power and status may be withdrawn as easily as they are given, and the loyalty of one's clients should be expected to readily switch to the new recipient of God's favor—whom they would know precisely by the fact of his obtaining power.

Messay (1999: 155, 203) puts power at the center of a moral value system built around submission to God, establishing power as a good in itself—provided that the powerful demonstrate sufficient generosity toward their subordinates. One submits to God because one loves God, or because it is good to do so (depending on whom you ask and what phrasing they choose). The same goes for saints and especially Mary. New Orthodox hymns are full of expressions of love for Christ, Mary, and the Archangel Michael, using both the passionate (*fik'ir*) and the tender or friendly (*meweded*) terms that can translate into English as 'love'. Take the following recent composition by Zemari Kibrom Marse:[2]

Mary, Mary, let me say to you,
My mother, let me say to you
My heart has been cured by your love [*fik'ir*]
Because your plea (on my behalf) has sustained me
I stood at your gate begging
Having faith in your motherhood
My wish was fulfilled
My heart has been filled with your love

There is much that is non-traditional in this hymn, especially the use of Amharic and its circulation on YouTube and on visual CDs. Traditional hymns use more figurative language but still talk about the love between the people, Mary, and God (Lee 2011: 225). This modern example calls on archetypal themes of human helplessness, Mary's intercession, and the fact that she does this out of love. Mary's efficacy as a loving protector is acknowledged and ratified by passionate statements of gratitude, submission, and loyalty made by the human supplicant. What is also implicitly acknowledged is that the boundlessness and perfection of Mary's love from above can never be fully reciprocated by the human party. Even though the language deployed is that of intimacy, this asymmetrical giving reinforces the hierarchical separation between the role of generous patron and that of helpless supplicant and debtor. Love, again, separates and differentiates while bringing closer.

This intercessional, healing model of love helps to establish the grounds for the model of justice that Messay (1999) describes, one based on loyal submission and generous rewards. In a discussion of why liberal models have failed in Ethiopia, Girma Mohammed (2012) makes a similar point when he describes Ethiopian thought across all religious groups as characterized by 'covenant thinking': a patron-client bond based on a foundational promise, which is integral to pan-Ethiopian notions of the good (Robbins 2013). According to Kaplan (1986: 10), this pattern is attested to throughout Orthodox hagiographic literature by the relationship between saints and devotees: "The image of the saint which emerges from the texts is not that of a pious pillar of morality and protector of the unfortunate, but rather of a powerful patron and jealous lord. The saint is celebrated not for his beneficent intervention in the affairs of mankind, but rather for the obvious favoritism he demonstrates towards those who are devoted to him." This favoritism has explicit analogues in contemporary political life. As one formerly politically active friend of Malara's describes it, rewards are achieved only with and through the long-term display of loyalty and submission. As this becomes established, the follower can expect rewards and favoritism of the kind described by Kaplan and Messay.[3]

In practice it is not so easy to differentiate between power that rewards its subjects justly and power that does not. For most Ethiopians, vertical power in daily life is an unfortunate fact of existence that must be lived with, rather than a moral model for society. The practical question then becomes how to engage with power (divine, political, or parental) so as to manage its excesses, gain advantage, or address the requirements to care and be cared for that constitute so much of everyday life.

Mediation and Hierarchy

In a society where religious and political relations between radically unequal parties are emphasized, the role of mediators is critical. Go-betweens can sometimes protect the weak from the powerful or make appeals on their behalf, so that relations are possible without turning into outright domination. In the Orthodox economy of salvation, saints, angels, and especially Mary have special importance as advocates. Part of the purpose of venerating a saint is so that when you are called to judgment, the saint will speak on your behalf. Saints can do so because they are closer to and more beloved of God than humans are, as Malara's fieldwork demonstrates. The logic of saintly mediating agency was explained by Belaynesh, a woman living in the capital, with the following example: "Who do you love more, me or your mother? You love your mother more. So if I am not very close to you, I will talk to your mother and ask her to beg you to do what I want from you. And you will do it because of the love that you have for your mother." Saintly mediation works the same way: saints are close to God and therefore can intercede with Him on others' behalf.

This is the logic of clientelism. Attaining favor from power is the outcome of fealty and submission; it is not simply due to moral righteousness on the part of the recipient. A classic illustration of the precedence of loyalty over righteousness can be found in the famous tale of the cannibal Belay Seb. Belay killed and ate his parents and almost every other person he ever met. The combination of patri/matricide and cannibalism makes him a paragon of evil. The exception was one leprous beggar who was begging by the roadside for water in the name of Mary. Belay, hearing the name, took pity and gave the beggar a single handful of water. Illustrations of the story in churches across Ethiopia depict Saint Michael weighing the murdered people against the single handful of water. In the panel, Mary can be seen casting her shadow over the side of the scale containing the water, causing it to outweigh the murdered people. And so, by having answered one request in the name of Mary, Belay is saved. This is a parable of Mary's love, but also of her efficacy as an advocate and of the 'weight' of her favor in the economy of salvation and mercy.

Thus, the advocacy of a good mediator (*amalaj*) can obtain mercy and protection for even the most heinous transgressions. When asked to differentiate Orthodoxy from Protestant 'heresy' (*menafík*), priests in Zege consistently say that mediation is the key point. In the Orthodox account, Protestants deny the intercessional power of Mary, saying that she 'does not mediate' (*attamaledim*). Protestants say that individuals pray directly to Jesus, while the Orthodox say that a saint or an angel must convey their prayers to God (Boylston 2012). By the account of one theologically educated friend, Hagos, to address Jesus by name or as a friend, as some Protestants do, suggests excessive self-confidence, as if you were putting yourself on his level. Friends of Malara living in Sirategna Sefer, a rather destitute district of Addis Ababa, would often comment that life in the city, and in contemporary Ethiopia in general, is often marked by different forms of moral compromise and that the ascetic efforts necessary to attain higher degrees of purity are hindered by a number of factors inherent to 'modern life'. One recurrent example of this was not having enough time to dedicate to church attendance because of one's work or family duties. In this case, seeking saintly mediation is an act of humility, the acknowledgment of one's imperfection. It allows busy, troubled people, who lack the time and energy to devote to what they consider proper religious practice, to enlist protectors to compensate for their imperfections and to seek forgiveness and redemption on their behalf.

According to Hagos, as well as many other informants of both authors of this chapter, when referring to Christ, one should use terms of deference such as *Gétachin* (Our Lord) or *Medhanítachin* (Our Savior). Even better is to ask intercession from Mary. As Hagos expressed it: "You can ask Mary, please tell your son to help me." Some people might even enlist a double mediation, asking a saint to petition Mary to intercede with Christ. In this way, mediation and deference are closely related. The Pentecostal heresy, as Orthodox Christians see it, consists in placing Christ too directly in contact with humanity, thereby exhibiting insufficient deference. As a priest in Addis Ababa put it: "Jesus is the one who is begged by mediators, but he is not a mediator himself. How can God mediate with God?" Every act of mediation, the priest reminded us, requires the non-identity of the parties involved. And, as our discussion illustrates, the differential status and positioning within the sacred hierarchy of supplicant, mediator, and intended receiver is the critical dynamic of asymmetric mediation.

As in many ritualistic systems, the main index of the value of hierarchy is in gestures of submission. Orthodox Christians practice *sigdet* ('worship' but also 'surrender') by bowing low and sometimes kissing the ground before an icon, or before the church, or simply at the roadside as one passes a church. The *sigdet* can be set as a penance by one's soul father, or it can simply be a part of daily religious practice. As both an act of submission and an identification with the suffering of Christ, the *sigdet* is a central performative index of sacred hierarchy. What Malara's informants stress, however, is that "to do what Christ did" can produce forms of identification that are only partial at best. Indeed, the faithful could never endure or understand the suffering that the Savior underwent. Such reasoning on the phenomenological limits of identification actively recreates distinction and encourages submissive dispositions by emphasizing human unworthiness and limitation as well as the ultimate incommensurability between divine and human.

The possibility of finding virtue in submission has received some attention recently as an important counterpoint to studies that focus only on the power-resistance dichotomy (Mahmood 2001a, 2001b; Walker 2012). As these writers note, to voluntarily submit to a power that is thought moral can be a form of agency or self-possession. As researchers, we do neither ourselves nor our informants any favors when we think of their relationships of submission purely in terms of subjection and dominance. For one thing, this would leave us little room to explain the passion and commitment that people often express for the powers and institutions to which they subordinate themselves. And yet it is no more helpful to swing the other way toward a conservative endorsement of hierarchy. Oppression and love are both integral to northern Ethiopian hierarchy; if they were not, it is hard to imagine how people would accept the system.

Abba Geremew, a senior priest, encapsulated this play of love and power when describing the role of icons in his own home. He explained that he keeps images of Mary and the Archangels Gabriel and Michael "because I need a mother and two soldiers." Saints and angels are very frequently depicted as violent warrior-protectors. Saint George, the national patron, is shown slaying the dragon or sometimes helping Ethiopian armies to vanquish foreign invaders. The archangels carry swords and smite demons. Some of them are known to be *k'ut'u* (short-tempered, angry). This capacity for violence and domination over demons is integral to their protective role. Sometimes it is what makes them worthy of love and devotion. Here, in the capacity for violence that inheres in relationships of protection, is the basis of the paradox of love, power, and hierarchy.

On Fathers and Other Great Men: Hierarchy and Submission in Daily Life

Tales of power, deference, and exploitation have dominated the sociology of Orthodox Ethiopia, but we should qualify these accounts by noting the numerous institutions and ethical codes of care and mutual support that exist in Orthodox society. The Hobbesian hierarchy is not the whole story (Messay 1999: 154); nonetheless, accounts of steep and open asymmetry capture something important about prevailing attitudes toward power and authority. Asymmetry is everywhere. It is understood not as a holistic map of a stratified society, but as a diffuse and fluctuating principle of power and asymmetry that is applicable to most social situations and relationships.

In a manner analogous to the veneration of saints, kinship is hierarchical and incorporates love and the ethics of care with steep power relationships. Generally, people tend to emphasize the disciplinary aspects of fatherhood and the nurturing facets of motherhood. A senior priest in Addis Ababa aptly expressed the ideal moral attitudes toward parents through a popular saying, "You love your mother and honor your father" (*inatih tiwedaleh, abatih takaberaleh*). The division of parenting labor is considered a foundational fact of the order of things. At the same time, looking after one's relatives and neighbors is paramount, for reasons no more complex than basic common feeling. The care of the sick is an ethical prerogative, as is the regular visiting of one's neighbors and the obligation to help those in need, if one is able to do so.

Apart from the disciplinary role of parents, especially fathers, children learn principles of hierarchy at meals: adult men eat first and together, while women and children eat afterward, depending sometimes on what is left. Children or women must carry water to wash the hands and (traditionally) feet of their seniors and guests before and after the meal. At the coffee ceremony with which people receive guests, it is the junior woman (servant, sister, daughter, or wife) who brews and serves the coffee, perched low to the ground below the guests (R. Pankhurst 1997). The micro-rituals of everyday life transmit and reproduce basic hierarchies of gender and seniority. A deep-seated principle, confirmed by many friends who had otherwise gained high degrees of practical independence, is that children do not contradict their fathers. When dealing with social superiors, beginning with one's father, the onus on silence and deference is extremely powerful.

If a son fails to contain his aggressive feelings, voicing openly his disagreement with his father or insulting him, his behavior is likely to be publically condemned, irrespective of the causes. Indeed, despite recognizing the tension implicit in the etiquette of obedience and deference, during our fieldwork friends and informants always spoke of familial hierarchical arrangements as being more or less divinely sanctioned facts. For many of them, patterns of deferential behavior have little to do with rational adherence to normative codes; instead, they are the naturalization and embodiment of such codes. Our friend Seyoum, the son of a notorious drunkard, expressed this point as follows: "Even if my father is drunk [*sekeram*] and annoying [*neznaza*], if he will ask me to fetch water for him, I will do it. Even if I am annoyed, even if I know he will forget tomorrow, I will still do it. I would not feel well otherwise. I would feel it here, in my stomach. It is heavy on me [*yikebdignal*]—you feel it here [on the shoulders]. I don't know how to explain it to you."

What informants of different ages and occupying different roles within a family all agreed upon is the importance of knowing one's place but also one's limits (*lik mawek'*). This phrase can be attributed a vast array of meanings according to the context of use. In the domain of familial relationships, it suggests the necessity of respecting the authority of those above you, of speaking properly or keeping silent when needed, and, in general, of acknowledging the limits of one's agentive possibilities.

The non-contradiction of one's seniors is a hierarchical rule that operates throughout social life; it reflects the fact that all are born into subordination to their fathers. Levine (1965: 83) writes: "Reverence for one's fathers is perhaps the key legitimating principle in the structure of Amhara morality. This is the outgrowth and foundation of a social system which makes children devoted servants of their fathers and keeps men under their fathers' control until they are fully adult." As Dawit, a young, educated Tigrayan put it: "An obedient child is honorable; a silent child is honorable" (*tazazh lij ch'ewa new; zimtegna lij chewa new*).

However, this authoritarian picture has its mediatory complement: if a child who has displeased her father is willing to apologize, the mother is likely to plead for her. Ashennafi, a young man from Addis Ababa explained: "If your father banishes you from the house, your mother will keep bringing food to you secretly. She will beg your father, 'Forgive your son.'" Mothers embody another modality of power, that of gentle persuasion. This power from below, which relies on humility, self-effacement, and begging, thus offers a counterpoint to the top-down, unanswerable, coercive power expected from men. The efficacy of mothers as mediators and go-betweens, their 'power', relies on a double proximity. As Dawit says: "Your mother is obviously closer to your father than you are, but of course she is also closer to you because she loves you." Many informants associate the mediating role of mothers within the familial hierarchical setting to that of 'peacemakers' (*astarak'i*). Inalienable maternal love is perceived as a sort of social lubricant for the intricate tapestry of hierarchical kinship (although in practice mothers can of course be strict disciplinarians). The gendered division of love and authority—and the mediation between them—is vital to Ethiopian Orthodox understandings of asymmetry. This is the basis of a general model of sociality, and the link between family and religious hierarchy is quite explicit. According to a senior priest in Addis Ababa: "God is the head of the Church; the Church is the head of the man; the man is the head of the woman" (*Igziyabihér ye béta kristiyan ras new; béte kristiyan ye wend ras new; wend ye sét ras new*).

The authority of fathers and the love of mothers are asymmetrical and complementary of one another. However, there still remains a crucial unresolved tension between moral authority and coercive authority. Apart from fathers, elders, and clergy, there is no strict calculus concerning whom one should show submission or deference to. Nonetheless, in meetings and associations and during daily encounters on the street, complex patterns of deference apply. The village in rural northern Ethiopia where Boylston has worked is comparatively relaxed about such things, due in part to being a market town that considers itself somewhat progressive. Yet even there, young informants explained how they must show respect to a *t'ilik' sew* (a 'great person' or 'big person'). Two main rules apply: one must bow, and one must "say *ishí* to them," *ishí* being the ubiquitous Amharic word denoting agreement and acquiescence. In Ethiopia, acquiescence is a critical index of power/authority, as Clapham (1969: 6) explains: "The respect for authority makes it very difficult to express any open opposition to a superior short of outright rebellion, for there has been no place for reasoned criticism of his proposals … It is certainly almost unthinkable for an inferior to refuse to obey an order … but it is very common for him to profess his obedience and then do nothing about it." What counts is the incontrovertible public acknowledgment of authority or greatness.

Complexities arise, however, when one asks what it is to be a great person. In Addis Ababa and in the village, multiple interlocutors of different ages, both men and women, agree that *t'ilik'net* (greatness), is a function of seniority and wisdom. It is not necessarily a direct correlate of age, for one may be old and foolish, but age tends to confer wisdom and status. A *t'ilik' sew* is the person who breaks up fights and mediates marital disputes. These interventions, like the intercession of saints, can be described as *amelajnet* (mediation). Mediation and greatness are linked in important ways across different spheres of authority. Monks are good examples of legitimate *t'ilik' sew* and are hence legitimate mediators. This is because of their accrued moral and spiritual authority, which arises in part from their asceticism (Kaplan 1984: 70–89). In rural Ethiopia, people often rely on monks to settle disputes.

More prevalent than the greatness that comes with self-effacement, however, is the greatness of the public man. At meetings of the parish or town council, a *t'ilik' sew* must be heard in full, no matter how baroque and tangential his locutions may become. As in other parts of the world, public lucubration is often itself an index of rank. True greatness also entails obligations: to show largesse, to give protection, and to prevent abuses of power by others.

In terms of this common definition, not all powerful people are great people. Many people become powerful by illegitimate means—be it through witchcraft or toadying or violence—without accruing the proper wisdom, seniority, or authority. The difference between power and greatness is widely recognized. However, and this is the important point, everybody equally recognizes that one's behavior toward a powerful person is exactly the same as toward a great person. You bow to them, and you say *ishí* (okay). The same goes for rich people. Wealth is categorically not in itself an index of greatness. Indeed, according to a woman who had returned to Addis Ababa after several years in the United States, the ostentation of wealth, of "not being able to handle wealth gracefully, ... is a shameful behavior typical of the new rich." Still, it is expected that the wealthy must be shown public deference. Seyoum explained that there are those you bow to out of respect and those you bow to out of fear. He added: "You hate those people. You really hate them. But you still bow to them." And no chapter on Ethiopian power would be complete without citing the famous proverb, "You bow in front and fart behind" (Levine 1965: 93). This blurring between legitimate authority and illegitimate power is where all the trouble lies. After all, gaining authority or greatness also increases one's coercive power, such that the two can never really be kept separate in practice.

One final note on this hierarchy: it is mainly inclusive, in that you may be subordinate to God or your father, but you are part of their household. This is part of the deal. You take a subordinate position in something bigger, and you get to feel part of its successes. But if the 'fluctuating hierarchy' in Ethiopia gives most people at least a sense that they could succeed, or that they are the same basic type of person as those at the top, other groups are totally excluded.

These groups, usually non-landowning, include potters, weavers, slave descendants, and the people known as Beta Israel. They have generally been forbidden from marrying outside their group, even to those with whom they share a religion. This has resulted in the phenomenon of underclass groups that persists today. Across Ethiopia, in both Christian and non-Christian areas, exist groups of people who have been firmly and irrevocably consigned to the bottom of society (A. Pankhurst 2003). In Zege, the Weyto canoe makers occupy such a position: Christians and Muslims will not marry them, share food or utensils, or allow for them to work as traders outside of their specified occupations. Here, the connection between religious and social hierarchy breaks down somewhat in the face of other complex and persistent stigmas.

The stigmatizing of the Weyto is thoroughgoing and contradicts all the usual ethics of care and hospitality. While one is usually compelled to offer food and coffee to a guest, Amhara in Zege and throughout the area will not share food with a Weyto. Whereas relations between parent and child, 'great person' and follower, saint and Christian, and emperor and subject are inclusive and incorporating, relations between Amhara and Weyto are exclusive. There is no sense that the Weyto should receive rewards for their subjection. It is not clear that these relationships even count as hierarchical. If hierarchy implies a relationship, the Amhara deny any kind of relationship with the Weyto and other outcast groups, who signify the alterity against which Amhara hierarchy defines itself. The distinction between relations of exclusion/stigma and those of inclusion/subordination seems critical, yet it may be missed in overgeneralized conceptions of hierarchy. The only mediation between mainstream Amhara and marginalized people is through commercial relations, for example, Beta Israel providing knives for the weddings of Christians, and Weyto selling canoes to people around Lake Tana. This is starkly different from those unequal relationships—between father and son or humanity and God—that can be mediated by love.

Conclusion

This chapter has been consciously light on references to Dumont. This is not because we reject Dumont outright, but because the specific problems of Ethiopian Orthodox hierarchy lead us to look for a different starting point and different perspectives. We have tried to ask what hierarchy looks like from the mundane perspective of everyday relationships, and how these relationships might then integrate (or not) with larger-scale societal values. Orthodox Ethiopia does not fit easily into Dumont's categories of holism/hierarchy and individualism/egalitarianism. From one perspective, prevailing local social theory looks absolutely holistic and totalizing, painting an orderly cosmos encompassed by God. From another, Orthodox society appears fragmented, fluid, and individualistic, premised more on the open practice of raw power than on an ordered Dumontian scheme of values (Donham 1986).

One way around this problem is to think less in terms of parts and wholes (individuals and societies) and more in terms of relationships (Strathern 1992). As we hope to have shown, Amhara Orthodox Christians tend to take a profoundly relational outlook on life. What is important and distinctive is that this relationality, in both its positive and negative aspects, usually takes an asymmetric form. Relationships—with family members, institutions, Church, and God—are shaped both by the circumstances of power and by notions of the good (the mercy and protection of God, the love of Mary, the authority of fathers). Since they convey authority, these notions of the good are often ripe for exploitation, which is why the selfless love of Mary and mothers is so important. But because of their selflessness, these kinds of love are also unequal and non-reciprocal.

Anthropologies of love, care, and submission can help us to move beyond the opposition of individual and society, whether that opposition is conceived in terms of encompassment or domination/resistance. Expressing faith, showing love, and caring for others are ways, as Klaits (2009: 3) writes, "of authorizing certain forms of intersubjectivity, rather than of asserting self-determining agency." Power is clearly present in these forms of intersubjectivity, but in moving from the classification of values to the practicalities of relating to people, we gain a much clearer impression of the forms that power takes. This concerns not just how values are articulated and authorized and how status is legitimized, but what kinds of relationships are thinkable and practicable. In Orthodox Ethiopia, most of the modes of legitimate and practical relationship building are asymmetrical. However, to extrapolate from this and to say that the society as a whole is based on domination alone misses much of the reality of how people build their lives together.

Without an account of vertical love and the daily practicalities of care and affection, it is difficult to see how a system based on naked domination, as Amhara is supposed to be, could ever be livable, or how claims about the values and virtues of hierarchy could ever be convincing. And yet people do submit willingly—even passionately—to hierarchical powers of many kinds.

This is not to apologize for hierarchy, but to acknowledge its political complexity. To this end, efforts to politicize the concept of love offer a new perspective on hierarchy. Love is not just personal, but a public concern. It is not just an egalitarian, unifying force, but a principle or a charter for relating that must cope with division, difference, and cases where commensurate return is impossible. Love can be instrumental without being any less emotively forceful, and love ideology has been a key aspect of quite a number of imperial as well as anti-imperial projects. But like hierarchy, love cannot be understood only with reference to totalizing social models. It is found in the way that people live out their relationships.

Love is an important part of the mediation of asymmetric relationships. It is a dynamic that has been called clientelism but that extends, as we have shown, well into the life of kinship and has registers other than the purely instrumental exchange of loyalty for favor and protection. When discussing mediation and intercession, our friends and informants repeatedly draw on idioms of love. Mary intercedes for us because she loves us, and God hears her pleas on our behalf because He loves her. Likewise, the loving mother who pleads with an angry father on behalf of her child is a trope of familial relations.

There is a widespread feeling that attempts to import Western-style individualistic liberal democracy to Ethiopia have not been successful (Maimire 2009; Messay 1999). For Girma (2012), this is because the asymmetric model of covenant thinking, based on pacts between patrons and followers, is the foundation of pan-Ethiopian social philosophy. Since covenants form the basis of Ethiopian understandings of what social morality is, to remove them in the name of a foreign individualism is simply anomic. Our argument is that any attempt to understand Ethiopian social philosophy is incomplete without an account of how people live with that philosophy. We have tried to demonstrate how affection, care, and the politics of love are inseparable parts of Ethiopian Orthodox hierarchy as it is lived. Critiques of hierarchy that fail to deal with asymmetric practices of love, care, and protection are missing a key aspect of how these systems function in practice.

Acknowledgments

We would like to thank Naomi Haynes, Jason Hickel, Anita Hannig, Lucy Lowe, Izabela Orlowska, and Dan Levene for their contributions to this chapter. Tom Boylston's research was funded by an ESRC 1 + 3 studentship and a British Academy Postdoctoral Fellowship. Diego Malara's research was supported by a PhD scholarship from the University of Edinburgh College of Humanities and Social Sciences and a Tweedie Exploration Fellowship.

Diego Maria Malara is a PhD candidate in the Department of Anthropology at the University of Edinburgh. His research looks at changing practices of religious mediation and emerging forms of urban subjectivity and relatedness among Ethiopian Orthodox city dwellers in Addis Ababa and Bahir Dar.

Tom Boylston is a British Academy Postdoctoral Research Fellow in Anthropology at the University of Edinburgh. He specializes in ritual, media, and materiality in Ethiopian Orthodox Christian society.

Notes

1. In this chapter, Amharic transliteration is based on the system used by Alula Pankhurst (1992), which we find most appropriate for non-specialists.
2. Titled *Maryam Maryam*, this *mezmur* (hymn) by Marse (2012) has been translated by the authors.
3. See Di Nunzio (2014) for a description of how this clientelism operates at the street level.

References

Abu-Lughod, Lila. 1986. *Veiled Sentiments: Honor and Poetry in a Bedouin Society*. Berkeley: University of California Press.
Bonacci, Giulia. 2000. *The Ethiopian Orthodox Church and the State 1974–1991: Analysis of an Ambiguous Religious Policy*. London: Centre of Ethiopian Studies.
Borneman, John. 1997. "Caring and Being Cared For: Displacing Marriage, Kinship, Gender and Sexuality." *International Social Science Journal* 49 (154): 573–584.
Boylston, Tom. 2012. "The Shade of the Divine: Approaching the Sacred in an Ethiopian Orthodox Christian Community." PhD diss., London School of Economics and Political Science.
Clapham, Christopher S. 1969. *Haile-Selassie's Government*. New York: Praeger.
Clapham, Christopher S. 1988. *Transformation and Continuity in Revolutionary Ethiopia*. Cambridge: Cambridge University Press.

Cole, Jennifer, and Lynn M. Thomas, eds. 2009. *Love in Africa*. Chicago: University of Chicago Press.

Di Nunzio, Marco. 2014. "Thugs, Spies and Vigilantes: Community Policing and Street Politics in Inner City Addis Ababa." *Africa* 84 (3): 444–465.

Donham, Donald L. 1986. "Old Abyssinia and the New Ethiopian Empire: Themes in Social History." In *The Southern Marches of Imperial Ethiopia: Essays in History and Social Anthropology*, ed. Donald Donham and Wendy James, 3–48. Cambridge: Cambridge University Press.

Donham, Donald L. 1999. *Marxist Modern: An Ethnographic History of the Ethiopian Revolution*. Berkeley: University of California Press; Oxford: James Currey.

Dumont, Louis. 1970. *Homo Hierarchicus: The Caste System and Its Implications*. Trans. Mark Sainsbury. London: Weidenfeld & Nicolson.

Dumont, Louis. [1980] 2013. "On Value." *HAU: Journal of Ethnographic Theory* 3 (1): 287–315.

Gell, Alfred. 2011. "On Love." *Anthropology of this Century* 2. http://aotcpress.com/articles/love/ (accessed 3 February 2015).

Girma Mohammed. 2012. *Understanding Religion and Social Change in Ethiopia: Toward a Hermeneutic of Covenant*. New York: Palgrave Macmillan.

Hannig, Anita. 2014. "Spiritual Border Crossings: Childbirth, Postpartum Seclusion and Religious Alterity in Amhara, Ethiopia." *Africa* 84 (2): 294–313.

Hardt, Michael. 2011. "For Love or Money." *Cultural Anthropology* 26 (4): 676–682.

Hoben, Allan. 1970. "Social Stratification in Traditional Amhara Society." In *Social Stratification in Africa*, ed. Arthur Tuden and Leonard Plotnicov, 187–224. New York: Free Press.

Hoben, Allan. 1973. *Land Tenure among the Amhara of Ethiopia: The Dynamics of Cognatic Descent*. Chicago: University of Chicago Press.

Kaplan, Steven. 1984. *The Monastic Holy Man and the Christianization of Early Solomonic Ethiopia*. Wiesbaden: Steiner Verlag.

Kaplan, Steven. 1986. "The Ethiopian Cult of the Saints: A Preliminary Investigation." *Paideuma* 32: 1–13.

Klaits, Frederick. 2009. "Faith and the Intersubjectivity of Care in Botswana." *Africa Today* 56 (1): 3–20.

Lee, Ralph. 2011. "Symbolic Interpretations in Ethiopic and Ephremic Literature." PhD diss., School of Oriental and African Studies.

Levine, Donald N. 1965. *Wax and Gold: Tradition and Innovation in Ethiopian Culture*. Chicago: University of Chicago Press.

Macfarlane, Alan. 1987. *The Culture of Capitalism*. Oxford: Basil Blackwell.

Mahmood, Saba. 2001a. "Feminist Theory, Embodiment, and the Docile Agent: Some Reflections on the Egyptian Islamic Revival." *Cultural Anthropology* 16 (2): 202–236.

Mahmood, Saba. 2001b. "Rehearsed Spontaneity and the Conventionality of Ritual: Disciplines of Ṣalāt." *American Ethnologist* 28 (4): 827–853.

Maimire Mennasemay. 2009. "The *Dekike Estifanos*: Towards an Ethiopian Critical Theory." *Horn of Africa* 27: 64–118.

Marse, Zemari Kibrom. 2012. "Maryam Maryam Lbelsh [Ethiopian Orthodox Mezmur]." Posted by "kiduel," 12 February. Video, 5:52 min. https://www.youtube.com/watch?v=VEzqWGvHu8c.

Mayblin, Maya. 2012. "The Madness of Mothers: Agape Love and the Maternal Myth in Northeast Brazil." *American Ethnologist* 114 (2): 240–252.

Messay Kebede. 1999. *Survival and Modernization—Ethiopia's Enigmatic Present: A Philosophical Discourse*. Lawrenceville, NJ: Red Sea Press.

Molvaer, Reidulf K. 1995. *Socialization and Social Control in Ethiopia.* Wiesbaden: Harrassowitz Verlag.

Muehlebach, Andrea. 2013. "The Catholicization of Neoliberalism: On Love and Welfare in Lombardy, Italy." *American Anthropologist* 115 (3): 452–465.

Pankhurst, Alula. 1992. *Resettlement and Famine in Ethiopia: The Villagers' Experience.* Manchester: Manchester University Press.

Pankhurst, Alula. 2003. "Introduction: Dimensions and Conceptions of Marginalisation." In *Peripheral People: The Excluded Minorities of Ethiopia*, ed. Dena Freeman and Alula Pankhurst, 1–26. Lawrenceville, NJ: Red Sea Press.

Pankhurst, Rita. 1997. "The Coffee Ceremony and the History of Coffee Consumption in Ethiopia." In *Ethiopia in Broader Perspective. Papers of the XIIIth International Conference of Ethiopian Studies, Kyoto, 12–17 December 1997*, ed. Katsuyoshi Fukui, Eisei Kurimoto, and Masayoshi Shigeta, 516–539. Kyoto: Shokado Booksellers.

Povinelli, Elizabeth A. 2006. *The Empire of Love: Toward a Theory of Intimacy, Genealogy, and Carnality.* Durham, NC: Duke University Press.

Reddy, William M. 2012. *The Making of Romantic Love: Longing and Sexuality in Europe, South Asia, and Japan, 900–1200 CE.* Chicago: University of Chicago Press.

Robbins, Joel. 2007. "Between Reproduction and Freedom: Morality, Value, and Radical Cultural Change." *Ethnos* 72 (3): 293–314.

Robbins, Joel. 2013. "Beyond the Suffering Subject: Toward an Anthropology of the Good." *Journal of the Royal Anthropological Institute* 19 (3): 447–462.

Schneider, Jane. 1990. "Spirits and the Spirit of Capitalism." In *Religious Orthodoxy and Popular Faith in European Society*, ed. Ellen Badone, 24–53. Princeton, NJ: Princeton University Press.

Strathern, Marilyn. 1992. "Parts and Wholes: Refiguring Relationships in a Post-plural World." In *Conceptualizing Society*, ed. Adam Kuper, 75–104. London: Routledge.

Teferi Abate Adem. 2012. "The Local Politics of Africa's Green Revolution in South Wollo." *African Studies Review* 55 (3): 81–102.

Vaughan, Megan. 2011. "The History of Romantic Love in Sub-Saharan Africa: Between Interest and Emotion." *Proceedings of the British Academy* 167 (1): 1–24

Walker, Harry. 2012. "Demonic Trade: Debt, Materiality, and Agency in Amazonia." *Journal of the Royal Anthropological Institute* 18 (1): 140–159.

Weber, Max. 1949. *The Methodology of the Social Sciences.* Trans. Edward A. Shils and Henry A. Finch. New York: Free Press.

Weissleder, Wolfgang. 1965. "The Political Ecology of Amhara Domination." PhD diss., University of Chicago.

Chapter 3

THE GOOD, THE BAD, AND THE DEAD
The Place of Destruction in the Organization of Social Life, Which Means Hierarchy

Frederick H. Damon

The opening and italicized question in Mauss's *The Gift* reads: *"What force is there in the thing given which compels the recipient to make a return?"* ([1925] 1967: 1). The facts I adduce in this chapter pose an analogous question: what quality is there in social life that makes destruction so often the condition of creation, the dead the lead-in to the good? The relationship between destruction and hierarchy is the problem, although in some social contexts hierarchy is desocialized into something often understood as accumulation.

Although it is given different meanings, the place of sacrifice in human organization cannot be contested. From the Moche in coastal Peru to the Cahokia proximate to contemporary St. Louis, pre-Columbian American polities seem to have run on the destruction of human beings. Some (e.g., Flannery 2001) would argue that the pattern persists into the present. Since Evans-Pritchard's (1956) *Nuer Religion*, Africa has been the classic place for

Notes for this chapter begin on page 72.

elaborating the essentials of Hubert and Mauss's paradigm (see Rigby 1971). Heusch (1985) wields the model to speculate upon continental orientations, an idea Rowlands (2003) reworks, and Taylor (1999) uses it to comprehend a late-twentieth-century holocaust. For millennia, China has been organized by the massive destruction of wealth in buried skilled labor. Now 'money' is burned,[1] tables of pigs slaughtered, and, in Taoist practice, texts destroyed— all this in a society that otherwise parades writing in universities, temples, and hillsides (Damon 2012: 176; Dean 1995: 181, 236n1; Elvin 2004). Exactly how analogues of a sacred/profane distinction are represented—whether they are combined or separated, who or what mediates, and to whom, what, and how benefits are distributed—varies by time and place. But everywhere destruction centers social reality.

This chapter's three parts assemble materials that I have been addressing for more than a decade concerning the place of destruction in organized social life. Part I elaborates the received model of sacrifice—from Hubert and Mauss, Evans-Pritchard, Lévi-Strauss—through basic ideas about destruction and hierarchy that I have learned from the Kula ring. There (Muyuw, Woodlark Island, in Milne Bay Province, Papua New Guinea) I have conducted more than 48 months of research since 1973, with my most recent visit taking place in 2014. Then I turn to Polynesia for a generalizable point from Dening (1992). While distilling a wide range of Polynesian data, Dening keeps returning to Europeans and the sacrificial connotations of hanging the *Bounty*'s mutineers. This leads to patterns of lynching in the American South, by way of historians drawing from classic anthropological perspectives.

The difference between dead pigs and live pigs organizes Part II. During my 1970s research, Muyuw people often complained about a newly enforced feature of their mortuary system.[2] An analysis generates a governing principal of this chapter—that destruction is the condition for the creation of significance, a kind of hierarchy. I elaborate on my principal point with the help of Gregory's (1982) *Gifts and Commodities* and Lévi-Strauss's (1963) *Totemism*.

Part III returns to our modern circumstances, looking specifically at the role of military spending in the United States and Europe. I draw on Dumont's (1970) *Homo Hierarchicus* and the direction Dumont took following that work, while taking a cue from Lévi-Strauss (1966: 238–239), who wrote: "When an exotic custom fascinates us in spite of … its apparent singularity, it is generally because it presents us with a distorted reflection of a familiar image, which we confusedly recognize as such without yet managing to identify it." Hubert and Mauss's ([1898] 1981) essay on sacrifice first appeared in *L'Année Sociologique* near the end of a century that reshaped religion as a bounded and separate domain of activity. This came after decades of increasingly intense and productive discussions about 'sacrifice' in the domain of religion in works such as Tylor ([1871] 1920), followed by writings from Robertson Smith and Frazer, and during a period when industrial capitalism spread and then spilled into World War I. Transposing an anthropological lens created in other places onto our own times argues for understanding 'sacrifice' as a story for the present.

Part I. Formal Integuments of 'Sacrifice'

In the Kula—*kun* in Muyuw³—the relationship between destruction and production is an explicit aspect of the formal exchange structure. Kula actors claim that kula activity, its very purpose, is to make their names rise, to make them visible over the horizon. Kula valuables come into one's possession from elsewhere. And they accomplish their purpose only by being thrown in the opposite direction from which they have come. If Kula valuables partake of the sacred, the institution works by getting rid of that reality. At least feigned anger is part of every exchange because by throwing a valuable to a partner the giver destroys part of his self. This is the immolation, the act of destruction central to the institution. A sign of that destruction is the loss of the person's name. Counter to the giver's experience, feigned or not, joy is at least part of every recipient's experience as his name rises. With a large valuable, the recipient might be stripped bare of his clothing; being made anew, he is returned to the initial condition. Other sacrificial moments frequently identified in the form's grammar—in reverse order 'invocation', 'consecration', and 'presentation'— could be described at length. Valuables are presented, for example, as soon as they have been hung up inside a house. There they are meant to be seen, their travels, attachments, and intentions absorbed by as many people as possible.

But this useful elicitation of the exchange/sacrifice order does not totalize what actually occurs because the iteration of the form is part of its very structure. For it is only by the valuable moving on to a third person that the giver's name is realized. On the beach of the initial exchange, the giver's name goes down, the receiver's goes up. This shift is repeated when the first receiver becomes a giver to a third person. But as his name goes down and the recipient's goes up, so also does the first person's name go up. So a person's name first goes down as he throws the valuable he has received, which becomes identified with him from the time he received it and then presented it; his name then goes up when that valuable has been thrown to a third person. Although he gains the name he sought, he does not regain the physical part that the valuable first carried away. His new rank is made as he is experienced elsewhere by means of somebody else's immolation. And it is explicit that this is accomplished by means of the physical depletion of the giver's body, effectively symbolized by the initial decline of his name. Men I have known for nearly 40 years like looking old, taking that appearance as a sign of their success. It is a fact—a painful fact, informants have stressed—that to be successful in the kula is to work hard, to expend one's powers, thus the visible sign of increased physical wear and tear. By means of shells from the sea, bodily stuff is transformed into a ranked name.

This kula depletion resembles the real destruction of bodies in Polynesia, at least from the thirteenth or fourteenth century when a now familiar Polynesian hierarchy appears in the archaeological record—a hierarchy arguably produced through sacrifice. The structural similarities with the Kula extend to the proximate beach location of so many of the Polynesian public structures.⁴ Dening (1992: 179) renders the important Tahiti marae, Taputapuatea, as "Sacrifices from Abroad." It was from there that bodies from the land were sent over the horizon to the heavens.[5]

Comparing the Kula and Polynesia, we may suggest this: the Kula is an expansion outward of the Polynesian social forms, the public structures, marae, which, by means of megalithic ruins, appeared in the Kula region earlier than Polynesia (see Bickler 2006). The open system of the Kula enables a broad and fluid ranking of social units by means of the exchange of shell wealth, materials brought into the human order from just beyond the beach. By contrast, the gifts—dead humans—to gods central to Polynesia appear as a contraction or condensation of Kula-like relations. And in this literal form of destruction, creations of the human order are sent beyond the beach to the gods.

A passage from Dening is now useful to invoke. His account of the *Bounty* drama passes back and forth between the likes of Oliver (1974) and Sahlins (1985) on Polynesian facts while making the history of the drama, that is, the Western experience, his central ethnographic focus. As Dening (1992: 228) puts it:

> In sacrifice, human actions—in the destruction of a living thing—are transformed by being given meaning. What is destroyed—a man, a pig, a plantain branch, a piece of unleavened bread—becomes something else: a victim, an offering, a gift, a scapegoat. The instruments of that transformation are always dramaturgical. There is always a play, a ritual, to present the meaning ... There are always things that, in their colour or shape or in their association, make an environment of signs. The sequence of actions draws their elements together ... But the significance of these plays is never automatically effective or static. The rituals are conditioned by all ... all the endless creativity of meaning construction. Above all, they are always historical: the meanings of the signs are always being changed by being read, by being interpreted.

So the gap is filled by words and images that attempt to make the experience of loss useful for the present. In the Kula, for example, people believe that they have depleted themselves physically by throwing a valuable. But that experience does not end with the transaction. Its details are often repeated, verbally, over and over again through time. Learning how to recite acts of giving is a major rhetorical form. In order to learn the practice, ambitious youths sit amidst elders as they recite stories of this and that kula. Even if the stories are made up, the ability to go on and on about the travels of the most important valuables—in order to counter somebody else's fabrication in fact—proves to the fabricator that a person knows something. Similarly, our popular culture is currently serving up a smorgasbord of books reworking and reliving the deeds of the twentieth century (e.g., Atkinson 2013; Beevor 2012; Hochschild 2011; Holland 2010; Perry 2009), drawing from the intimacies of individuals but placing them in the global constructs that leave us with our present, thus supporting Dening's claim that "the meanings of the signs are always being changed by being read, by being interpreted." Evans (2012) touches on this quality in a recent review: "Popular fascination with World War II in particular continues to be led by an enthusiasm for experiencing vicariously the heroic struggle of the

The Good, the Bad, and the Dead | 63

democracies and their armed forces against the barbarism of the Nazi forces and the sadism of the Japanese military."

Films provide more visceral experiences of this reliving. The sequence is unstinting, from *Saving Private Ryan* in 1998 to *United 93* in 2006 about the events of 9/11. More recently, there is *Fury*, directed by David Ayer and starring Brad Pitt. Drawing on 50 years of Hollywood's depiction of World War II, this 2014 film runs along two tracks: one celebrates the nobility of men who sacrifice their lives for their created community so that others may live; the other shows the necessary initiation into a society predicated on power that can shift to the indiscriminate. This is not just popular fascination with a past that is conceived as more heroic. These films play out our cosmology. Dumont (1986: 85) captures this structure in an early contribution:

> In this theory, the social is to a great measure reduced to the political. Why? The reason is very clear in Hobbes: starting from the *individuum,* or the individual, social life will be necessarily considered in terms of consciousness and force (or "power"). In the first place, one can pass from the individual to the group only in terms of "covenant," i.e. in terms of conscious transaction or artificial design. It will then be a matter of "force," because "force" is the only thing the individual can bring into the bargain: the opposite of "force" would be hierarchy, the idea of the social order, the principle of authority; and this is precisely what the contracting individuals will more or less unconsciously have to bring forth synthetically from the common pool of their forces or wills. Hierarchy is the social obverse, force the atomistic reverse, of the same coin. This is how an emphasis on consciousness or consent immediately issues into an emphasis on force or power. Modern political theory, in the best case, is an individualistic manner of dealing with society. It involves an *indirect* acknowledgement of the social nature of man.

Designed to parallel my Melanesian inquiries, I teach a course on US/Western culture, a portion of which is devoted to nineteenth-century social transformations. The interest in sacrifice eventually brought me to lynching, which, after the Civil War (1861–1865), became increasingly a white/black phenomenon. Hale (1999) works along one line of thought regarding the practice. In her model, by the end of the Civil War there had been much intermarriage among distinguishable sets of people. So, given the new forms of ranking that were spreading during the nineteenth century in which egalitarianism was replacing hierarchical notions more or less equivalent to the Great Chain of Being, a way of demarcating people was needed. Hale provides insight on a 'presentation' aspect of these forms (ibid.: 206–207):

> The 1893 murder of Smith [in Paris, Texas] was the first blatantly public, actively promoted lynching of a southern black by a large crowd of southern whites. Adding three key features—the specially chartered excursion train, the publicly sold photograph, and the widely circulated, unabashed retelling of the event by one of the lynchers—the killing of Smith modernized and made more powerful the loosely organized, more spontaneous practice of lynching that had previously

prevailed. In what one commentator aptly termed a "neglected feature of railroading," from 1893 on railroad companies could be counted on to arrange special trains to transport spectators and lynchers to previously announced lynching sites.

Publically destroying a representative body and then distributing its parts among the witnesses—either the real parts of dismembered bodies or those on picture postcards (at the time, a new form of communication)—served to distinguish who was who and who was dead. The dead brought life, the vibrancy of a rite of passage, to the living.[6]

The logic of this argument is this: continuity needs to be replaced by tangible discontinuity (or differentiation). The same argument works in the Kula. There are two kinds of kula valuables that can be equated by means of the *kitoum*, the personally owned category that facilitates the movement of one form into the other. But generally all *mwals* (armshells) are the same, as are all *veiguns* (necklaces); therefore, all members of each of these sets can be, and are, ranked from lowest to highest.[7] It is the same with people. Although kula actors are acutely aware of the intra-cultural ranking and practice intercultural ranking games with gusto, the institution's structure enables the formal equation of all people and the inversion of all such ranking principles across the region. I vividly remember one of the first such transactions I saw in 1973 when a young man aged 25 severely scolded and practically walked over the biggest man in the southeast corner of the Kula ring. The possibility of similarity, however, is transformed into rank by means of kula exchange.

I shall return to this argument about the formal dissolution of continuity by means of instigated discontinuity, but there is another, and I think preferable, way to fathom late-nineteenth- and twentieth-century lynching. As Garry Wills (2003) observes, until the Civil War, the South ran the United States.[8] That war destroyed the South's place atop the country, just as, not coincidentally, Northern interests sought to change the US's rank order in the world system from a periphery to a competing core member. In his historical ethnography *Rockdale*, Anthony Wallace ([1978] 2005) documents this transformation, showing how, during the US's 'second Great Awakening', the social system reorganized itself so that it could compete with the hegemonic power of the time—England. The South's system serviced the European core powers. The interests that came together in the North, eventually leading to the Civil War, changed that dynamic.[9] What then became increasingly prominent after that war was the substantiation of the difference between white and black by means of piacular rituals when blacks were conceived to enter the white domain. Drawing on Julian Pitt-Rivers's discussions of honor and grace in anthropology, historian Bertram Wyatt-Brown (1982, 2001)[10] brilliantly explicates the problem of honor in the South in the years following the Civil War.[11] Lynched and dismembered bodies distributed across the countryside restored, to the participants, what some thought was their appropriate social standing.[12] This was a question of hierarchy, and dismembering a body made visible a relation that had been all but destroyed by the Civil War. As Wyatt-Brown (2001: 287) puts it: "Just as there were once saints' relics, white lynchers seized the victims' knuckles, bones, skull or some other part of the body and treated them as icons to be treasured and proudly displayed."

This is a significant pattern in American culture. John Dower (1986: 65; footnotes omitted) describes the same thing about World War II, concerning the Pacific War:

> [I]n Asia it was Allied combatants who collected ears. Like collecting gold teeth, this practice was no secret. "The other night," read an account in the Marine monthly *Leatherneck* in mid-1943, "Stanley emptied his pockets of 'souvenirs'— eleven ears from dead Japs. It was not disgusting, as it would be from the civilian point of view. None of us could get emotional over it." Even as battle-hardened veterans were assuming that civilians would be shocked by such acts, however, the press in the United States contained evidence to the contrary. In April 1943, the *Baltimore Sun* ran a story about a local mother who had petitioned authorities to permit her son to mail her an ear he had cut off a Japanese soldier in the South Pacific. She wished to nail it to her front door for all to see. On the very same day, the *Detroit Free Press* deemed newsworthy the story of an underage youth who had enlisted and "bribed" his chaplain not to disclose his age by promising him the third pair of ears he collected.

A safe generalization suggests that wars, at least in the US, frequently generate piacular activities, with 9/11 consequences providing a recent set of examples.

Part II. What Is 'the Lie'?

My question is this: why is so much social life constructed by destruction?[13] Two texts animate the background inquiries for these speculations.

The first is C. A. Gregory's (1982) *Gifts and Commodities*. I draw on his suggestion that the only way there can be real accumulation in gift societies is when the means of exchange (sooner or later congealed value), and thus the possibility of repayment, are destroyed. This idea becomes particularly intriguing if one looks at the contemporary world through the eyes of Wallerstein's (1974, 2004) modern 'world-system'. Although none of his major volumes suggest knowledge of anthropology's exchange literature, Wallerstein's model is essentially a gift system. Units in the system become ranked by their ability to produce and exchange certain kinds of products. As in the Kula, the problem is who produces and exchanges what ranked values, not the price of the products exchanged.[14] If you produce raw materials, you are at one end of a spectrum; if you produce high-quality products, that is, items that congeal massive amounts of human creativity, you are ranked highly. In this model, the fact of exchange does not lead to accumulation. Only, perhaps, the destruction of exchangeable things, including bodies, seems to manage that.

My second text comes from Lévi-Strauss, primarily *Totemism* (1963). This book and Lévi-Strauss's (1966) *The Savage Mind*, both published in France in 1962, contain a plethora of extremely suggestive quips. They also have led to a reorganization of our consideration of the logic inherent in social life. It is probably less well known that the two raise the status of the organizational significance of 'totemism', an illusionary category, while dismissing 'religion', much less illusionary. Lévi-Strauss (1966: 95) thinks religion is impoverished and considers 'sacrifice' a nonsensical form of communication (ibid.: 228). The Dening quote above was probably designed to counter Lévi-Strauss's views, although its widespread pertinence supports what Lévi-Strauss suggests, namely, that sacrificial structures are similar everywhere. Yet what interests me is how he understands the condition of totemism. Drawing from Ojibwa and Tikopian myths, Lévi-Strauss (1963: 26) writes: "[T]otemism as a system is introduced as *what remains* of a diminished totality, a fact which may be a way of expressing that the terms of the system are significant only if they are *separated* from each other, since they alone remain to equip a semantic field which was previously better supplied and into which a discontinuity has been introduced." In this interpretation, reduction is the condition for significance. Put differently, destruction is its condition. This is standard linguistic analysis: (making) difference is a condition for communication. Hale's (1999) argument approaches this logic.

What is 'the lie'? I refer to the gossip that carried the day during mortuary rituals when I was first doing research. People complained that others[15] forced them to gather a lot of pigs for their definitive mortuary ceremony, generically *sagal*, specifically *anagin ta valam* (the fruit of our crying). However, most of the pigs would be traded rather than killed and cut up as pork for immediate consumption (the fruit). Killing everything was the normal practice, and destroying live animals by turning them into distributable pork remains a significant part of the process today. The dead and distributed pigs are either returns on old debts or new debts. If a pig debt cannot be returned, some other productive resource, garden land and sago orchards being foremost, must take its place. By contrast, if the pigs are traded immediately, nothing is at stake. That is why people classed this practice as 'the lie'. Dead pigs contest people's ability to produce (and reproduce). The destruction of pigs in a ritual either represents the production of replacement pigs or engages the receiving unit to so orient its activities. The pigs are real, but they are also mimetic instances of productive activities that include building up horticultural (yams and taro) and arboricultural (sago orchards and betel nut) resources for several years leading up to the ritual. These activities make these rituals the pressing social occasions that they are. The tense, furtive reality that lurks beneath the gaiety of mortuary rites is the concern for relative, that is, ranked, futures. The rites leave those futures in the balance, and that is why everyday life in the region is a continuous discussion about the coming and going of pigs. The dead pigs animate life; they make life count, and counting makes life. These rituals have a symmetrical cast about them for they structure the exchange of equivalents. But it is no accident that the most successful, powerful people—*guyau*, the proverbial Melanesian big men—perform these rites with respect to one another. They are ranking devices.

I do not think this form is unique. So let me close this section by picking up on an observation in Ernest Mandel's (1975) *Late Capitalism*.[16] Mandel attempted to employ Marx's production departments—the production of the means of production versus the production of articles of consumption—to model certain aspects of our social system between the middle of the nine-teenth century to the middle of the twentieth century. But he observed it was impossible to make the model plausible unless he added a third production department, that of destruction. Although building weapons is common across cultures,[17] Mandel felt that the increase in armaments expenditures—and, one might wish to add, certainly now, the contribution that such spending makes to society—leapt to a new level. For the US, this seems counter-intuitive because it practically disarmed after the Civil War. However, slowly it started to build a navy. In the 1880s, Carnegie and his adviser mulled over whether or not to go into the production of cannons for battleships. They decided in the negative because the English and French were so far ahead of the Americans. And the problem with cannons, unlike the shells they consume (mostly in practice), is that you do not need many of them, so they went into shell production. This is not just cute. The United States went into serious production of a navy—think of all the steel in those ships—at the same time that the country was suffering a continual overproduction problem with railroads and all the steel that went into the rails, bridges, and steam engines. The overproduction crises of this time—during the 1870s and beyond[18]—enabled Carnegie's consolidation of the US steel industry. There is a real empirical question here: over and above the technical advances that came to shipping as the US decided to move from a third-rate to a first-rate naval power between about 1880 and 1910, how much surplus production did those ships absorb? (It is over these decades that the anthropological discussion of 'sacrifice' becomes productive.) I used to think that the Kondratieff upswing that started circa 1894 was brought to a prema-ture end by the financial crisis of 1907 and then World War I in 1914. But that was certainly not the case in the United States. World War I led to the realiza-tion of all those rail lines and factories that had been built up from 1890: their value was absorbed by fashioning the material for trench warfare in Europe. In relation to that otherwise incomprehensible slaughter, life was enabled. Those dead bodies were like dead pigs, giving vitality to the living.[19]

Destruction relationships similar to these mark human sociality. Of Southeast Asia's expanding production of tin, Anthony Reid (2011: 28) writes: "China's demand for Southeast Asian tin expanded greatly during its prosperous eigh-teenth century, partly to make the tinfoil burnt as joss paper in offerings to the ancestors."[20] Dana Priest and William Arkin's (2011) *Top Secret America: The Rise of the New American Security State* would seem to show the same engagement of technical and human capital—the problem of absorbing the fantastic amount of creativity generated with respect to computers since 1980. The events of 9/11 cre-ated more dead pigs. Death, removal from a social context, gives people meaning.

Part III. Conclusion: Is Killing Not Killing?

We are familiar with Dumont's notion of hierarchy. The religious contrast between the pure and impure not only contains a contrary but encompasses the social system, providing its paramount value. Subsequent to his India period, ending about 1962, Dumont addressed the Weberian problem of showing how religious values constitute the fundamental dynamic in Western social life. As his work extended over the years, he became increasingly wedded to the idea of a role for Christianity in the West analogous to the Brahmanical role in India—one that is generative. So far as I know, however, Dumont did not attempt to reveal something like a contained contrary as central to the Western experience, although he believed it was central to India. The Western 'structure' appears rather flat. In his comparative project this is important because the Indian form enables a profusion of varying value systems, whereas, it seems, in the Western model there is the idea that there should be just one. Iteanu (2009) has a forceful statement about this difference in orders. The implicit comparative propositions in these proclamations require considerable work, given the 'regionalism' that now forms our apprehension of social reality. The ethnographic world we need to analyze is much different from the one of Dumont's generation. India was never an isolate. Hierarchical forms existed in many places. In any case, the broader idea here is that certain ideological constructs give actionable shape to a whole set of relations. Following Dumont and Sahlins, these are what Robbins, in many publications, calls 'paramount values' (see, e.g., Robbins 2009).

That paramount values orient many if not all social systems seems patent. Yet in our work these structures too often appear as unordered incantations, independent of social analysis. During a recent rereading of *Homo Hierarchicus*, I was taken aback at Dumont's attempt to read successive changes in the nature of sacrifice in the Indian data over the millennia; for his times, it was a complex historical argument. I want to piece together an interpretation of that argument to plea for the centrality of destruction-generating social forms, not just in India but in the place to which Dumont turned—the contemporary West.

The important passages in *Homo Hierarchicus* draw from the German writer Alsdorf concerning "the evolution of living sacrifice and the consumption of meat from the Veda to Hinduism; and the development of the idea of *ahimsā* ('non-violence', or rather absence of the will to kill) and of vegetarianism in Jainism and Buddhism" (Dumont ([1970] 1980: 147). But the beginning of the sequence is deceptive (ibid.):

> Grazing played a large part in the life of the Vedic Indians, and it may be supposed that like many other pastoral peoples they killed cattle only when there were good reasons, sacrificial reasons, and only the meat of sacrificed animals was eaten. In other words, there was a religious attitude towards cattle, which is not surprising, and which is to be taken as the starting-point for what was later to become the veneration of the cow, the cow having already been extolled in Vedism as a cosmic symbol, the universal mother and source of food, etc. It was the 'sacred animal most preferred for sacrifice' (Alsdorf) ... At the same time, in the sutras of the domestic ritual and of the dharma, a cow is killed on certain ritual occasions: in ancestor worship, and to honour a distinguished guest (the guest is called *goghna*, 'cow killer' by the grammarian Panini); a bull is sacrificed in a specific sacrifice.

Although ostensibly located in a specifiable time in the history of the subcontinent, I suggest that the real time here is 1956, the publication date of *Nuer*

Religion.[21] A central problem in that book is the identification between humans and cattle. Evans-Pritchard explains that relationship not by the fact of their mutual production, amply illustrated in his other work on the Nuer, but by the external category *kwoth,* or God—in short, religion. However, just as Evans-Pritchard divorced cattle and people from the facts of their mutual production, so Dumont, I believe, has divorced the domain of religion from other activities, a kind of necessity if it is going to be turned into a causative relation. But the relation is already there. I suggest that the terms 'distinguished guest' and 'ancestor' must index relative relations of rank, and that it is precisely the capacity to take cattle out of existence and transform them into a different substance (or relation) that creates ranking and signification in the social order. In other words, ritual order is not removed from the social process but constitutive of it. It is not religion that gives these actions their significance; rather, these actions—the destruction of valued, produced relations—generate the experience of contained orders that we call religion.

I must stress a point here. Working from Hubert and Mauss, and in Evans-Pritchard's footsteps, Dumont illustrates and extends a line of analysis that arguably has not been surpassed to this day for its ability to delineate forms of thought and social action. Over the next decade or so, this kind of analysis blossomed. To this day, Beidelman's (1966) work on Swazi royal rituals remains a rich, useful model, as does Rigby's (1971) on another pastoralist group's understanding of cattle. In an odd sort of way, however, these brilliant essays never locate their analyses in equally subtle understandings of their social milieus.

This point seems more than paradoxical with respect to Dumont, for in other respects he most certainly does what I am asking. I just think he ignores what can be derived from what he has witnessed. A long passage in *Homo Hierarchicus* makes clear a productive order at issue. In a chapter titled "Hierarchy: The Theory of the 'Varna,'" Dumont ([1970] 1980: 67–68) writes:

> Thanks to Hocart and, more precisely, to Dumézil, the hierarchy of the varnas can be seen as … as a series of successive dichotomies or inclusions. The set of the four varnas divides into two: the last category, that of the Shudras, is opposed to the block of the first three, whose members are 'twice-born' in the sense that they participate in initiation, second birth, and in the religious life in general … Let me simply say here that the lot of the Shudras is to serve, and that the Vaishyas are the grazers of cattle and the farmers, the 'purveyors' of sacrifice, as Hocart says, who have been given dominion over the animals, whereas the Brahmans-Kshatriyas have been given dominion over 'all creatures' … the Kshatriya may order a sacrifice as may the Vaishya, but only the Brahman may perform it. The king is thus deprived of any sacerdotal function. It can be seen that the series of dichotomies on which this hierarchy rests is formally somewhat similar to caste hierarchy, and it also is essentially religious; but it is less systematic and its principles are different.

This is an order of exchanged products, a productive order, and the top is reserved for the category that can take a product out of the system while converting it into something else.[22] As Dumont explains: "Today the Brahman lineages are graded in virtue of the rank of the castes they serve as domestic priests ... the highest being the learned Brahmans who do not serve at all" (ibid.: 70). The very top of the system effectively removes itself from the social order. And I would suggest that removal—the destruction of relation—bequeaths the social order.

These passages reveal a line of argument that can be used for our own social system. From the holocaust of Hiroshima much of our world is now lit up. One may claim that everyday life is afforded due to the vast sums of money that our social system spends on extraordinarily expensive and wasteful, or wasted, weapon systems. Some of these, in particular recent fighter planes, are so intricate that they can hardly be used.[23] Yet materials developed from research that went into making Soviet and US spy planes since the 1950s now fashion many Boeing and Airbus airplanes. The killing is not killing, to echo aspects of the Indian ideology.

Garry Wills's (2010) *Bomb Power* describes a radical institutional transformation in the US political structure effected by the country's reaction to World War II. From that war's experienced necessities, the US president now assumes a near absolute power to destroy the world.[24] But more than that, 'bomb power' organized similar activities, largely opaque institutional structures that are nevertheless determinative and defining, to some extent coming up to the present (Jacobsen 2011). Summarizing his book's thesis, Wills (2010: 4) writes:

> Cheney was right to say that the real logic for all these things is the President's solitary control of the Bomb. He was also right to say that something like what the Bush administration did was tried, adumbrated, or justified by other Presidents, going all the way back to the creation of the Manhattan Project, without any authorization, funding, or checks by the Congress. That was the seed of all the growing powers that followed ... Executive power has basically been, since World War II, Bomb Power.

That pattern for creating and harnessing scientific discoveries fueled the transportation systems leading into the twenty-first century. It made a new, mad divine. Wills quotes Rhodes concerning the Manhattan project: "[Los Alamos] 'bore no relation to the industrial or social life of the country; it was a separate state, with its own airplanes and its own factories and its thousands of secrets. It had a peculiar sovereignty, one that could bring about the end, peacefully or violently, of all other sovereignties'" (ibid.: 31).

So we are back to separation, destruction, and from both the making of the significant, the possible in everyday lives. The digital watches that organize our lives derive from the intercontinental ballistic missiles of the 1950s and 1960s, many junked and transformed into radioactive waste. Arguably, the logic our ancestors revealed in sacrificial orders surrounds us. If we can manage to identify it, can we change the circumstances of our condition?

To deal with a pervasive aspect of human sociality, this chapter attempts to combine two ideas forged together with one of our discipline's classic models. It is a fact that humans use destruction—more metaphoric there, more real here—to create their existence. The myth Lévi-Strauss employs to suggest that reduction, and therefore destruction, is necessary for a viable order applies too literally to a portion of space and time in the United States.[25] Gregory's (1982) idea about destruction leading to accumulation in gift societies seems a reach for looking at the contemporary West. But it is a fact that defense spending is the leading research component in the country that has been the defining order for nearly a century. Unfortunately, wasting money on military expenditures, and occasional wars, seems to be our bridge to progress.

This kind of analysis raises important questions about the order of 'is' versus 'ought' in human affairs. But right now it seems to me that the question we are best prepared to answer is, what is the human condition? It is quite often, as we might consider it, "'sacrilegious'" (Lévi-Strauss 1966: 225).

Acknowledgments

I have presented various aspects of the problem that this chapter poses, including earlier versions in Hong Kong and Paris in 2004 and a reworked version for the Department of Anthropology at the University of Bergen in November 2011. The immediate genesis for its current form was the Louis Dumont Centennial Conference, "Diversité des sociétés et Universalisme idéologique" organized by André Iteanu and Cécile Barraud, held in Paris in September 2011. That draft was revised for the 2012 American Anthropological Association session organized by Jason Hickel and Naomi Haynes. That work went through a further revision for the April 2013 workshop "Sacrifice in Different Civilizations," which was organized by Wang Mingming and Yang Zhengwen with the assistance of members of the Anren Exhibition of Ethnography, sponsored by the Center for China Sociological Research and Development Studies of Peking University; the Southwest University for Nationalities in Chengdu; the exhibition of ethnography of Sichuan Anren Town, sponsored by Old Mansion Culture Development Co., Ltd.; and the Mengyangshan Anthropological Association of Peking University. Participants in all these settings responded critically and creatively to what I have attempted here. This final version is much improved due to comments from Jason Hickel and Naomi Haynes.

Frederick H. Damon completed his PhD in Anthropology at Princeton University and is Professor of Anthropology at the University of Virginia. He has conducted research on Muyuw, Woodlark Island, in Papua New Guinea for a total of 48 months from 1973 to 2014. He has initial research experience in China and has been teaching courses on contemporary US society since the late 1970s. Originally focused on questions of exchange and production, with attention to ritual orders and the orders that rituals create, his current work is concerned with large-scale temporal and spatial comparisons.

Notes

1. Damon (2014) presents a version of this chapter that was addressed to a Chinese audience concerned with Chinese sacrifice. Another version (Damon 2016) emphasizes its Dumontian ties.
2. For its typically Melanesian shape, see Damon (1989; 1991: chap. 4).
3. For more background information on Muyuw, see, among other publications, Damon (2002).
4. Bickler and Damon (n.d.) instantiate this assertion. Oliver (1974), Sahlins (1985), and Valeri (1985) do not argue that activities make rank, but the point rises from their descriptions. If the destruction of persons is metaphorical in the Kula, it was real in Polynesia.
5. Dening (1992) argues for the liminal beach location, but other ethnographers do not. Oliver (1974: 70) maintains: "Trees especially favored by spirits ... were the *tamanu* (*C. Inophyllum*), *miro* (*Thespesia populnea*) and *'aito* (*Casuarina equisetifolia*). These trees grew in many settings." Irrespective of "many settings," these are trees of the littoral.
6. In the 1970s, anthropologist Peter Stone carried out extensive research with people who had experienced lynchings, showing that lynching was in a set with brideless weddings and minstrelsies. These rituals played on gender and sex, the unreal and the real, with lynchings combining features of the others. Most lynchings after 1870 were 'about' a black person entering a white domain: the rite, thus piacular, was intended to reverse the intrusion.
7. For Kula valuable ranking, see especially Campbell (1983), Damon (2002), and Munn (1983). My logic follows Crocker (1969) and Barnett (1976).
8. In his volume, Wills cites historian Leonard Richards (2009: 9): "In the sixty-two years between Washington's election and the Compromise of 1850, for example, slaveholders controlled the presidency for fifty years, the Speaker's chair for forty-one years, and the chairmanship of House Ways and Means [the most important committee] for forty-two years. The only men to be reelected president—Washington, Jefferson, Madison, Monroe, and Jackson—were all slaveholders. The men who sat in the Speaker's chair the longest—Henry Clay, Andrew Stevenson, and Nathaniel Macon—were slaveholders. Eighteen out of thirty-one Supreme Court justices were slaveholders."
9. In the sequel to *Rockdale*, titled *St. Clair*, Wallace (1988) documents intense rivalry between the US and England. This tale continues in Steil's (2013) account of Bretton Woods, where England loses it last claim to hegemonic status—the City of London as the world's financial center—to Americans.
10. In *Southern Honor*, Wyatt-Brown (1982) draws on Pitt-Rivers (1977). In *The Shaping of Southern Culture*, Wyatt-Brown (2001) harkens to Peristiany and Pitt-Rivers (1992).
11. One might suggest that the dynamic continues today, as evidenced by the geographical distribution of incarceration and execution rates.
12. As Wyatt-Brown (2001: 284) relates: "Photographs of white crowds stolidly and unashamedly facing the camera with a black body dangling from a nearby tree limb reveal their collective sense of having done a righteous and honorable deed." This practice inverted a double inversion, the North over the South and some blacks being considered equal to or superior to whites. Pulling into its vortex the whole Southern order, lynching replaced the more elite dueling as the primary honor ritual.
13. Although my argument shares ideas found in Weiner (1992) and Godelier (1999), Gregory (1982) is my inspiration.

14. Regions inside Muyuw participated in the Kula little, if at all, and they were disparaged (Damon 1983). A Melanesian 'deep structure' is its regional specialization and attendant rank.

15. In this history, the others—people from the Kula ring's southeastern corner—enforced this change. If correct, this took place under the umbrella of the colonial order and is part of that order's devaluation of indigenous modes of production and exchange.

16. In the April 2013 presentation of these ideas in Chengdu, Stephan Feuchtwang reminded me that Paul Sweezy and Harry Magdoff were saying things similar to Mandel. The issues here concern the absorption problem, that is, overproduction crises.

17. Note the character for spear in the traditional Chinese term for country: 國, 戈, gē.

18. In Western economic history, this time is understood as a Kondratieff long wave cycle, roughly analogous to the now better-known 'trough' of the 1920s to 1930s.

19. Hochschild (2011: 93) comments on the life-giving properties of war: "The French minister of the interior sent word to local police chiefs *not* to arrest anyone listed in Carnet B … He guessed right: 80 percent of them would eventually do military service. Even in Austria-Hungary, with its restless mix of ethnic groups to whom mobilization orders had to be issued in more than half a dozen languages, the authorities were amazed that so few men refused the call-up. In the end, as the historian Barbara Tuchman wrote, 'The working class went to war willingly, even eagerly, like the middle class, like the upper class, like the species.'" See Perry (2009) for an account of Australian soldiers leading themselves to death at Gallipoli. These are ritual forms, collected action. The destructive force is similar to what Wyatt-Brown (2001: 287) describes of the South in the 1890s.

20. To this sentence, Reid (2011: 28) adds "but also for packaging the booming tea trade."

21. Dumont references *The Nuer* and another item from Evans-Pritchard, but he was in Oxford in the early 1950s.

22. *Punya* and *dan* do not appear in *Homo Hierarchicus*, and they do not become central categories of analysis until Rhaheja and Parry publish in the 1980s. They neglect to note that *punya* flows opposite *dan*; the receiver of *dan* has to be a source of *punya*.

23. On armaments expenditures and the international social system, see Chandrasekaran (2013). See also the Cato Institute's line on defense spending (Preble 2012). Journalistic literature on this topic is enormous and expanding (see, e.g., Risen 2014).

24. Wills (2010: 3–4; emphasis added) quotes Vice President Dick Cheney: "'The President of the United States now for fifty years is followed at all times … by a military aide carrying a football that contains the nuclear codes that he would use, and be authorized to use, in the event of a nuclear attack on the United States … *He doesn't have to check with anybody, he doesn't have to call the Congress, he doesn't have to check with the courts.*'"

25. In *St. Clair*, Wallace (1988) devotes a chapter to the Mollies. Other Northern labor situations should be compared to lynching in the South.

References

Atkinson, Rick. 2013. *The Guns at Last Light: The War in Western Europe, 1944–1945.* New York: Henry Holt.

Barnett, Steve. 1976. "Coconuts and Gold: Relational Identity in a South Indian Caste." *Contributions to Indian Sociology* (n.s.) 10: 133–156.

Beevor, Antony. 2012. *The Second World War.* Boston: Little, Brown and Company.

Beidelman, T. O. 1966. "Swazi Royal Ritual." *Africa: Journal of the International African Institute* 36 (4): 373–405.

Bickler, Simon H. 2006. "Prehistoric Stone Monuments in the Northern Region of the Kula Ring." *Antiquity* 80, 307: 38–51.

Bickler, Simon, and Frederick H. Damon. n.d. *"Remember the Massim: Monumentalism in the Context of Pacific History and Sociality."* Unpublished.

Campbell, Shirley. 1983. "Attaining Rank: A Classification of Shell Valuables." In Leach and Leach 1983, 229–248.

Chandrasekaran, Rajiv. 2013. "F-35's Ability to Evade Budget Cuts Illustrates Challenge of Paring Defense Spending." *Washington Post,* 9 March.

Crocker, J. Christopher. 1969. "Reciprocity and Hierarchy among the Eastern Bororo." *Man* (n.s.) 4 (1): 44–58.

Damon, Frederick H. 1983. "On the Transformation of Muyuw into Woodlark Island: Two Minutes in December, 1974." *Journal of Pacific History* 18 (1): 35–56.

Damon, Frederick H. 1989. "The Muyuw Lo'un and the End of Marriage." In *Death Rituals and Life in the Societies of the Kula Ring,* ed. Frederick H. Damon and Roy Wagner, 73–94. DeKalb: Northern Illinois University Press.

Damon, Frederick H. 1991. *From Muyuw to the Trobriands: Transformations Along the Northern Side of the Kula Ring.* Tucson: University of Arizona Press.

Damon, Frederick H. 2002. "Kula Valuables: The Problem of Value and the Production of Names." *L'Homme* 162: 107–136.

Damon, Frederick H. 2012. "'Labour Processes' across the Indo-Pacific: Towards a Comparative Analysis of Civilisational Necessities." *Asia Pacific Journal of Anthropology* 13 (2): 163–191.

Damon, Frederick H. 2014. "Productive Destruction: Observations about Destruction as the Central Organizing Form to Social Life, 民族学刊 *(MínZúXuéKān)." Journal of Ethnology of the Southwestern Min Zu University* 5 (3): 4–6. Chinese Summary, 88–105, English version.

Damon, Frederick H. 2016. "The Problem of 'Ultimate Values': Charting a Future in Dumont's Footsteps." In *Puissance et impuissance de la valeur: L'anthropologie comparative de Louis Dumont,* ed. Cécile Barraud, André Iteanu, and Ismaël Moya, 217–233. Paris: CNRS Editions.

Dean, Kenneth. 1995. *Taoist Ritual and Popular Cults of Southeast China.* Pbk ed. Princeton, NJ: Princeton University Press.

Dening, Greg. 1992. *Mr. Bligh's Bad Language: Passion, Power and Theatre on the Bounty.* Cambridge: Cambridge University Press.

Dower, John W. 1986. *War without Mercy: Race and Power in the Pacific War.* New York: Pantheon Books.

Dumont, Louis. 1970. *Homo Hierarchicus: The Caste System and Its Implications.* Trans. Mark Sainsbury. Chicago: University of Chicago Press.

Dumont, Louis. 1986. "Genesis II: The Political Category and the State from the Thirteenth Century Onward." In *Essays on Individualism: Modern Ideology in Anthropological Perspective,* 60–103. Chicago: University of Chicago Press. Originally published in 1965 as "The Modern Conception of the Individual: Notes on Its

Genesis and That of Concomitant Institutions." *Contributions to Indian Sociology* 8: 13–61.

Elvin, Mark. 2004. *The Retreat of the Elephants: An Environmental History of China.* New Haven, CT: Yale University Press.

Evans, Richard J. 2012. "The Truth about World War II." *New York Review of Books* 59 (15): 52–56.

Evans-Pritchard, E. E. 1956. *Nuer Religion.* Oxford: Clarendon Press.

Flannery, Tim. 2001. *The Eternal Frontier: An Ecological History of North America and Its Peoples.* New York: Grove Press.

Godelier, Maurice. 1999. *The Enigma of the Gift.* Trans. Nora Scott. Chicago: University of Chicago Press.

Gregory, C. A. 1982. *Gifts and Commodities.* London: Academic Press.

Hale, Grace E. 1999. *Making Whiteness: The Culture of Segregation in the South, 1890–1940.* New York: Vintage.

Heusch, Luc de. 1985 *Sacrifice in Africa: A Structuralist Approach.* Trans. Linda O'Brien and Alice Morton. Bloomington: Indiana University Press.

Hochschild, Adam. 2011. *To End All Wars: A Story of Loyalty and Rebellion, 1914–1918.* New York: Houghton Mifflin Harcourt.

Holland, James. 2010. *The Battle of Britain: Five Months That Changed History, May–October 1940.* London: Transworld Publishers

Hubert, Henri, and Marcel Mauss. (1898) 1981. *Sacrifice: Its Nature and Functions.* Trans. W. D. Halls. Chicago: University of Chicago Press.

Iteanu, André. 2009. "Hierarchy and Power: A Comparative Attempt under Asymmetrical Lines." In Rio and Smedal 2009, 331–348.

Jacobsen, Annie. 2011. *Area 51: An Uncensored History of America's Top Secret Military Base.* New York: Little, Brown and Company.

Leach, Jerry W., and Edmund R. Leach, eds. 1983. *The Kula: New Perspectives on Massim Exchange.* Cambridge: Cambridge University Press.

Lévi-Strauss, Claude. 1963. *Totemism.* Trans. Rodney Needham. Boston: Beacon Press.

Lévi-Strauss, Claude. 1966. *The Savage Mind.* Chicago: University of Chicago Press.

Mandel, Ernest. 1975. *Late Capitalism.* Trans. Joris de Bres. London: New Left Books; Atlantic Highlands, NJ: Humanities Press.

Mauss, Marcel. (1925) 1967. *The Gift: Forms and Functions of Exchange in Archaic Societies.* Trans. Ian Cunnison. New York: W. W. Norton. Originally published in 1925 as "Essai sur le don: Forme et raison de l'échange dans les sociétés archaïques." *L'Année Sociologique* (n.s.) 1: 30–186.

Munn, Nancy D. 1983. "Gawan Kula: Spatiotemporal Control and the Symbolism of Influence." In Leach and Leach 1983, 277–308.

Oliver, Douglas L. 1974. *Ancient Tahitian Society.* 3 vols. Honolulu: University Press of Hawaii.

Peristiany, J. G., and Julian Pitt-Rivers, eds. 1992. *Honor and Grace in Anthropology.* Cambridge: Cambridge University Press.

Perry, Roland. 2009. *The Australian Light Horse: The Magnificent Australian Force and Its Decisive Victories in Arabia in World War I.* Sydney: Hachett Australia.

Pitt-Rivers, Julian. 1977. *The Fate of Shechem, or the Politics of Sex: Essays in the Anthropology of the Mediterranean.* Cambridge: Cambridge University Press.

Preble, Christopher A. 2012. "Lies, Damned Lies, and Defense-Job Statistics." *Foreign Policy*, 5 November. https://www.cato.org/publications/commentary/lies-damned-lies-defensejob-statistics.

Priest, Dana, and William M. Arkin. 2011. *Top Secret America: The Rise of the New American Security State.* New York: Little, Brown and Company.

Reid, Anthony. 2011. "Chinese on the Mining Frontier in Southeast Asia." In *Chinese Circulations: Capital, Commodities and Networks in Southeast Asia*, ed. Eric Taglia-cozzo and Wen-Chin Chang, 21–36. Durham, NC: Duke University Press.

Richards, Leonard L. 2000. *The Slave Power: The Free North and Southern Domination, 1780–1860*. Baton Rouge: Louisiana State University Press.

Rigby, Peter. 1971. "The Symbolic Role of Cattle in Gogo Ritual." In *The Translation of Culture: Essays to E. E. Evans-Pritchard*, ed. T. O. Beidelman, 257–291. London: Tavistock.

Rio, Knut M., and Olaf H. Smedal., eds. 2009. *Hierarchy: Persistence and Transformation in Social Formations*. New York: Berghahn Books.

Risen, James. 2014. *Pay Any Price: Greed, Power, and Endless War*. New York: Hough-ton Mifflin Harcourt.

Robbins, Joel. 2009. "Conversion, Hierarchy, and Cultural Change: Value and Syncre-tism in the Globalization of Pentecostal and Charismatic Christianity." In Rio and Smedal 2009, 65–88.

Rowlands, Michael. 2003. "The Unity of Africa." In *Ancient Egypt in Africa*, ed. David O'Connor and Andrew Reid, 39–54. London: University College London Press.

Sahlins, Marshall. 1985. *Islands of History*. Chicago: University of Chicago Press.

Steil, Benn. 2013. *The Battle of Bretton Woods: John Maynard Keynes, Harry Dexter White, and the Making of a New World Order*. Princeton, NJ: Princeton University Press.

Taylor, Christopher C. 1999. *Sacrifice as Terror: The Rwandan Genocide of 1994*. Oxford: Berg.

Tylor, Edward B. (1871) 1920. *Primitive Culture: Researches into the Development of Mythology, Philosophy, Religion, Language, Art, and Custom*. 2 vols. London: John Murray.

Valeri, Valerio. 1985. *Kingship and Sacrifice: Ritual and Society in Ancient Hawaii*. Trans. Paula Wissing. Chicago: University of Chicago Press.

Wallace, Anthony F. C. (1978) 2005. *Rockdale: The Growth of an American Village in the Early Industrial Revolution*. Rev. ed. Lincoln: University of Nebraska Press.

Wallace, Anthony F. C. 1988. *St. Clair: A Nineteenth-Century Coal Town's Experience with a Disaster-Prone Industry*. Pbk ed. Ithaca, NY: Cornell University Press.

Wallerstein, Immanuel. 1974. *The Modern World-System: Capitalist Agriculture and the Origins of the European World-Economy in the Sixteenth Century*. New York: Aca-demic Press.

Wallerstein, Immanuel. 2004. *World-Systems Analysis: An Introduction*. Durham, NC: Duke University Press.

Weiner, Annette B. 1992. *Inalienable Possessions: The Paradox of Keeping-While-Giving*. Berkeley: University of California Press.

Wills, Garry. 2003. *"Negro President": Jefferson and the Slave Power*. New York: Hough-ton Mifflin.

Wills, Garry. 2010. *Bomb Power: The Modern Presidency and the National Security State*. New York: Penguin Press.

Wyatt-Brown, Bertram. 1982. *Southern Honor: Ethics and Behavior in the Old South*. New York: Oxford University Press.

Wyatt-Brown, Bertram. 2001. *The Shaping of Southern Culture: Honor, Grace, and War, 1760s–1880s*. Chapel Hill: University of North Carolina Press.

Chapter 4

CIVILIZATION, HIERARCHY, AND POLITICAL-ECONOMIC INEQUALITY

Stephan Feuchtwang

Instead of amplifying Louis Dumont's (1972) *Homo Hierarchicus* as the *locus classicus* of the anthropological conception of hierarchy, I shall take his work back to an earlier publication by another French master, Marcel Mauss. In doing so, I argue that we should understand Louis Dumont's conception of hierarchy as encompassment and ideology to be a starting point for an anthropology of comparative civilizations and their histories. Combining Mauss with Dumont offers a conception of civilization that in itself is not evaluative or ethnocentric, but is *about* evaluation, centricity, encompassment and ideology. I shall argue that Dumont's ideal type of hierarchy, based on Brahmanic priestly purity, should be treated as merely one of many different types of human hierarchy and, thus, that instead of an ideal type, we can conceptualize the basic ingredients of all human hierarchies and include them in the concept of civilization. Hierarchies can and should be compared, but not in a single structure of type and anti-type as Dumont does. I shall argue that what he took to be an anti-hierarchy—the ideology of egalitarian individualism—is in fact hierarchical with all ingredients present. But that is not the comparison I shall mount with extended examples. Drawn from civilization in China, the examples I discuss will illustrate the great value of a concept of civilization, which is to reintroduce into anthropology the historical processes of transformation that last for hundreds or even thousands of years and that may or may not present sequences that are repeated in other civilizations elsewhere in the world.

A further point in my treatment of Dumont and the concept of civilization that I will elaborate is his differentiation of hierarchy from power and economic inequality. Hierarchy and civilization are obviously affected by political economy and its changes, but hierarchy and civilization are at the same distinguishable as affecting and encompassing those changes. Classes are reconceived and experienced through the ideologies and encompassments of hierarchy. I hope to illustrate this with my Chinese examples.

Mauss on Civilization

Mauss wrote: "The form of a civilisation is the sum ... of the specific aspects taken by the ideas, practices and products, which are more or less common to a number of given societies ... We could also say that the form of a civilisation, is everything which gives a special aspect, unlike any other, to the societies which compose this civilisation" ([1930] 2006: 63). In the technical terms of Mauss's (and Durkheim's) sociology, a civilization is the geographic spread of collective representations and practices. Collective representations are the shared imaginary and material symbols of social relations that, when combined, make up total social facts. In his essay on civilization, Mauss calls them "ideas, practices and products." He says that these are 'arbitrary', by which he means they are not universal but preferred (by a 'collective will', to use his term) modes of making and doing things. In other civilizations, the same things are done in different ways.

To make what Mauss says explicit, that is, to claim that a variation of ideas, products, and practices belong together as a civilization, is to infer from archaeological, ethnographic, and documentary evidence a common set of forms, practices, and meanings—not one dominant characteristic, design, or thing, but the way they all hang together—and to trace their evolution over time and their variation in space. To make these inferences is to mark boundaries of civilizational spread. Beyond them, further spreads of traded goods can be seen, but they are distinct by being regarded as strange or exotic, rather than accepted for the symbolic meanings or purposes that their producers attach to them. On the other hand, within a civilizational spread there are other boundaries of more coherent structures and their centers: polities, cultures, societies. These enclose and differentiate themselves from others in similar ways that each can recognize because they characterize a shared civilization. To draw out further the implications of Mauss's concept, civilization is a way of defining inside and outside. It gives societies and cultures a mode of self-definition and internal coherence. Local centers, or larger centers of more coherence, differ from their neighbors as an inside to an outside. The variation among them increases with greater geographical distance until a civilizational border region is reached where even greater differences are to be found, namely, differences between civilizations. But even there on these borders, local societies and cultures will be creative mixtures of civilizations, related to both or more sides and their centers. And what comes from elsewhere through these border regions may well be absorbed into those centers. Civilizations are centered mixtures.

Civilization in this conception is like 'culture', but it emphasizes the *spread* of culture, of "constant borrowings and evolutions," as Mauss says ([1930] 2006: 68). It is like 'society', but it is more loosely systemic than is a society. Not just at their borders, where it might first occur, but at their centers, even as they make them their 'own', civilizations are transformed by additions from elsewhere, from other civilizations. 'Civilization' is a grand but not a totalizing concept of social, moral, cultural, and material life.

'Civilization' in Mauss's conception therefore calls for an anthropology of processes of transformation and of diffusion, a critical return to the long term and to comparison over wide geographical spaces. But this would be done with evidence from archaeology and documentation, informing inferences from ethnographic observations and rejecting ethnocentric assumptions such as those made by many of the evolutionary theorists and diffusionists of Mauss's time. Such a renewal and reconception of 'civilization' in anthropology is something of a movement, whose main figures currently include Johann Arnason and Jan Assmann. Ulf Hannerz (1997) had already alerted us to the importance of flows of culture across social boundaries, to borders, and to hybrids, which I think are all much better conceptualized under the Maussian category of civilization.

Such moves in anthropology have their equivalent among historians calling for a reconfigured return to the *longue durée*. Armitage and Guldi (2014) celebrate the new possibilities of computed analysis of huge databases covering long periods of time as tests of ideas that would make history into a critical social science again, whereas my concern is first of all with developing a critical analytic concept of long-term transformation. Note too that I am interested in transformation, in continuity through radical change, not just in duration and its end, although of course what has endured can have an irreversible end as well as irreversible transformations.

Lastly, as Mauss ([1930] 2006: 71) points out, we come upon the evaluative element that is carried in common usage but must also be included in any concept of civilization. Every civilization, except that of the most exigently egalitarian societies, is a hierarchy of distinction, of standards of wealth, comfort, strength, skill, order, organization, etiquette, and civility (this is Mauss's list). In other words, civilization is ideological and aspirational. It ranks and distinguishes 'fine' art from 'popular' art, a great tradition from a little one, what merits distinction and what is experienced as failure, and within all this, for Mauss, is the formation of the person as a moral being. The governing ideology may exclude subjects of that civilization from realizing themselves according to its aspirations, standards, and evaluations, treating them as less than or not even civilized. This is a central topic for the study of civilizations in terms of the concept Mauss offers, but the concept endorses none of them.

Whereas insiders describe their own centricity and differences from others in evaluative reflections on their habits and practices in certain ways, the concept of civilization analyzes but does not endorse the ways in which people define themselves and distinguish themselves from others. For instance, insiders' knowledge of others is both informative—in that it can provide evidence of what was in their border regions and beyond—and indicative of their idealizations of themselves. However, we cannot rely solely on this self-definition and knowledge of others. We add all other sources of knowledge to see what else might characterize the ways that the familiar center and the wild periphery, the known and the unknown, the high and the low are differentiated. Similarly, when the evaluation marks out high from low in the vertical conception of spatial marginalization, the etic conception of civilization takes such evaluations as data, but not as criteria of what is 'civilization'. There may indeed be several evaluative hierarchies, or heterarchies, in any one civilization and its spread, co-existing and complementing each other, let alone distinguishing themselves from other civilizations. This is all the more so for the anthropology of civilizations, in which no one civilization and no one evaluative hierarchy can be the prototype. The possibility of such an anthropology brings me to the work of Dumont—its rigor, its indispensability for a conception of hierarchy—but also to the problems that make it an obstacle to comparison.

Historical Human Types: Dumont and Hierarchy

In *Homo Hierarchicus*, Louis Dumont (1972) describes a pair of ideologies: those of *homo aegalis* (or *homo minor*) and *homo hierarchicus* (or *homo major*). The latter is a hierarchy of endogamous sub-castes constituted by rules of propriety and a division of labor among them, a hierarchy from the lowest to the highest, the most polluted to the purest, in which aspiration to rise in the hierarchy can be realized only by sub-caste mobility. Mobility is achieved, for instance, through political and economic domination being converted into caste, or by acquiring higher caste accomplishment while changing or disguising one's natal status, or by locally establishing a caste as dominant. Political-economic relations of class inequality and dominance are contained by hierarchy, or rather encompassed as the contrary of hierarchy. *Homo aegalis* is for Dumont purely political economy, lived and produced by the striving of individuals who are formally equal.

Dumont elaborates the Enlightenment philosophies of individual rationality and describes these as a general counter-type to 'hierarchical' humanity. He makes no distinction between this European tradition and the traditions of small-scale egalitarian societies. Crucially, he reserves his concept of 'ideology', which describes the evaluative core of hierarchy, for his Indian prototype, ignoring the fact that small-scale egalitarian societies have ideologies of egalitarianism that keep them egalitarian and that the European cult of individualism is also an ideology, but does not maintain equality at all. It is the ideology of equality of opportunity: individuals and families might move up and down, according to ideals of merit in learning and its accomplishment, of risk taking and its just rewards, and of work and its just fruits. I maintain that this is an ideology, since the detractors of factual inequality use the same ideology to denounce reality, just as Brahmanic hierarchy is used to denounce found failures to live up to it. In the ideology of merit and reward, inequalities are justified by using ideas of natural and inherent incompetence, a racial theory of class, or an ethnic idea of outsiders as inferior. The inequality justified by the ideology of merit and market is a hierarchy of status groups, and it encompasses by justifying the top, the elite. Thus, it encompasses and justifies or denounces class inequalities just as the caste hierarchy does.

Encompassment is also achieved by the collective version of the same ideology, now not individual self-realization but a more or less nuanced and multiple but nevertheless essentialized popular self, identified with a territorial sovereignty. This collective self, or unified diversity of selves with claims to representation, is found repeatedly in the rhetorical invocation and measurement of public opinion and in the historical myths and wars that sort the world into 'us' and 'others'. Its self-realization is this ideology's future-oriented temporality, accounting for the past of its emergence, its current travails, and the future generations as its hope. These are ideals, dominant ideals (which Dumont calls 'ideology'). The reality of class relations is not a realization of these ideals either in India for *homo hierarchicus* or in Europe (or North America, or anywhere else in the world) for *homo aegalis*.

A related problem shadowing Dumont's account of these two ideologies is how they are affected by—or in turn themselves affect—the processes of political economy. Critically, it must be asked whether their *non*-realization produces other ideologies, variants upon them among the very same population. Such variants could eventually become new or transformed ideologies affecting the relation of rule. The relation between Brahmans and kings is particularly important in this respect (Fuller 1992). The pairing and separation of Brahmanic responsibility for the cosmos, on the one hand, and sovereign responsibility for rule, on the other, are for Dumont an encompassing structure and its contained opposite. Their separation meant that there never was a single Brahmanic empire, just kingdoms linked by the Brahmanic hierarchies of caste and ritual. Brahmanic ideals bred critiques of the world as an impure realm of mundane reality, the red dust of the suffering world. It is inherently possible that such critiques, either from below or from above, could produce movements of transformation in both political and ideological realities, the key example being the rise of Buddhism in India. Dumont's account offers no way of saying how hierarchy might be subject to such transformations and have been the result of structural transformation, such as the struggles between classes and status groups that, as Norbert Elias ([1939] 1994) shows in *The Civilizing Process*, have resulted in the national character of civilization and its ideology of individualism and equality in Europe from the eighteenth century.

In addition to this serious limitation, there is a vexing comparative problem. Dumont uses the structuralism of complementary opposition to set up binary opposites: not just purity versus pollution, but also *aegalis* versus *hierarchicus*, in which *aegalis* stands for modernity, now globally spread in a chronology that he acknowledges, while *hierarchicus* presents a pre-modern form without a chronology of emergence except in India. India is generalized to become 'hierarchy' as such. We should, I think, do two things with these binaries. One is to accept certain characteristics of the way Dumont describes hierarchy, namely, that it is ranking in status and scale through an ideology with material exemplary objects of encompassment. But we should hold in reserve the structuralist imperative of a totality constituted by encompassment and its negation. Structural analysis serves well to expound the ideology of purity and pollution, but it may serve other ideologies less well. The other option, as I have already suggested, is to reject Dumont's contention that hierarchy is confined to something designated as traditional or pre-modern.

All this adds up to the possibility of defining several such *homo* as long-persisting human types, of which equal-opportunity-*aegalis* and Indian-purity-and-pollution are just two, each of them a product of and subject to a history. I feel justified in this because Dumont himself felt it necessary to refer to a civilization and therefore, by implication, to others, each one having its own temporality and also its own history. Dumont (1972: 242) states: "In fact, the search for fundamental constants in Indian civilization—renunciation, specific place of royalty, hierarchy with its implications mentioned here—yields correspondingly a certain idea, a certain form, of historical development." Typically, he invokes civilization in order to identify constants, a society revealing itself through its history, as he puts it. I would in addition search for transformation of whatever remains constant.

Instead of proposing that one civilization, the Brahmanic, is an ideal type, as Dumont does, I think it would be better to avoid holism but to accept encompassment, not only for hierarchical but also for egalitarian civilizations. In a hierarchy, this is possible only if all those underneath, in the lower reaches of the hierarchy, accept the principle of ranking that makes the top the encompassing embodiment of all that is below. The principle that a hierarchy and its top are *ideologically* justified as encompassing can be accepted while insisting on its historical contingency. More pertinently, those in encompassing ranks may betray the ideals of the hierarchy, and therefore the same or alternative realizations of the ideology may be critically espoused by the lower ranks. In other words, precisely the evaluative content of a civilization, the ideals internally accepted as such, has a critical function. That critical function can work itself out without altering the hierarchy, but probably with some civilizational admixtures, it can also, in aggregate and over a long period, work out as a transformation of hierarchy (as I will show in my Chinese case study), with some continuity of what Dumont refers to above as "constants." In any case, all civilizations, hierarchical and non-hierarchical, and all ranks in a hierarchy are self-fashioning, according to the norms of the ideology of encompassment.

So, returning to my point about there being many hierarchies, or historical human types, I include all human cultures in the broader and more linked-up concept of civilization as a structure of practices of self-fashioning constraint. Elias seems to contend that the civilization of the bourgeois mimesis of court manners was the first to engage self-restraint over violent impulses. But Hadza hunters and foragers are as self-constrained—in their case, to be generous and to share—as any other civilization (Woodburn 1982).

Hierarchy can be shallow, as in Highland New Guinea Big Man civilization or Australian Aborigine ritual knowledge civilization, or steep, as in Brahmanic and class statuses of meritocratic equal opportunity. Rio and Smedal (2009: 35–41) demonstrate that Melanesian egalitarianism is encompassed by a striving of each to gain access to life-giving substances and is therefore hierarchical: its ideology is an aspiration to become a person whose will is a greater version of the will of every other person. This and other shallow hierarchical civilizations feature totalizing and encompassing objects such as, in this instance, a Big Man. Another example of an encompassing object is an outrigger canoe and its material, including its analogical relations to gardens and islands of forest, in the Kula system of the circulation of valuables (Damon 2008).

In what Woodburn (1982) refers to as demand-sharing, immediate-return economies, there is no hierarchy. But to judge from the work of Jerome Lewis, I would argue that there is both encompassment and a realized ideology of egalitarianism that involves collective sanctions, especially those conducted by women, against domination, against the failure to share, and even against being too successful in hunting. Such anti-hierarchical hunter-gather societies exist in all parts of the globe, and Lewis (2014) lists them. They are hunter-gatherers without horticulture or pastoral production. The Mbendjele BaYaka Pygmies in central Africa, an example he gives, have initiation rituals in which the myth of the gender division of social organization is enacted and ancestors recalled, but they do not have age grades. Significantly, they perform polyphonic music in what Lewis calls 'spirit plays', which act as a model of egalitarian division of labor and of being part of a "society of nature" (ibid.: 86) that involves listening to and mimicking the forest and its fauna, which also listen to each other. Masks representing this relation with the surrounding forest are an important part of this singing of spirit plays, and I would argue that the mask and the euphoric experience of the collective performance are encompassing objects. In sum, in this case egalitarianism is evaluatively endorsed by its encompassment as an anti-hierarchical civilization. Lewis argues well, citing others' evidence, that this is a civilization of immense duration, but one whose transformations he cannot delineate except for its duration through recent transformations of juxtaposition with agrarian populations.

Every civilization conveys ideas about an encompassing and evaluative reality. In many cases, particularly but not only in steeper hierarchies, these ideas include practical condemnations of those who exist in the lower reaches of the hierarchy as well as erecting permanent impediments to rising within it. The most drastic impediments—from the most shallow to the steepest hierarchies, but not the anti-hierarchical hunter-gatherers—are those of gender and of captivity, especially their combination, as a result of raids and wars, although there is the possibility of being included in the kin of the conquerors and thus of rising in the hierarchy. In describing them, the anthropology of civilizations does not of course endorse these ideas or the steeper hierarchical ideologies of inequality as a universal standard, even though in their own terms all pre-modern civilizations claim to be universal. The important point is that a civilization is a transmission of aspiration to the ideals of an ideology. Once they involve evaluative ranking, they often include mobility over a time frame (which may include many generations or simply a life-course), but also a reproduction of the impediments to aspiration. For myself and for my colleague Mike Rowlands, with whom I am working on a book that seeks to reintroduce the concept to anthropology, 'civilization' is thus (1) usually hierarchical; (2) aspirational but with impediments to rising in the hierarchy; (3) evaluative, inasmuch as it is a promotion of moral and aesthetic good; and (4) the basis of internal critiques of that civilization, its centers and tops of hierarchy.

Hierarchy and the 'Axial' Civilizations

One quite elementary ranking occurs when someone is accepted as a leader because he or she conveys grace or divinity or has access to hidden forces. To these traits must be added the knowledge of how to conduct rites. The invisible world of the dead and of the spirits has gateways accessible to those with ritual expertise in the world of the living, which is the world of seasonal life cycles and mortality. What is more, as the great Weberian sociologist S. N. Eisenstadt (1986, 2003) first noted, the middle phase of rites of passage, which Victor Turner named the 'liminal' stage, is experienced as an apprehension of a world or of a cosmos and its genesis, a sense of the giving of life. The final phase, if we follow Maurice Bloch's (1992) interpretation of Van Gennep and Turner, is then the reconquest of the world of the living—a reinforcement of an authoritative ideology of the source of life and the authority to take life.

But Eisenstadt and his followers conceive of civilization as the articulation and disclosure of a world and of the practices of being in the world as an elite articulation reliant on writing. For them, with their stress on hermeneutical sociology, civilization as such is potential or latent but not yet a fact until it is a self-professed and distinct level of articulation, institutionalized through writing and all that it implies. In short, we cannot speak of 'civilization' until transcendence replaces or transforms immanence. There have been modifications of Karl Jaspers's original thesis on the emergence of 'axial' religions as the foundation of both civilization and humanity. One important instance is Eisenstadt's own finding that Japanese civilization was not axial but nevertheless produced a modernity. Another is Arnason's (2010a, 2010b) stress on the 'archaic' civilizations, so called although they long preceded the axial age. Nevertheless, Eisenstadtians maintain the framework of the Weberian teleology of what might lead to 'modernity' as a single civilization. For them, the axial moment comes when an ideology and ideal of transcendence and its disciplines, including reading and writing, generates a stance capable of criticism of mundane reality.

Eisenstadtians are therefore prone to using civilization in the singular and telling its history with modernity as a current end result. Such singular histories need not be sanguine or progressive. For instance, Franz Steiner ([1938] 1999) describes a process of civilization as a way of organizing the avoidance of danger and contagion in a history of increasing domination, not over nature, but over other people and peoples. The least civilized, least dominating situate danger and others on their borders. Danger and otherness are ambivalently strange, wonderful, and demonic for these lesser civilizations. The most civilized, most dominant civilization is the one imposed on and extending across the world from Europe, in which the demonic and dangerous, as well as its policing, are internal (ibid.).

I am for keeping civilizations plural, comparing them, and asking what happens to each in their encounter with the ideology and political economy of Europe-generated 'modernity'. Challenges to the Weberian dichotomy between traditional and modern ideal typical models of authority have been too many to review here. I will just say that it is still possible to identify the modernization project with an ideology and a civilization that has by now been absorbed and modified by civilizations all over the world. Furthermore, I accept that the invention of writing introduces a capacity (not a necessity) of religions that advocate renunciation of the world to set a pattern of transcendence over the world of the living and therefore to question it. The disciplines of writing and reading encourage retreat into solitary contemplation in addition to preserving a past knowledge or a set of rules or a truth that is related to but distinct from a present reality. But it needs also to be said that patterns of non-textual rituals, the generality of rituals that perform a reconquest of the world of the living, are just as civilizational. They are just as much evaluative as those that use writing. The significance of the emergence of literate elites is the steepening of hierarchies of aspiration and exclusion. The liturgies and handbooks of rituals and their compilation in texts such as those of the methods and results of divination add a level of authority over other claims to ritual expertise. Writing aids the formation of states and their capacity to subject populations, on the one hand, and to canonize 'cultural memory' (Assmann 2006), on the other. Lévi-Strauss's (1961: 292) hypothesis still has validity: "[T]he primary function of writing, as a means of communication, is to facilitate the enslavement of other human beings."

The realization of the potential effects of writing and other transformations of hierarchy takes a long time, and sometimes we have sufficient materials, including written records, to trace them. The topic of 'civilization' alerts us to such temporally lengthy transformations and continuities. But does the description and comparison of civilizations and their hierarchies need to be confined to the 'axial' and the written? Surely, this is to accept the point of view of the elites. It is to fall short of a more analytical comparison of hierarchical civilizations and their evaluative ideologies.

In an attempt in the 1950s–1960s by anthropologists and historians at a comparative historical anthropology of cultures and civilizations, organized and heavily influenced by Robert Redfield and his concept of Great Traditions, every civilization was seen top down. Redfield (1948) studied peasants, what was below, and transformed the study of villages and peasant-farmers by making clear that they are not isolates but what he called 'part-societies', that is, parts of a larger economy of marketed commodities and of an encompassing civilization, which he called a Great Tradition, of which peasants lived a Little version.

Including the ideas, products, and practices of peasants or anyone else at the bottom of hierarchies is surely a good and necessary thing to do, but it should be done without endorsing or prioritizing textual traditions, high-status practices, capital cities, and tops of hierarchy. It is more important to see the work of transmission of ideology at all levels and to ask how or if those levels work together. Indeed, the facts are that the main centers accommodate themselves to less powerful centers within their regimes as well as to those on the frontiers of their regimes. They show the reverse of so-called Little and Great Traditions in terms of agency. Contrary to the Great Tradition concept of civilization, I would not reserve the term 'civilization' for a description of the top echelons, the courtliest, the most literate. Rather, I think it is preferable to refer to aspirations toward ideals of cultivation, and that includes quite ordinary habits of eating, of preparing food, and, especially, of rituals of offerings to gods or ancestors and of hospitality to others, including spirits, and how that otherness is conceived and played out in practice, at all levels of hierarchy.

To sum up, 'civilization' as a usage is always ideological, which is to say it is contentious. But that does not mean we, as anthropologists, should not use this word and develop it as a concept for its analytic use. Its ideological usage is a key point of interest. Civilization is a descriptive term for the depiction of habitual and transmitted aspirations for self-realization and hierarchical mobility during a life-course or over several generations of self-cultivation. Such aspirations are shared and also disputed, with others professing to share the same or similarly formulated and identified standards of aspiration.

For the analyst, the concept of civilization is descriptive and not ideological, even though it is about ideology. It does not endorse or validate the standards it describes in each case. My use of the word 'civilization' therefore describes evaluational encompassment, ideology, aspiration, and self-fashioning, all of which are at once continuous historically and at the same time transformed. Civilizations have histories, partly because they can be self-critical, partly because they have to absorb the contingencies of political relations, wars, influences from other civilizations, and the political economies that they encompass. I emphasize that the concept of civilization can be used critically as well as descriptively, exposing the ideological usage that justifies the continuation of privilege and denies the civilizational aspirations of others in the hierarchy.

I turn now to an example of a hierarchy and its civilization not envisaged by Dumont, namely, that which emerged with the imperial unification of civilization in China. First, I will date and describe its emergence. I will then describe some of the long-term processes of its transformation, including the absorption and remaking of Buddhism from India.

Civilization and Hierarchy in China

In a period of roughly two millennia from about 4000 BCE, archaeological evidence without writing indicates steepening hierarchy in what is now China. As soon as we encounter ranks of tombs, judged by their size and contents, we also encounter fortified villages, then towns, and then cities (Zhao Hui 2012). Within them we also encounter a theme: the relation between offerings to ancestors and offerings to other spirits and how each might establish claims to authority and to property in land and surplus (gift or tribute) derived from powers to contact divinities. Based on the largest tombs, we can infer that rulers were shamans and military leaders and that their successors treated their forebears as mediators to more powerful spirits.

I do not know how to define exactly a point in this development of towns where we can speak of the formation of states (note the plural). Once fortified towns or cities with artisans and rulers' courts had emerged, along with palaces, walls, and large tombs, then certainly we can say that there were states and that this was part of a long process of the steepening of hierarchy.

From 2000 BCE on, goods accompanying coffins became increasingly elaborate (Wu Hung 2010: 21–25), now with writing. They exemplify a hierarchy in a world invisible to the living, created and deliberately hidden inside tombs, and also suggest the importance of burial in the civilization emerging over this period. The steepening of hierarchy appears to have resulted in 'shaman-ancestor' becoming 'ancestor' pure and simple, with shamans remaining as advisers to rulers who turned to a quest for immortality as sage rulers of patrilineal noble descent. The encompassing object was the fortified city and palace as well as the shamanic reference upward to a supreme deity, called Di late in this emergence of states. This long process occurred in many centers, among which a ruler might have hegemony but did not establish a single ruling center. Unlike Mauss's starting point of civilization spreading out from a single center, instead we find similarities of practice and product, along with significant variation, among several centers. Three things drove this transformation. One was the Neolithic revolution of agriculture and the domestication of animals. A second was the import and imitation of metalworking and its products, including armor and personal weapons for sovereigns, from Central Asia. The third was the invention of writing, first on pots, then for the interpretation of divination by oracle bones, and then for inscription on bronzes to establish noble status. In other words, an increasing hierarchy of valuables, gifts, and traded objects were introduced into an encompassed political economy, and its effect was the transformation of shallow into steep hierarchies.

But then, from the third century BCE onward, a single center was established through military conquest by one of the preceding centers, the Qin, making itself both the cosmological and the political capital, a pattern followed by all subsequent dynasties. The capital city changed location several times in the course of the empire's history, and the empire was often divided into rival dynasties, but always with the claim to form a single cosmological and political center. The center was in fact invigorated from its outer regions and according to the cosmology of the universe known as "Tianxia (All under Heaven)" (Wang Mingming 2014: 3). Tian/Heaven was by now the encompassing and supreme reference, the encompassing dome and seat of virtue in this civilization. The center of mediation by humans between Earth and Tian/Heaven was the political capital, but its sources of strength and divinity, including closeness to Tian, were mountains in its outer regions, from which numinous power was brought into the center.

The act of conquering rival states and forming an empire, and the subsequent imperial sponsorship of the synchronization of several systems of ritual, divination, physical, and moral knowledge, established the unification and singularity of political and civilizational centricity. In this unified cosmology, accompanied by writing, humanity was not transcendent. On the contrary, this was a cosmology of humanity that mediated by ritual means and by knowledge gained through divination, including the imperial issuing of calendars that were also almanacs of the circuits of vital energy (*qi*) that mark constant movement, cyclical and transgressive, and are manifest in the forms of Earth, solid and fluid, and in the bodies of Heaven, bright and stellar. According to the revered ritual manual, *Li Ji*, sage rulers should take this "as a pattern for the black-haired people" (cited in Puett 2008: 208–209),[1] who are thus distinguished from other, less civilized people. The mandate of Tian/Heaven to the emperor as 'son' of Heaven meant that the emperor was the supreme mediator between Heaven and Earth. A poor ruler allowed his officials to be self-seeking, his court to be extravagant, and the common people to seek the aid of spirits and so to attempt to find their own mediations to Tian. This was an admission that from their lower levels and centers, commoners aspired to communicate with the ultimate center, Tian. For the ruler and his advisers, on the other hand, in a phrase often cited, 'cutting the [lay] communication between Heaven and Earth' was the ideal. Through his sacrifices, the ruler, aided by ritual experts, ordered both the places of the spirits in Tian/Heaven and the places of men on Earth, according to the fourth-century BCE text *Discourses of the State* (*Guoyu*), while the ruled simply revered the spirits and obeyed. Yet a later Han dynasty classical compilation titled the *Writings of Master Guan* (*Guanzi*), which includes texts of the same period as the *Discourses of the State*, asserts that each person has an essence of vital energy that can be cultivated as a spirit, and that through such cultivation sagehood can be achieved. This was the other principle of civilization in China besides sage rule that had emerged by the third century BCE, namely, that knowledge and the attainment of sagacity was not a question of descent by birth, as in succession to an imperial dynasty. It was an attainment by means of learning, discipline, and technique in a system of discipleship and a line of masters.

Hierarchy in this civilization was not of caste but of status, including sage or divine status. But it depended on literacy, which was an exclusively narrow achievement for those with wealth in land and mercantile accumulation. In the early centuries of this civilization, such wealth was the privilege of nobility and magnates of inherited and large landed estates, despite the ideology that aspiration to perfection through self-cultivation was open to all. There was no separation of responsibility for rule as there was in the Brahmanic hierarchy in India. Sage rule by an emperor who was the son of Heaven unified cosmological rule with political rule. Only inherited large-scale landlords and the literate could make ancestors of their dead and aspire to the accomplishments of the 'consummate man' (*junzi*), the subject of the writings of the Confucian tradition and of the rites and propriety of filial hierarchy that became the imperial canon of cultural memory.

Two Further Examples of Long-Term Civilizational Change

The dynamic of the processes of civilizational change that I shall now add in outline are, again, political and economic. From the Tang dynasty (618–905) onward, imperial codes protected private land ownership for all peasants and instituted equal inheritance among sons, thus breaking up landed estates that were not lineage, princely, or monastic trusts.

The Tang period was one of the most open periods of Chinese civilization— open to the influences of other civilizations while retaining its own centrality in the universe. Indeed, it expanded the extent of imperial rule to its greatest point westward, achieved again only by the last dynasty, the Qing. Like the Qing rulers, who were Manchu, the Tang rulers were not from the central areas of civilization in China, nor were they fully Chinese ethnically, being of mixed Turkic and Chinese parentage. In this they repeated a pattern begun before and continuing with the very formation of the unified empire under the Qin: the military and inspirational sources of renewal came from outside the centered polity. The Tang capital cities Chang'an (present-day Xi'an) and Luoyang (in northern China) were full of Turkic, Persian, Central Asian, Arabic, and other nationalities (Hansen 2000: chaps. 4 and 5).

Most notable was the great number of Buddhist monasteries that had been founded over the long period of six centuries from the initial introduction of Buddhism to China. There were several Indian Buddhist monks, two of whom were also alchemists, who provided to the emperor the means to prolong life and achieve immortality (Forte 1985). The most famous Buddhist was the Chinese monk Xuanzang, who spent 16 years traveling through Central Asia to India. He lived there learning Sanskrit and Hindi in order to bring back to the Chinese capital a large collection of Buddhist scriptures, which he proceeded to translate. Indian Buddhists at the same court had long before also been engaged in this work of translation alongside their Chinese brothers. This relationship to India as the land of the Buddha, and its revered King Ashoka (268–232 BCE) as the model of Buddhist monarchy, marginalized China as outside the area in which the Buddha had lived. Xuanzang felt the need to respond to the amazement of his Indian brothers in Nalanda, the center of learned Buddhist life in India, at his wish to return to China, which they saw as a land of barbarians. He countered by asserting that the Chinese empire was a land of exemplary rule and wisdom. But this mutual marginalization between centers of the world and of civilizations set up what Forte (ibid.) calls a 'borderland complex' for the Chinese Buddhists highly favored by the Tang court. The court's and their response was to compose new Buddhist sutras, in Sanskrit and in Chinese, hailing China as the land of Buddha.

The next major transformation in this history came during the second half of the Tang dynasty after a reaction against the landed power of monasteries.[2] In a revival of Han dynasty Confucianism, Buddhist monasteries were attacked, and monks and nuns were forced to work on the land and to pay taxes. The revenues thus acquired by the court helped to pay Turkic generals and their armies who had been assigned to fight off other Altaic- or Turkic-speaking pastoralists and their federations threatening invasion.

Finally, the Khitans, an Altaic tribal federation, took control of the northern region of Chinese provinces, exercising a dual rule that was federal and tribal facing north, but city-centered on the Tang model facing south. The reconquest of some, but not the far north, of Tang China in the tenth century by the forces of the new Song dynasty remained in a similarly threatened relation to the successors of the Khitans and then the Jurchen (Mongol) federation, which eventually took a much larger northern swath of land and formed its own Chinese dynasty, taking over the Song capital Kaifeng and forcing the Song south to a new capital, Hangzhou. All these centuries of northern invasion had forced Chinese farmers and landowners to move south of the Great River, the Yangzi, where they drained and irrigated rice-growing lands and built new cities. The Song emperors increased the powers of civil officials who specialized in the passing of civil service examinations and argued over the way to rule and what should be learned in the examinations. The way to rule meant, eventually, to stimulate commerce as a tax base for revenue. The Song emperors, aware of the danger to their rule from their own generals, avoided armed attack as a response to the northern threat. Instead, they resorted to diplomatic gift exchange with the tribal federations to ward them and other federations off. In addition, the results of this Song ruling strategy, that is, making commerce and the production of commodities respectable, brought about a rise in the literacy of artisans and merchants and, as before, an increase in self-cultivation in a number of traditions, including the one associated with Confucius, but also those of Daoism and of Buddhism, with their own hierarchies of the accomplishment of sagehood. Expanded literacy was accompanied by an increase in candidates for the examinations. All these were results of symbiotic relations between militarily strong pastoral and trade-controlling outsiders and the agrarian inside. It replayed the dynamic of transgression and adaptation by the self-proclaimed civilizational centers of sage rule.

The absorption of indigenous local cultures and the Southern Song reliance on commerce, as well as an enlarged and opened civil administration, had the unintended consequence of a strong tendency to celebrate local officials and elite ancestors. This was interwoven with the building of local shrines to deities from elsewhere, often Daoist adepts who had achieved perfection and could bring rain or heal illness (Hymes 2002). Another element of this localism of the high elite was a parallel building of academies to study the works of commentators and reformers of the Confucian classics. Local academies that honored famous scholars of 'the way of the learned' (rujiao), mountain temples and abbeys in which Daoists who had achieved perfection were worshipped, and others where Buddhists also sought personal and world salvation were the institutions of the literate, although the abbeys and monasteries were also destinations of commoner pilgrimage. At the same time, local temples to deities who embodied both virtue and the power to act in the visible world spread among commoners. During the Southern Song (1127–1229), local elites promoted such temples and their gods for endorsement by the imperial court in increasing numbers (Hansen 1990). Privileges of birth for entry into the imperial bureaucracy were abolished completely in this period. In addition, commoners, partly as a result of the long absorption of Buddhism, acquired for themselves the privilege of worshipping ancestors at their graves, an extension of the shrines they had already been building at the graves of their forebears for the Buddhist salvation of their souls.

A scholar named Zhu Xi from Wuyuan, in what is now the southeastern Chinese province of Jiangxi, had become a major figure in one of the new local academies. He advised the emperor to introduce as imperial orthodoxy what had been forbidden to those who were not great land-owning families or of noble birth as a way of cultivating virtue in the population. He advocated discipline by rites (*li*), such as those already observed by commoners seeking Buddhist salvation for their dead, to be applied to corrupt magnates and nobility (Ebrey 1986). The renewed, officially endorsed rites had as their aim the cultivation of hierarchic social relations that are summarized as filial: respect and affection between sons and fathers, loyalty and responsive care between subjects and rulers, propriety between rulers and ministers, differentiation between husband and wife, precedence between elder and younger brothers, trust between friends, fidelity between business partners.

Dynastic rule through its ancestral cult was challengeable by having an ancestor buried in a particularly auspicious grave, which was a matter of good locational selection, not privileged birth. These and other arts and exercises of self-cultivation centered body and location in relation to others in fields of vital forces, which I have already described as the immanent forces of this civilization that created microcosms and relations to various externalities, insides to various outsides. This was the cosmology consolidated during the first Han imperial administration and its centralization of civilization in China. But now it had become the cosmology of a shared commoner and *literati* self-cultivation.

North and south were reunited and brought into a tight imperial system of command and control by a Mongol conquest and its dynasty, the Yuan (1271–1368), which fixed the mix of civilizations under the imposition of a settled version of Mongol pastoral command. The collapse of the Yuan dynasty—preceded by the terrible epidemic of plague that the cross-steppes migratory movements and trade brought to China, as it did to Europe, and succeeded by the even more terrible devastation of civil war—ended with the establishment of Chinese rule. The resulting Ming dynasty used its military garrisons over the whole territory of the empire to impose more fiercely than any previous Chinese empire a single, homogeneous civilization. It tightened borders and treated all within them as a single interiority—'inside flourishing cultivation' (*huanei*)—with renewed tax administration, a completed Great Wall in the north, and a single system of state cults. This extended all the way down to rural territorial communities (*she*), their land shrines, their ancestors, and their orphan dead, and in cities it involved the same territorial units inherited from the Mongol dynasty. But this homogeneity did not last, and by mid-Ming the proliferation of both urban and rural territorial deities and their cults, local academies, and all the other locally varied aspirations to cosmological centeredness and mobility up the imperial ladder of success flourished, along with increased commerce and market centers. Literacy expanded further, and so did the revelation through dreams and divinatory writing of new texts for moral salvation, the 'precious scrolls' (*baojuan*) (Overmyer 1985). The reading out loud of these scrolls in congregations and the rising popularity of syncretic cults tracing all teachings back to the cosmogonic originator, the Ancient Mother Who Was Not Born (Wusheng Laomu), constituted a new surge in commoner aspirations to salvation now— not just salvation of their souls and those of their dead, but also of the world.

These redemptive societies combined the textual traditions of the officially recognized teachings into a revelatory return to an earlier origin for them all. The societies had their own liturgies for the rites of death and other life-cycle and annual occasions. They are further evidence, in addition to the Buddhism of earlier centuries, of those with lower or no forms of literacy seeking to realize their aspirations for themselves and, in a critical way, asserting the values of the civilization in which they lived.

In the same period, and especially from the tenth century onward, the cults of local territorial protectors proliferated. They reached their widest proliferation in the periods of the last two dynasties (fourteenth to nineteenth centuries). Each locality was defined by being centered on such a cult, with or without a temple. It differed from its neighbors in a spread of similarities, including the sites of pilgrimages to mother temples—a spread of increasing differentiation of insides from outsides that reached the border zones of the imperial and now national territory.

These are examples of slow change that brought about a transformation of hierarchy, which in each case was an increase in the capacity of commoners to realize civilizational aspirations, including cosmological and filial salvation and moral or cosmological renewal from their own centers. These transformations at once confirmed centricity and the high authority of texts, but at the same time challenged the actual civilizational and political authority. Like all civilizational critiques coming from the higher or the lower ranks, they preserved continuity by the fact that transformational movements and reforms were posited as a return to origins and a keeping of the configurations in palaces and temples of the vertical axis reaching to the encompassing Tian/Heaven.

Conclusion

From the demand-sharing of the Mbendjele hunter-gatherers and the masks of their spirit plays to the shallow hierarchies of the Big Men of Melanesia or the chiefs engaging in the Kula, to Indian rulers and Brahmans, from Chinese emperors and their ritual experts, including lay preachers and their texts, to the civilization of individual and popular self-realization as meritocratic and market success, it is evident that a civilization's core characteristics are restraint, self-cultivation, and an encompassment that is also an evaluation that shapes aspirations. But the occurrence, nature, and ranking of hierarchy and the extent of exclusions from realizing the highest achievements in it are varied.

The placing—juxtaposition or ranking—of ancestors with gods, the privileging of ancestral lineage, and the canonization of gods are functions of steepening hierarchy in China. Writing adds to this steepening. Ritual practices for achieving immortality as an ancestor or as a god or as a person, in some material sense, may be common to many other civilizations. But the cosmology and cosmocracy described in the ritual practices found in China are distinctive, for instance, in combining cosmological with political functions.

In China, civilization in its own terms is an activity of centering, and this may be true of other, if not all, civilizations. What is distinctive about the civilization of imperial China is its conception of humanity, of human being as relational and hierarchical and as a mediation of the laws and moral principles of constant change located in Tian/Heaven. The principles and positions in the encompassing cosmos are historicized in deities and other kinds of human spirit. Dwellings and cities are centered in orientation to the changing material forms of earth and sky. Both Heaven and Earth are substantiations of flows of materiality—*qi*—from the finest to the most solid that make up the universe. These relations are made visible in proper conduct, including rites, or else in destructive abandon or possession by malign *qi*, resulting in chaos and confusion that require moral and physical renewal and readjustment.

The condition of civilization that I wish to highlight with this example is that it is hierarchical and ideological, as Dumont says, but not like the prototype he expounded by the complementary oppositions of his elegant structuralism.[3] Civilization is often hierarchical, but it is a more comprehensive term than hierarchy. It is a transmission of ideals through habits, rituals, performances such as spirit plays, and eventually texts. Further, claims to the same civilization are made from several centers: they can be complementary but different hierarchies of self-fashioning and encompassment, and can be potentially critical of the established center. Civilization is not only a spread of styles, norms of conduct, distinction, and knowledge. It is also an arena of contention to the same spread, from several centers of the same civilization, in the same way that the charismatic promise of a religious tradition is taken up outside its established centers. Finally, I think my examples from China show that anthropologists can and should ask questions and seek answers about the processes of very long-term structural transformation, which are in this case also long-term processes of changes of hierarchy.

Acknowledgments

I would like to thank the editors of this volume for their care and patience in prompting me to work out the argument of this chapter. I also thank Jerome Lewis for his indispensible help in correcting mistakes in an earlier draft and for providing me with examples of egalitarian practices that I have chosen to conceive as civilizations, with ideology and encompassment but without hierarchy.

Stephan Feuchtwang is Emeritus Professor in the Department of Anthropology, London School of Economics. His main area of research has been China, but recently he extended it to the comparative study of the transmission of great events of state violence in China, Taiwan, and Germany. This research was published in *After the Event* (2011). He has been working with Michael Rowlands for the past 10 years on a book, now nearing completion, on civilization, reintroducing the long term in a comparative approach to civilizations defined as spreads and mixtures with many centers, not as cultures that clash.

Notes

1. I am most grateful to the author for the gift of this book.
2. For much of the history in this and the following paragraphs, I rely on Hansen (2000).
3. At least, my analysis does not support Dumont's prototype. I do not exclude the possibility that others might refine it into a more elegant structure made up of sets of oppositions.

References

Armitage, David, and Jo Guldi. 2014. "The Return of the *Longue Durée*: An Anglo-American Perspective." *Annales. Histoire, Sciences Sociales* 69: 367–678.

Arnason, Johann P. 2010a. "The Cultural Turn and the Civilizational Approach." *European Journal of Social Theory* 13 (1): 67–82.

Arnason, Johann P. 2010b. "Introduction: Domains and Perspectives of Civilizational Analysis." *European Journal of Social Theory* 13 (1): 5–13.

Assmann, Jan. 2006. *Religion and Cultural Memory*. Trans. Rodney Livingstone. Stanford, CA: Stanford University Press.

Bloch, Maurice. 1992. *Prey into Hunter: The Politics of Religious Experience*. Cambridge: Cambridge University Press.

Damon, Frederick H. 2008. "On the Ideas of a Boat: From Forest Patches to Cybernetic Structures in the Outrigger Sailing Craft of the Eastern Kula Ring, Papua New Guinea." In *Beyond the Horizon: Essays on Myth, History, Travel and Society*, ed. Clifford Sather and Timo Kaartinen, 123–144. Helsinki: Finnish Literature Society.

Dumont, Louis. 1972. *Homo Hierarchicus: The Caste System and Its Implications*. London: Paladin.

Ebrey, Patricia B. 1986. "The Early Stages in the Development of Descent Group Organization." In *Kinship Organization in Late Imperial China, 1000–1940*, ed. Patricia B. Ebrey and James L. Watson, 16–61. Berkeley: University of California Press.

Eisenstadt, S. N., ed. 1986. *The Origins and Diversity of Axial Age Civilizations*. Albany. SUNY Press.

Eisenstadt, S. N. 2003. *Comparative Civilizations and Multiple Modernities*. Vol. 1. Leiden: Brill.

Elias, Norbert. (1939) 1994. *The Civilizing Process*. Trans. Edmund Jephcott. Oxford: Polity Press.

Forte, Antonino. 1985. "Hsi-chih (fl. 676–703 AD), a Brahmin Born in China." *Estratto da Annali dell'Instituto Universitario Orientale* 45: 106–134.

Fuller, C. J. 1992. *The Camphor Flame: Popular Hinduism and Society in India*. Princeton, NJ: Princeton University Press.

Hannerz, Ulf. 1997. "Flows, Boundaries and Hybrids: Keywords in Transnational Anthropology." *Mana* 3 (1): 7–39. Published in Portuguese as "Fluxos, fronteiras, híbridos: Palavras-chave da antropologia transnacional."

Hansen, Valerie. 1990. *Changing Gods in Medieval China, 1127–1276*. Princeton, NJ: Princeton University Press.

Hansen, Valerie. 2000. *The Open Empire: A History of China to 1600*. New York: Norton.

Hymes, Robert. 2002. *Way and Byway: Taoism, Local Religion, and Models of Divinity in Sung and Modern China*. Berkeley: University of California Press.

Lévi-Strauss, Claude. 1961. *A World on the Wane*. Trans. John Russell. London: Hutchinson.

Lewis, Jerome. 2014. "BaYaka Pygmy Multi-modal and Mimetic Communication Traditions." In *The Social Origins of Language*, ed. Daniel Dor, Chris Knight, and Jerome Lewis, 77–91. Oxford: Oxford University Press.

Mauss, Marcel. (1930) 2006. "Civilisations, Their Elements and Forms." In Marcel Mauss, *Techniques, Technologies and Civilisation*, ed. and intro. Nathan Schlanger, 57–74. New York: Berghahn Books.

Overmyer, Daniel L. 1985. "Values in Chinese Sectarian Literature: Ming and Ch'ing *Pao-chüan*." In *Popular Culture in Late Imperial China*, ed. David Johnson, Andrew J. Nathan, and Evelyn S. Rawski, 219–254. Berkeley: University of California Press.

Puett, Michael J. 2008. "Human and Divine Kingship in Early China: Comparative Reflections." In *Religion and Power: Divine Kingship in the Ancient World and Beyond*, ed. Nicole Brisch, 199–212. Chicago: Oriental Institute of the University of Chicago.

Redfield, Robert. 1948. *Folk Culture of the Yucatán*. Chicago: University of Chicago Press.

Rio, Knut M. and Olaf H. Smedal. 2009. "Hierarchy and Its Alternatives: An Introduction to Movements of Totalization and Detotalization." In *Hierarchy: Persistence and Transformation in Social Formations*, ed. Knut M. Rio and Olaf H. Smedal, 1–63. New York: Berghahn Books.

Steiner, Franz. (1938) 1999. "On the Process of Civilisation." In *Orientpolitik, Value, and Civilisation: Franz Baerman Steiner Selected Writings*, vol. 2, ed. Jeremy Adler and Richard Fardon, 123–128. New York: Berghahn Books.

Wang Mingming. 2014. *The West as the Other: A Genealogy of Chinese Occidentalism*. Hong Kong: Chinese University Press.

Woodburn, James. 1982. "Egalitarian Societies." *Man* (n.s.) 17 (3): 431–451.

Wu Hung. 2010. *The Art of the Yellow Springs: Understanding Chinese Tombs*. London: Reaktion Books.

Zhao Hui. 2012. "The Dawn of Chinese Civilization." *The History of Chinese Civilization*. Vol. 1: *Earliest Times–221 BCE*, ed. Yuan Xingpei, Yan Wenming, Zhang Chuanxi, and Lou Yulie. Cambridge: Cambridge University Press. Originally published in Chinese in 2006.

Chapter 5

ISLAM AND PIOUS SOCIALITY
The Ethics of Hierarchy in the Tablighi Jamaat in Pakistan

Arsalan Khan

In recent decades, Pakistan has witnessed the dramatic rise of Islamic revivalist forces, including Islamic piety movements, political parties, new Islamic schools, televangelists, NGOs, corporations, and banks. These Islamic revivalists draw their legitimacy from the idea that they are creating—or, in their terms, recreating—the conditions for a virtuous Islamic community in Pakistan. In this flurry of Islamic revivalist activity, the Tablighi Jamaat, a transnational Islamic piety movement, stands out, not only for the dramatic growth that it has experienced in recent decades, but also due to the zealous commitment of its practitioners to their own distinct form of face-to-face preaching (*dawat*). Tablighis can be seen traveling through Pakistan's villages, towns, and cities in groups of 10 or 12 men, dressed in the traditional *shalwar kameez*, with their pant legs raised above their ankles, wearing Muslim skull caps and sporting long, flowing beards—an image that is immediately discernible as an iconic representation of

Notes for this chapter begin on page 112.

the Prophet. Itinerant Tablighis, who live in mosques for periods up to a year, travel from house to house, 'calling' Muslims to the mosque and exhorting them to fulfill their ritual duties and live according to Islamic ideals.

Tablighis insist that *dawat* must be conducted in the Prophet's way (*rasool ka tariqa*) in order to be efficacious and that all other ways of spreading Islam are doomed to failure. Tablighis are especially critical of Islamist political activism, which they see as not only ineffective in terms of spreading Islam but actually inimical to Islamic virtue. Tablighis say that Islamists have confused religion (*din*) and the world (*dunya*) and are therefore creating moral chaos (*fitna*). The Tablighi critique of Islamists stands out when we consider the fact that Tablighis and Islamists share basic doctrinal commitments to Sunni Islam and also draw on the same reformist tradition of Islam that rejects popular forms of Sufism organized around the intercessionary powers of saints and the sacred genealogies of the Prophet. Tablighis and Islamists also agree that it is each individual Muslim's duty to strive to create the ideal Islamic community as it was realized at the time of the Prophet. The difference is that while Tablighis say that Islam is spread only through *dawat*, which they regard as divinely given, Islamists have long insisted that the best way to create an Islamic society is by wresting control of the state from unIslamic forces and creating an Islamic state governed by Islamic law (*shariat*), one that enforces Islamic codes and injunctions and actively creates the space for Muslims to live according to Islamic precepts. While Islamism, a political and religious revival movement within Islam, has had an overwhelmingly statist orientation in Pakistan, in recent years Islamists have shifted toward creating and controlling institutions like corporations and NGOs (Iqtidar 2011a). They have also become an active presence in mass media, such as radio, television, newspapers, and, increasingly, social media like Facebook and Twitter.[1]

In this chapter, I use the Tablighi critique of Islamism as a wedge into a significant ideological cleavage within the Islamic revival in Pakistan. I argue that while Islamists have adopted a modernist conception of religion that stresses the content of religious doctrine and belief, Pakistani Tablighis insist that religious practices like *dawat* must fulfill the conditions of a sacred practice (see Asad 1993). Much like the Islamic pietists in Egypt examined in the work of Saba Mahmood (2005) and Charles Hirschkind (2006), Tablighis understand *dawat* to be a sacred means for the cultivation of ethical selves. I make two central claims in this chapter. First, I argue that Tablighis regard *dawat* as a religious practice (*dini amal*) because it entails a model for ethical action in which a person cultivates pious virtue by submitting to the authority of pious others and by being 'acted upon' by those more pious than oneself (cf. Mittermaier 2011). In other words, Tablighis acquire pious virtue by living in a world of pious sociality structured by an ethics of hierarchy. Second, I argue that this contrasts sharply with the Islamists, who have adopted an ethics of egalitarian individualism that places ultimate value on individual autonomy, authenticity, and agency. Tablighis understand this ethics of egalitarian individualism to be one characterized by hubris and willfulness, which they associate with the immoral attribution of agency to the self rather than to God. Not only is this ethics an obstacle to the cultivation of a virtuous self, it destroys virtue and is therefore a primary source of moral chaos in Pakistan. Tablighis aim to create a world of pious sociality shaped by an ethics of hierarchy in order to offset the danger of moral chaos posed by egalitarian individualism in both liberal and Islamist varieties.

Dawat, Discipline, and Ethical Personhood

The Tablighi Jamaat began in the 1920s in North India, but it now has a major presence in many parts of the world, especially where there are large South Asian populations. Pakistan is one of the four major centers of Tablighi activities, with the others being India, Bangladesh, and England. Hundreds of thousands of Muslims from Pakistan and around the world attend the annual congregation (*ijtima*) in Raiwind as well as other annual congregations in cities across the country. Since the 1980s, the Tablighi Jamaat has grown dramatically in Pakistan, as evidenced by the large mosque complexes (*markaz*) that have sprung up in all the major cities in Pakistan. These complexes serve as key institutional nodes in a network of mosques that are informally affiliated with the movement.

Tablighis travel for specified periods of time from mosque to mosque and house to house, 'inviting' (the literal meaning of the word *dawat*) fellow Muslims to the mosque to pray and listen to sermons with the ultimate aim of getting them to commit to *dawat*. Tablighis say that *dawat* is the duty of every individual Muslim and cite passages from the Qur'an in support of this claim, like the following: "And let there be [arising] a nation from you inviting [all that is] good, enjoining what is right and forbidding what is wrong, and those will be the successful" (Ṣaḥeeḥ International [1997] 2004: 57). Tablighis interpret this and other passages to mean that it is their duty to preach to fellow Muslims who have abandoned religion and have been led astray by the world. Tablighis insist that their method of preaching (*tariqa-e-tabligh*) follows the Prophet's way, and therefore, like all of the Prophet's actions (*sunnat*), is divinely inspired. Some early Tablighi accounts suggest that this method came to the founder of the movement, Muhammad Ilyas, in a dream, implying that it was a direct gift from God. Ilyas said that *dawat* is a blessing from God and that "the closeness and the help and blessings [of God] is [sic] not to be found in the case of other methods" (cited in Sikand 2002: 131). The efficacy of *dawat* in soliciting God's aid and spreading Islamic virtue depends on it being conducted in precisely the form that it was prescribed and fulfilled by the Prophet and his companions (*sahaba*).

The Tablighi Jamaat falls squarely in the tradition of Islamic reform that grew to prominence in the late nineteenth and early twentieth centuries in South Asia, centered at the Dar-ul-Uloom seminary at Deoband in North India. Muhammad Ilyas, the founder of the Tablighi Jamaat, was a scholar (*aalim*) trained at this seminary and a proponent of what came to be known as the Deobandi tradition. In this tradition, ultimate truth is embodied in the Qur'an (understood as the direct word of God) in the Prophet's example, as it has been documented in the hadith literature (*sunnat*), and in Islamic law, as it has been developed by Islamic scholars (*ulema*). The Prophet was a perfect human, incapable of sin (*maasoom*) and the model for the exemplary Islamic life. All of his actions—from everyday minutiae, like dressing, eating, and sleeping, to major decisions, such as how to marry, conduct business, wage war, or govern—qualify as religious practices (*aamaal*), and all Islamic practices, according to my interlocutors, have hidden qualities that elude human reason. The fulfillment of these practices draws God's favor and brings with it moral, political, and economic well-being. The Devil continuously attempts to draw Muslims away from Islamic practice, so Muslims must continuously stave off the Devil's advances by cultivating faith (*iman*).

The central claim of the Tablighi movement is that *dawat* is not only for the benefit of others but, crucially, is for the reform or correction (*islah*) of the self. *Dawat*, I was repeatedly told, is designed to grow one's own faith and create in each Tablighi the 'passion' and 'desire' to fulfill his or her religious duties. Tablighis explained to me that preaching *dawat* on the virtues of a specific practice produced or 'gave birth' to the desire in oneself for that specific practice. According to one Tablighi I interviewed: "If you preach the merits of the mandatory prayers, you yourself will want to do your prayers; if you preach to others the merits of fasting, you too will want to do fasting. People think that you should not preach if you do not do something yourself, but this is not right. We give *dawat* to others so that we realize ourselves the virtues of practice." This transformative power of *dawat* was recounted in countless narratives like the following:

> A young man who was clean-shaven was going to Canada for studies, and he was worried about his faith, so he decided to go visit the Imam of his mosque to ask what he should do to not lose his faith. "Imam *sahib*, I am very worried that I will go abroad and be drawn away from Islam. What should I do to protect my faith?" Without hesitation, the Imam said, "Spend time with Muslims and give *dawat* to others. Invite them to come to the mosque for prayers." The young man agreed. A few years later, the young man returned to his mosque, and the Imam was very pleased to see him. The man now had a beard and wore his pant legs above his ankles. He had become pious (*dindaar*). The Imam asked him if he had remembered to give *dawat*, and the young man nodded. "What happened?" the Imam inquired. The young man replied, "I felt uncomfortable at first, but because I had made a commitment, I continued to do it." "Did anyone ever come to the mosque?" asked the Imam. The man replied, "No, not many, but I began praying five times a day, and the rest you can see."

In such stories, a young man of the kind who is most prone to losing his way, with a modest level of faith indicated by his lack of a beard and his generally 'unIslamic' appearance, would be departing to a foreign country where he would likely be further influenced by unIslamic ways. The young man goes abroad, but instead of coming back less pious, as one might expect, he actually comes back a much more devout and practicing Muslim than he was before he left. This transformation is attributed to the power of *dawat* in cultivating his faith.

This understanding of *dawat* fits well with the descriptions of Islamic pietists in Egypt by Mahmood (2005) and Hirschkind (2006). These scholars show that rituals in Islam, far from being merely representations of an already given state of piety, are actually understood to be disciplinary practices that cultivate virtuous dispositions in the practitioner. They show that Islamic rituals, such as the mandatory prayer, Qur'anic recitation, and sermon listening, cultivate morally laden affective dispositions like humility, pious fear, patience, and love, which are the basis for an ethical life. As Hirschkind (ibid.: 9) notes, sermon listening is not merely about understanding the 'content' of sermons; it is understood as a disciplinary practice that 'hones the senses' and "attune[s] the heart to God's word and incline[s] the body toward moral conduct." Similarly, Tablighis describe *dawat* as a disciplinary practice that produces the interior state of faith and therefore lays the ground for all other Islamic practice. Because *dawat* 'gives birth' to faith, Tablighis often refer to it as the 'mother of practices' (*umm-al-aamaal*). *Dawat* is, therefore, the basis for an Islamic life.

The relationship between ritual, discipline, and piety must be understood through broader Islamic understandings of personhood. In popular understandings, the person is comprised of three components: a lower self (*nafs*), the spirit (*ruh*), and reason (*aql*) (Kurin 1981). Spirit is understood to be a divine faculty, possessed by all animate beings—angels, humans, *jinn*, and animals. Angels are unique, however, because they are made of pure spirit. They are simply conduits for God's will and are incapable of breaking divine commandments. Animals also have a spirit, but their spirit is understood to be weak and relatively insignificant to their being. Animals mostly act as their base instincts tell them. Humans have both a spirit and a lower self, the latter understood as the seat for animalistic desires and passions, including the passion for sex and other bodily needs. The lower self is not altogether bad; it is a necessary and even valued part of life, but it must be molded and brought in line with divine commandments (*hukm*) as they are embodied in revelation. This requires the discipline of *dawat*.

Dawat is what Birgit Meyer (2011) has called a 'sensational form', that is, a sacred means to create a relationship with transcendental power, and it is through this relationship that Tablighi acquire Islamic virtue. Three features constitute *dawat* as a ritual. First, *dawat* must be conducted in a face-to-face—or, as Tablighis say, 'heart-to-heart'—manner. Tablighis draw on a broader Islamic tradition of what Brinkley Messick (1993: 25) calls "[r]ecitational logocentrism" in which the human voice is seen as unmediated and direct and the most reliable means for conveying the truth. Second, Tablighis say that *dawat* requires sacrifice (*qurbani*) in three forms: physical energy or life force (*jaan*), wealth (*maal*), and time (*waqt*). The more sacrifice that a person has made in *dawat*, the more he elicits God's power to create transformations in both himself and others. Third, and crucially, *dawat* is a 'collective practice' (*ijtimai amal*) rather than just an 'individual practice' (*infaraadi amal*), which means it draws its force from being conducted in a group (*jamaat*). These three features are, to borrow an apt phrase from J. L Austin (1975), the 'felicity conditions' of *dawat*. In practice, this means that Tablighis travel and live together in mosques in order to 'directly' preach the virtues of Islamic practice to fellow Muslims. The close proximate living is said to produce ties (*jor*) between Muslims that are based on the good (*achei pei*) or ethical relationships, which in turn keep a person on the right path. Hence, while *dawat* creates an ethical self, this self is a product of ethical relationships forged through the ethical work of *dawat*. Understood through the idioms of love, care, and concern, these ethical relationships, I argue, are structured hierarchically.

Pious Sociality: *Dawat* as an Ethics of Hierarchy

Tablighis say that *dawat* is a practice that simultaneously brings Muslims into a relationship with both other Muslims and God. Through the collective ethical work of *dawat*, the congregation draws divine vitality (*barkat*) from God, which creates bonds between them that allow them to "stand together on the good." It is hard to overstate the significance of these ethical relationships in Tablighi discourse. Tablighis told me frequently that because they spend time with good Muslims, they find it hard to break God's commands. These relationships remind them of their commitment to God and to the Islamic community. When asked what these relationships entail, Tablighis described them in terms of love, respect, care, and concern, affective dispositions that "God puts in one's heart." Indeed, God's presence is felt in these relationships, which is why one must always be in the company of other pious people. It is these ethical relationships that discipline a person and keep him from drifting away from the congregation. Tablighis say that this is why *dawat* is a collective practice rather than simply an individual practice.

These relationships are primarily male relations, and they are modeled on kin relations between brothers, on the one hand, and between brothers and fathers, on the other. Tablighis add the title 'brother' (*bhai*) before each other's names, and they confer paternal authority on the leaders of the movement, whom they refer to endearingly as 'the Elders' (*buzurg*). These kin terms connote hierarchy associated with South Asian, especially North Indian, models of kinship in which younger siblings pay deference to older siblings by referring to them with various honorific titles like 'brother' that follow their names. Tablighis apply the title 'brother' before rather than after the name to mark a 'religious' kinship, but the hierarchical connotations of the term persists. As one Tablighi noted, "We are all brothers because of our shared relationship with the Prophet, but remember brothers are never equal." Similarly, the relationship between the congregation and the Elders is modeled on the precepts of hierarchical relations between fathers and sons and older and younger generations.

The fact that the Tablighi congregation is overwhelmingly a male space and that these bonds are conceptualized primarily in terms of brother-brother and father-son relationships is a central aspect of life inside the congregation. It is beyond the scope of this chapter to fully address the basis for Islamic gender norms, but a few words are in order. Tablighis uphold and adhere to broader Islamic norms of gender segregation (*pardah*) in which only men and women who are either married or unmarriageable (*mehram*) can and should interact. Women incite male passions and sexual impulses and should be avoided except in legally sanctioned relationships. Women are understood as a 'temptation' or *fitna*, a word that also means a state of moral chaos of which women are widely understood to be the primary source. Gender segregation is therefore a basis for moral order. Itinerant Tablighis make all efforts to avoid or at least limit any contact with women by lowering their gaze or averting their eyes—to the point of facing a wall—when women cross their path. Some Tablighis even avoid telephone conversations with their female kin because, in pulling them back to the world, they are understood to be an obstacle to the realization of pious virtue.

Women do travel on *dawat* tours called *mastooraat*, a term that means both 'women' and 'the hidden part'. Women's tours are significantly less frequent than those of men, and women must be accompanied on these trips by a legally sanctioned male, usually a husband, brother, or father. Itinerant women preach to other women within a host's home, while men live and preach in a mosque. Women are barred from giving sermons even to each other. Each evening, a designated man delivers the sermon to the women in the house from behind a curtain—a position that establishes women as 'listeners' to a male 'speaker'. While men's bodies and words should resonate across the country and even around the world, women's bodies and words should be confined to the home. One finds here a set of homologous hierarchies: male/female, mosque/home, religion/world, and spirit/lower self. These distinctions are understood in both temporal and spatial terms in that male-religion-spirit are enduring and spatially expansive, while female-world-lower self are fleeting and spatially circumscribed. This gender hierarchy in which men encompass women is a foundational structure of the Tablighi Jamaat.

However, to speak about hierarchy between men in the Islamic tradition runs up against long-standing assumptions about the fundamental egalitarianism of Islam. For example, a prominent scholar of medieval Islam, George Makdisi (1983: 85), writes that Islam, more so than any other religious tradition, is "characterized by the basic equality of all Muslims in the eyes of the law, as God's submissive servants." Anthropologists studying Islam in South Asia, especially those focused on popular forms of Sufism organized around the intercessionary powers of Sufi saints, have contested this perspective (Basu 1998; Werbner 2003; Werbner and Basu 1998b). Genealogical descent from the Prophet is central to the delineation of religious hierarchy in the Sufi tradition (Ho 2006; Sanyal 1996). But the Tablighi Jamaat draws on a tradition of Islamic reform that explicitly rejects both saint intercession and the notion that Prophetic descent confers special status on an individual Muslim. Tablighis draw on a model of male ontological egalitarianism in which men are differentiated only by their deeds (*hasb*) rather than by their lineage (*nasb*) (Metcalf 2004). Despite this male ontological egalitarianism, the conception of persons as divided between the lower self and spirit and the understanding of the transformative power of *dawat* inscribe the social world with what Tablighis understand to be differences of 'spiritual rank' (*darja*) (see Messick 1993). Through practice, one strengthens one's relationship to God and becomes increasingly spiritual (*roohani*), which is understood as 'closeness' to God. The longer one sacrifices in *dawat*, the closer one becomes, and this closeness induces what Tablighis call 'spiritual power' (*roohani quwwat*). Closeness to God, Tablighis say, makes one's words 'heavy' and 'powerful', so that when others hear these words, they are moved by them and are drawn toward Islam. The more pious a person, the greater that person's reach and influence should be.

The Tablighi congregation is organized through a distinction between old companions (*puranei saathi*), those who have conducted the four-month *dawat* tour, and new companions (*nai saathi*), those who have not. The four-month tour is given great significance as a spiritual threshold. It is understood as three consecutive 40-day tours (*chilla*), a period that in the Sufi tradition is understood to be a time of seclusion for fasting and prayer and a basis of spiritual renewal (see Ewing 1997). Tablighis frequently compared the *chilla* to each phase of a child's development in the mother's womb, and the four-month mark as the point at which God blows the spirit into the child. Here, one clearly finds the notion of *dawat* as a form of spiritual 'rebirth'. *Dawat* tours are, as one Tablighi explained, like 'incubators' for creating pious persons. The notion that *dawat* is the 'mother of practices' because it 'gives birth' to faith, then, is not merely metaphorical. Rather, it refers to a bodily transformation.

Decision making inside *dawat* tours and in each local mosque generally happens on the basis of consultation (*mashwarra*), during which each person offers his opinion, but old companions nevertheless make key decisions. The ultimate decision, both during *dawat* tours and at the local mosque, falls to the leader (*amir*), who must be an old companion. More significant than decision making, however, is the pervasive sense that by conducting the four-month tour, one inhabits the pious virtues that allow one to faithfully transmit knowledge without distortion or innovation (*biddat*) to others. Old companions, therefore, are those who train new companions in the Prophet's ways. Given the significance placed on speech in the movement, one might say that the movement from new to old companions is thought of in terms of those who are principally listeners to those who are primarily speakers.

This is most evident in the reverence for the Elders, the pinnacle of religious achievement and spirituality (*roohaniat*) in the movement. The Elders sit on the city, regional, national, and international councils (*shura*) of the movement. The Elders speak from the pulpit at the annual congregation in Raiwind, Punjab, which attracts hundreds of thousands if not millions of Muslims, as well as at other major congregations. At these events, Tablighis spend three days listening to sermons given by the Elders. Tablighis frequently told me that the words of the Elders would readily sink into a person's heart because they were "heavy" and "powerful." The annual congregation, therefore, provides unprecedented opportunity for self-transformation, turning Tablighs into a collective body of pious listeners relative to the Elders. One Tablighi told me that the Elders "are a channel for words that come directly from God." Not everyone agreed with this, but the notion that the Elders have a close relationship with God was well accepted. The Elders are the beneficiaries of guidance (*hidayat*), a divine gift that brings with it the secure presence of God in one's life, in one's actions, and in one's words. Guidance means that God readily accepts one's supplications, another sign of powerful words. This close relationship confers other spiritual powers, including, some said, the power to be able to peer into or recognize what is in others' hearts. The ability to see the hidden/interior (*batin*), especially in contrast to the apparent/outer (*zahir*) to which everyone else is confined, is a characteristic traditionally associated with Sufi spiritual guides or sheikhs (see Gilsenan 1982), but here it is understood through the ideology of *dawat* as a power acquired through sacrifice in the service of God. This power makes the Elders a source of great knowledge about what is hidden from ordinary Tablighis, who are said not to know what lies in their own hearts. Hence, ordinary Tablighis are dependent on the Elders for realizing pious virtue.

The Tablighi congregation is structured by a pedagogical discipleship based on spiritual rank in which new companions take instruction from old companions and Tablighis collectively take instruction from the Elders. Pedagogical discipleship is evident in both formal and informal ways in all aspects of congregational life, especially in the receiving and giving of sermons. New companions give sermons primarily to non-Tablighis on *dawat* tours, old companions give sermons to larger congregations of Tablighis in the local mosque, and the Elders give sermons to the entire Tablighi congregation at the grand mosques. Put differently, lower-ranked Tablighis are speakers relative to non-Tablighis and lower-ranked Tablighis, but they are listeners relative to higher-ranked Tablighis and the Elders. Becoming a proper Islamic subject requires that a Tablighi must learn how to live in a hierarchically structured social world as both giver and recipient of Islamic knowledge (cf. Malara and Boylston, this book).

My analysis confirms the broader understanding of Islamic piety as a form of self-mastery achieved through ritual practice (Asad 1993; Hirschkind 2006; Mahmood 2005), understood here as the subordination of the lower self to the spirit. But I add the notion that a particular understanding of *dawat* as a ritual of transcendence also gives definite substance and form to what Tablighis recognize as pious sociality structured by hierarchical relationships. Piety is thus conceived not only as an internal disposition but also as an ethical social order within which ethical selves are cultivated. My argument is close to Brian Silverstein's (2011) analysis of the Islamic notion of a *sohbet* in a Naqshbandi Sufi order in Turkey. The term *sohbet* (*sohbat* in Urdu) has the same root as the word for companion (*sahaabi*) of the Prophet and is a term used widely in the Tablighi congregation. For the Naqshbandi Sufis in Silverstein's work, spiritual realization or the cultivation of ethical dispositions requires mystical techniques that involve 'companionship' with the sheikh. "For the proper formation of character, then," Silverstein writes, "one should try to always be with 'good people,' defined as those who seek the approval of God, and only God, and are not led astray by such things as popular fashion, prestige, or power" (ibid.: 144). The Tablighi Jamaat draws on this Sufi model of Islamic companionship, but while Islamic authority in the Sufi model is transmitted through the authorization (*ijaazat*) of a sheikh, in the Tablighi Jamaat, *dawat* is the duty of all Muslims, and Islamic authority can be created by anyone through participation in the movement and companionship with pious others (cf. Metcalf 2003).

My use of the term 'hierarchy' here differs from the classic formulation of hierarchy in Louis Dumont's (1980) *Homo Hierarchicus*. For Dumont, caste hierarchy assumed a distinction between purity and pollution that was intrinsic to the relationship between castes, whereby each caste had a more or less given place relative to others. My use of the term implies a progression toward an ideal and a movement of proximity to transcendental power and is therefore closer to what Dumont described as 'rank'. As a ritual of transcendence, *dawat* elevates a person up a system of spiritual rank, which is generated and sustained through continuous enactments of piety. *Dawat* is a culturally specific mode of creating and realizing value, the value of pious virtue, which Tablighis understand in the idiom of the sacrifice of life force, wealth, and time. The creation and realization of higher forms of value understood as spiritual-divine (*dini*) require destroying and forsaking lower forms of value understood as material-worldly (*dunyavi*) (Graeber 2001; Munn 1986). The process of submitting to pious authority is the means through which more highly valued objects like heavy and powerful speech are acquired, and hierarchy also provides a model for the larger Islamic order that *dawat* aims to create. In this sense, the ethics of hierarchy is both a means and an end, a characteristic of ultimate ethical values (Lambek 2015).

Dawat against *Politiks*: Fetishism, the Self, and the Inversion of Virtue

The Tablighi concern about Islamism was forcefully brought to my attention one evening at the weekly Thursday congregation. Three Tablighi friends were discussing their mutual acquaintance, a young man in his early twenties who occasionally stayed after prayers to listen to sermons and participate in other mosque activities. He had potential, they insisted, because of his "passion" for Islam. When he suddenly stopped participating in mosque activities, they became concerned about his well-being and began seeking him out. They spoke with his family members and were told that he was busy with his studies. For reasons to which I was not privy, they arrived at the conclusion that he stopped his limited participation in the congregation because he had joined an Islamist political party at his university. They all agreed that they should try to intervene, but they were worried that their intervention would drive him further away from Islam. They agreed that one of the three would visit him at his home on Friday evenings to do what in Tablighi parlance is called a special tour (*khasoosi gasht*), a kind of religious intervention that targets specific people who are seen as being sympathetic to the movement but are now drifting away. I asked why they were so worried about him if they believed he was pursuing his passion for Islam, and one of them promptly explained: "He has passion, but he is very far from practice!" Such undisciplined passion, it seemed, was a dangerous thing.

I had the opportunity to discuss the tension between Tablighis and Islamists with a few Islamist political party workers as well. When interviewing a member of the Islamist party Jamaat-ud-Dawa, I asked what he thought about the religious work of the Tablighi Jamaat, and he responded: "We do not have any issue with them on religious grounds, but I don't understand why they don't get involved in *politiks* [using the English word]. Sometimes you have to do some things for yourself."[2] This was characteristic of Islamist critiques of *dawat*: by relying exclusively on *dawat*, Tabighis did not take any responsibility for their own circumstances. Islamists see *dawat* as a weak and ineffective form of intervention. The Tablighis' stance against *politiks* makes little sense if the purpose is to create an Islamic society, which requires wresting control of powerful institutions like the state away from unIslamic forces. In an interview I conducted with another Islamist, this time of the Jamaat-i-Islami party, he explained the situation succinctly: "Pakistan is full of problems, and these Tablighis only want to preach about religion [*mazhab*]. Religion is right in its own place, but we need an Islamic system [*nizam*] here to fix our problems, and that requires getting people involved in *politiks*. People have to take responsibility. They cannot leave everything to Allah." He then proceeded to explain that *politiks* is itself "religious" if it is being done in "defense of Islam." What matters is not how it is being conducted but whether it is effective in bringing about an Islamic system. This is the kind of instrumentalist approach to Islam that Tablighis find inimical to Islamic virtue.

There are a few important points to highlight about the modernist epistemology evident in these statements by Islamists. First, Islamists locate 'true' Islam in the content of religious texts and have little concern for the form of religious practice itself, which is considered ancillary and largely incidental to the meaning of the texts. Hence, even as Islamists acknowledge that Tablighis are on sure grounds in terms of doctrine, they see no reason why *dawat* must take a specific ritual form. Second, this leads Islamists to claim that what they are referring to as *politiks* is itself 'religious' as long as it is done with the correct end in mind, that is, the creation of a society governed by Islamic law. The means should be judged solely by their effectiveness. Third, they believe that the form of *dawat* is largely ineffective in addressing the concerns of Muslims in Pakistan and is a type of inaction. Taking responsibility for oneself requires doing *politiks*, which has instrumental value in a way that ritual and prayer do not. Combined, these assumptions mean that Islamists treat the forms that Tablighis deem necessary for *dawat* to qualify as an Islamic practice to be mere ritualism. Islamists accuse Tablighis of conflating the medium for the message, form for meaning, and signifier for signified. In doing so, Islamists are reproducing a modern language ideology that privileges referential functions of language over the pragmatic and relational aspects of speech (Jakobson 1957; M. Silverstein 1976) and a religious framework that stresses religious belief and doctrine over materiality, embodied practice, and form (Asad 1993; see also Engelke 2010).

When I told a longtime Tablighi about the Islamist statements, he proclaimed definitively: "They have no faith! They want to do this on their own. They don't understand that only Allah can fix these problems, and the only way to bring Allah to our aid is through *dawat*." He then went on to dismiss *politiks* not only as ineffective but also as dangerous because it is the "worship of the self" (*khud parasti*). The above statement implies not only that *politiks* is unauthorized by the authoritative textual sources, a point Tablighis made frequently, but also that the Islamist perspective evidences a lack of faith in God's power and an improper assumption of one's own power. Faith, the Tablighi explained, is the "certainty that everything comes from God and nothing comes from another." This includes, it appears, from one's own self. It is the failure of Islamists to live out this principle and their belief in the agency of their own self or that of some others, like their political leaders, that Tablighis see as central to *politiks*, which replaces faith in God with a faith in man, a form of idolatry that destroys Islamic virtue. For Tablighis, *politiks* is a form of 'negative value' creation that undermines the basis for Islamic virtue (Munn 1986; see also Graeber 2001: 83–84).

The conflict between Tablighis and Islamists brings to mind Webb Keane's (2007) description of the conflict between Calvinists and Sumba practitioners in the missionary encounter in Indonesia. Calvinism, Keane argues, was predicated on a semiotic ideology that drew a sharp separation between subjects and objects, persons and things, and immaterial and material domains. For Calvinists, the Sumba located agency in material objects, including ritualized words and actions, and therefore failed to locate agency in the self, the ultimate source of value. This directly parallels the Islamist critique that Tablighis fail to take responsibility for their own world. But Keane astutely notes that fetishism is a "two-way street" (ibid.: 184), and if Calvinists accused Sumba practitioners of projecting agency onto objects, Sumba practitioners countered this with the charge that Calvinist insistence on their own agency represented a form of hubris. For the Sumba, practices that fail to solicit powers beyond themselves were "dangerous and ineffective" (ibid.: 194). Like the Sumba, Tablighis accuse Islamists of hubris. By locating agency in the self rather than in divine power, Islamists conflate cause for effect, source for issue, signified for signifier. They thus fall prey to a fetishism of the self.

Tablighis claim that *politiks* is not only ineffective but also dangerous because it destroys the basis for Islamic virtue. Maqsood, a taxi driver and seasoned Tablighi, summed up the problem:

> I knew this young man who was a member of some party, and he would go off to these rallies each day, and sometimes, like us, he would even go to the villages, not for *dawat* of course, but he said he was going for Islam. But he would come back, and he would fight with his family, with his wife and beat his children, even fight with his parents, and he never had any peace at home. His neighbors were all scared of him. Everyone said that he was an angry person with hardness of temperament … he has passion for Islam but he is home fighting with his parents and wife. His passion is just his lower self speaking, and this is what gives birth to anger and aggression in him. How is someone like this going to bring others to Islam? When we come back home from *dawat*, we come back with a sense of peace. *Dawat* creates softness of temperament and makes us feel calm and cool … *dawat* awakens your spirit and brings Allah's support.

Because it fails to take proper ritual form, Islamist *politiks* is not only ineffective but also threatens to produce undisciplined subjects who claim to speak for Islam. In Maqsood's narrative, the lower self is "speaking" rather than the spirit, and this is producing passions and dispositions that are precisely the opposite of what are induced by *dawat*. Contrasts of high/low, soft/hard, calm/wild, and cool/hot are inverted, with the former valuable term being subordinated to the latter. *Politiks* inverts the value generated in *dawat*, creating a person who is incapable of caring for those below (wife and children) and respecting those above (parents)—in other words, a person who fails to understand and disregards his role in an Islamic hierarchy. This tendency to fetishize the self threatens harmonious relations in the family, between families and neighbors, and in the Islamic community more generally, creating the conditions for moral chaos.

Politiks creates an undisciplined subject characterized by arrogance, self-centeredness, and willfulness, whose lower self speaks through him and who either commits himself to false authorities like political leaders or simply locates authority only in himself. This person rejects or is incapable of recognizing legitimate forms of authority. Such people are not only themselves 'far from Islam' but also lead others away from Islam. They are therefore a threat to an Islamic order. *Dawat*, by contrast, produces a disciplined subject whose spirit speaks through him. Such a person is characterized by humility (*khushu*) and pious fear (*khauf*) and is capable of love (*mohabbat*) and care (*khidmat*) for other Muslims. These qualities allow him to recognize his place in an Islamic hierarchy and fulfill his obligations to those below and above himself. Such a person is capable of not only living an Islamic life but also drawing others to Islam.

For Tablighis, the problem of Islamist *politiks* is embodied not only in persons but also in institutions, especially the Islamic state. Tablighis reject the Islamist preoccupation with the Islamic state because, as one Tablighi noted, "the government cannot put love in people's hearts. Only Allah can put love in people's hearts." Islamist *politiks*, he explained, was the pursuit of "the greatest idol," the idol of the state. But Tablighis are not opposed to an Islamic state. Like Islamists, they say society should be governed by Islamic law, or *shariat*. However, Tablighis say that *shariat* is not just a set of rules that can be imposed on people but a 'way of life' (*zindagi ka tariqa*) that one must learn to live. This gives credence to the claim in the literature on Islam that *shariat* has not always meant 'law' in the narrow sense of codes of behavior enforceable by the state, but is better understood as a broader framework of ethics that includes alternative conceptions of the state and political power (Ahmad 2009; Alam 2004; Hallaq 2013). Tablighis presuppose the anthropological wisdom that 'the state' is an 'effect' of specific forms of practice (Mitchell 2006), and for the state to be substantially Islamic, it has to be created from Islamic practice, which the current Pakistani state, according to Tablighis, is certainly not. When I asked Tablighis what they meant by *shariat*, they invariably pointed to how Muslims lived with each other in the Prophet's time and how Tablighis live in *dawat* as exemplifying this sacred past. *Dawat* is a metonym for *shariat*. When Muslims come to live and govern according to *shariat*, 'the state' will become a conduit for God's will, and it will be able to create moral, political, and economic well-being for all Muslims. The Pakistani state, however, is defined by *politiks* and is thus an embodiment of the fetishism of the self, making the state "the greatest idol." This logic is not limited to the state; it is also applied to other modern institutions claiming Islamic legitimacy, such as corporations and NGOs. The proliferation of idols is the fundamental problem of modernity.

To summarize my argument, then, while both Tablighis and Islamists claim to be creating a society based on the doctrinal principles of Islam, they conceive of religion in rather different ways. For Tablighis, religion entails not only a set of doctrinal principles but, importantly, an ethics of hierarchy through which those very principles and their ethical entailments come to be embodied. Islamism, by contrast, has adopted a modernist approach to religion, which stresses religious content over religious form, message over medium, and belief over practice. In the former case, Islam must be spread through a ritualized form that materializes a set of ethical relationships. In the latter, religion becomes a set of propositions or a code that does not need to take any particular material form. This latter approach treats the embodied forms of religious practice that Tablighis deem necessary as secondary and inessential to religious doctrine and belief (Asad 1993). For Tablighis, the Islamist preoccupation with *politiks* is a fetishism of the self that destroys the Islamic virtue engendered by *dawat*.

Pious Sociality as Islamic Counterpublic in Times of (Neo-)liberal Chaos

The Tablighi Jamaat has experienced remarkable growth since the 1980s, a fact that is evidenced by the large mosque complexes associated with the movement that have sprung up across the country. Yet the Tablighi Jamaat is only one of a dizzying array of Islamic forces shaping Pakistan's public sphere today. The Islamization of Pakistan is often directly attributed to the policies of the state and specifically to the martial regime of General Zia-ul-Haq (1977–1988), which linked state sovereignty to Islam and cultivated a climate in which countless Islamic revivalist currents, including militant ones, thrived. But one cannot attribute everything to the Islamizing policies of the state. The loosening of government regulations on private media and the general liberalization of the economy since the early 2000s have created space for the rise of many popular televangelists, radio broadcasters, new educational institutions, online communities, companies, and organizations that claim the mantle of Islamic legitimacy.

Facilitated by new information technologies, this upsurge in Islamic revivalist activity has meant that the Islamic public sphere is increasingly experiencing what Eickelman and Piscatori (1996) have called the 'fragmentation of authority', whereby traditional religious authorities like the *ulema* and prominent sheikhs now share space with a host of other contenders. Tablighis regard this fragmentation of authority as symptomatic of moral chaos. The most significant aspect of what Tablighis dismiss as Islamist *politiks* is the struggle Islamists wage for recognition and legitimacy in the arenas of formal democracy and through the mass media. Tablighis insist that the ceaseless appropriation of

Islam for *politiks* not only distracts people from Islamic practice but also generates endless and unresolvable argumentation, criticism, and conflict. In other words, it is the egalitarian linguistic sensibilities cultivated in this new Islamic public sphere that Tablighis see as anathema to Islam. It is not surprising, then, that the most significant aspect of *politiks* is that it is a form of 'talk' that is all the more dangerous because it claims Islamic legitimacy and thus leads Muslims astray. Joel Robbins (2001) has argued that modern language ideology assumes that language is capable of transmitting intentionality and therefore places a high premium on sincerity, the communication of an individual's true inner state through words and gestures. Anchored in egalitarian individualism, this language ideology encourages each person to have a position on the truth at the same time that it eschews ritual, which appears insincere because it originates outside the individual. These features combined turn religion into a form of talk. Tablighis position their own ritualized form of *dawat* as a remedy to what they see as this growing penchant for 'talk' in modernity.

Charles Hirschkind (2006) has described how an 'ethics of listening' is central to what he calls the 'Islamic counterpublic' in Egypt, one that stands in opposition to the dominant liberal-secular public sphere. What Tablighis describe as *politiks* references the egalitarian sensibilities that increasingly characterize public discourse in Pakistan, sensibilities that cut across liberal and Islamist ideologies, particularly as they are exhibited in the mass media. For instance, Tablighis point to rancorous shouting matches on the now ubiquitous political talk shows on television as embodying the problem of *politiks*: the failure to listen and the incessant desire to speak. The central problem of modernity for Tablighis is that Muslims fail to listen and take instruction; they lack receptivity and refuse to be acted upon by pious others and God. Piety born out of pious listening produces the ability to speak, to communicate, and to 'convey' (the literal translation of the word *tabligh*) without leading others astray. How to speak, when to speak, where to speak, whom to speak to, whom not to speak to—all these are questions that preoccupy Tablighis. In other words, an ethics of listening furnishes the grounds for an ethics of speaking, and an ethics of speaking produces the faith that is the condition for listening. This dialectic of speaking and listening is central to *dawat* as a total ethics of conveying Islamic truth, affect, and knowledge. Crucially, this ethics of conveying involves assuming a position in a sacred hierarchy in order to learn how to be both a speaker and a listener, someone who gives instruction and receives it, someone who acts on others and is acted upon. Rather than locate agency within a self-contained, bounded individual who exists prior to and separate from society, agency here is distributed through a network of ethical relationships that act upon people and keep them on the path of the Prophet (see Strathern 1988). The ethical self, then, is an effect of ethical relationships and emerges through the shared ethical work of *dawat*.

When I began my research, I assumed that the dramatic growth of the Tablighi Jamaat reflected a broader neo-liberal turn within the Islamic revival away from state institutions toward a focus on individual autonomy, authenticity, and agency. This, I thought, was evidenced by the Tablighi rejection of traditional hierarchies based on genealogy, the stress on individual duty, and the emphasis on a direct relationship between an individual and God, common features of modern religious and semiotic ideologies (Eisenlohr 2011; Engelke 2007; Keane 2007). The impact of this modernist framework on Islamic movements can be found in many parts of the world (Bayat 2013a; Roy 2004; Rudnyckyj 2009), including Pakistan (see Iqtidar 2011b, 2013). However, the sharp distinction Tablighis draw between practice (*amal*) and talk (*batein*), *dawat* and *politiks*, and religion (*din*) and the world (*dunya*) and the formidable Tablighi critique of Islamism suggest an opposite movement, one that centers on the form of religious practice and the importance of hierarchical relationships within the community. For Tablighis, the modernist understanding of religion anchored in egalitarian individualism is one of the principal sources of moral chaos as it authorizes every individual to interpret and speak for Islam and thus generates argumentation, divisiveness, and fragmentation. By creating a world of pious sociality shaped by an ethics of hierarchy, *dawat* is an effort to counter the threat of moral chaos posed by egalitarian individualism in both liberal and Islamist varieties.

Acknowledgments

I am grateful to the editors of this book, Jason Hickel and Naomi Haynes, for their invaluable feedback on earlier drafts. My gratitude also extends to Richard Handler, who helped me clarify key points in previous formulations of the argument, to Eve Danziger and Saba Mahmood for their comments on an earlier draft, and to two anonymous reviewers. A Dissertation Fieldwork Grant from the Wenner-Gren Foundation provided the funding for the research on which this chapter is based. Any shortcomings of the present work are of course entirely my own.

Arsalan Khan is an Assistant Professor in the Department of Anthropology at Union College in Schenectady, New York. His research examines the intersection of ritual, gender, and ethics in the Islamic revival in Pakistan and addresses the broader relationship between Islam, secularism, and modernity.

Notes

1. My focus is on the Tablighi critique of Islamism rather than Islamism itself, so I leave open the possibility that some aspects of Tablighi piety are present in Islamist groups as well. Tablighis acknowledge some overlap, but they say that Islamists devalue religious practice, which is precisely the problem with Islamists.
2. I mark the term *politiks*, which Tablighis often use interchangeably with the Urdu term *siyasat*, to draw attention to the specific meanings Tablighis assign to the category.

References

Ahmad, Irfan. 2009. "Genealogy of the Islamic State: Reflections on Maududi's Political Thought and Islamism." *Journal of the Royal Anthropological Institute* 15 (S1): S145–S162.
Alam, Muzaffar. 2004. *The Languages of Political Islam: India 1200–1800*. 1st ed. Chicago: University of Chicago Press.
Asad, Talal. 1993. *Genealogies of Religion: Discipline and Reasons of Power in Christianity and Islam*. Baltimore: Johns Hopkins University Press.
Austin, J. L. 1975. *How to Do Things with Words*. 2nd ed. Ed. J. O. Urmson and Marina Sbisà. Cambridge, MA: Harvard University Press.
Basu, Helene. 1998. "Hierarchy and Emotion: Love, Joy and Sorrow in a Cult of Black Saints in Gujarat, India." In Werbner and Basu 1998a, 117–139.
Bayat, Asef. 2013a. "Introduction: Post-Islamism at Large." In Bayat 2013b, 3–34.
Bayat, Asef, ed. 2013b. *Post-Islamism: The Changing Faces of Political Islam*. Oxford: Oxford University Press.
Dumont, Louis. 1980. *Homo Hierarchicus: The Caste System and Its Implications*. Rev. ed. Chicago: University of Chicago Press.
Eickelman, Dale F., and James Piscatori. 1996. *Muslim Politics*. Princeton, NJ: Princeton University Press.
Eisenlohr, Patrick. 2011. "Introduction: What Is a Medium? Theologies, Technologies and Aspirations." *Social Anthropology* 19 (1): 1–5.
Engelke, Matthew. 2007. *A Problem of Presence: Beyond Scripture in an African Church*. Berkeley: University of California Press.
Engelke, Matthew. 2010. "Religion and the Media Turn: A Review Essay." *American Ethnologist* 37 (2): 371–379.
Ewing, Katherine P. 1997. *Arguing Sainthood: Modernity, Psychoanalysis, and Islam*. Durham, NC: Duke University Press.
Gilsenan, Michael. 1982. *Recognizing Islam: Religion and Society in the Modern Middle East*. London: Croom Helm.
Graeber, David. 2001. *Toward an Anthropological Theory of Value: The False Coin of Our Own Dreams*. New York: Palgrave Macmillan.
Hallaq, Wael B. 2013. *The Impossible State: Islam, Politics, and Modernity's Moral Predicament*. New York: Columbia University Press.
Hirschkind, Charles. 2006. *The Ethical Soundscape: Cassette Sermons and Islamic Counterpublics*. New York: Columbia University Press.
Ho, Engseng. 2006. *The Graves of Tarim: Genealogy and Mobility across the Indian Ocean*. Berkeley: University of California Press.
Iqtidar, Humeira. 2011a. "Secularism Beyond the State: The 'State' and 'Market' in Islamist Imagination." *Modern Asian Studies* 45 (3): 535–564.
Iqtidar, Humeira. 2011b. *Secularizing Islamists? Jama'at-e-Islami and Jama'at-ud-Da'wa in Urban Pakistan*. Chicago: University of Chicago Press.
Iqtidar, Humeira. 2013. "Post-Islamist Strands in Pakistan: Islamist Spin-Offs and Their Contradictory Trajectories." In Bayat 2013b, 257–276.
Jakobson, Roman. 1957. *Shifters, Verbal Categories, and the Russian Verb*. Cambridge, MA: Harvard University, Russian Language Project.
Keane, Webb. 2007. *Christian Moderns: Freedom and Fetish in the Mission Encounter*. Berkeley: University of California Press.
Kurin, Richard. 1981. "Person, Family, and Kin in Two Pakistani Communities." PhD diss., University of Chicago.

Lambek, Michael. 2015. *The Ethical Condition: Essays on Action, Person, and Value.* Chicago: University of Chicago Press.

Mahmood, Saba. 2005. *Politics of Piety: The Islamic Revival and the Feminist Subject.* Princeton, NJ: Princeton University Press.

Makdisi, George. 1983. "Institutionalized Learning as a Self-Image of Islam." In *Islam's Understanding of Itself*, ed. Speros Vryonis, Jr., 73–85. Los Angeles: University of California Press.

Messick, Brinkley. 1993. *The Calligraphic State: Textual Domination and History in a Muslim Society.* Berkeley: University of California Press.

Metcalf, Barbara D. 2003. "Travelers' Tales in the Tablighi Jamaat." *Annals of the American Academy of Political and Social Science* 588 (1): 136–148.

Metcalf, Barbara D. 2004. *Islamic Contestations: Essays on Muslims in India and Pakistan.* New Delhi: Oxford University Press.

Meyer, Birgit. 2011. "Mediation and Immediacy: Sensational Forms, Semiotic Ideologies and the Question of the Medium." *Social Anthropology* 19, no 1: 23–39.

Mitchell, Timothy. 2006. "State, Economy, and the State Effect." In *The Anthropology of the State: A Reader*, ed. Aradhana Sharma and Akhil Gupta, 169–189. Blackwell.

Mittermaier, Amira. 2011. *Dreams That Matter: Egyptian Landscapes of the Imagination.* Berkeley: University of California Press.

Munn, Nancy D. 1986. *The Fame of Gawa: A Symbolic Study of Value Transformation in a Massim (Papua New Guinea) Society.* Cambridge: Cambridge University Press.

Robbins, Joel. 2001. "God Is Nothing but Talk: Modernity, Language, and Prayer in a Papua New Guinea Society." *American Anthropologist* 103 (4): 901–912.

Roy, Olivier. 2004. *Globalized Islam: The Search for a New Ummah.* New York: Columbia University Press.

Rudnyckyj, Daromir. 2009. "Market Islam in Indonesia." *Journal of the Royal Anthropological Institute* 15 (S1): S183–S201.

Ṣaḥeeḥ International. (1997) 2004. *The Qur'ān: English Meanings.* Trans. and ed. Ṣaḥeeḥ International. Jeddah: Al-Muntada Al-Islami. https://asimiqbal2nd.files.wordpress.com/2009/06/quran-sahih-international.pdf.

Sanyal, Usha. 1996. *Devotional Islam and Politics in British India: Ahmad Riza Khan Barelwî and His Movement, 1870–1920.* Delhi: Oxford University Press.

Sikand, Yoginder. 2002. *Origins and Development of the Tablighi Jama'at (1920–2000): A Cross-Country Comparative Study.* London: Sangam Books.

Silverstein, Brian. 2011. *Islam and Modernity in Turkey.* New York: Palgrave Macmillan.

Silverstein, Michael. 1976. "Shifters, Linguistic Categories, and Cultural Description." In *Meaning in Anthropology*, ed. Keith H. Basso and Henry A. Selby, 11–55. Albuquerque: University of New Mexico Press.

Strathern, Marilyn. 1988. *The Gender of the Gift: Problems with Women and Problems with Society in Melanesia.* Berkeley: University of California Press.

Werbner, Pnina. 2003. *Pilgrims of Love: The Anthropology of a Global Sufi Cult.* Bloomington: Indiana University Press.

Werbner, Pnina, and Helene Basu, eds. 1998a. *Embodying Charisma: Modernity, Locality and the Performance of Emotion in Sufi Cults.* New York: Routledge.

Werbner, Pnina, and Helene Basu. 1998b. "Introduction: The Embodiment of Charisma." In Werbner and Basu 1998a, 3–30.

Chapter 6

DEMOTION AS VALUE
Rank Infraction among the Ngadha in Flores, Indonesia

Olaf H. Smedal

Taking up the issue of whether the study of values is best served by monist or pluralist accounts, Joel Robbins (2013: 102) notes that debates over these issues center on the nature of the relations between values. Inspired by Louis Dumont, especially *Homo Hierarchicus* (1980), Robbins suggests that unlike philosophers, anthropologists can fruitfully explore such relations empirically. As values tend to be played out and sometimes contested in social life, it is only to be expected that different values—even or perhaps just precisely opposite ones—are dominant in separate social spheres. Obvious candidates for such differently valorized social spheres would be the ritual and the secular, the religious and the economic, and men's activities and women's, to mention just three sets. In an effort to open the way for anthropological investigations of how different values operative in separate spheres relate to each other in concrete settings, Robbins (2013: 106–111) usefully distinguishes between four alternative constellations: monism, monism with stable levels, (relatively) stable pluralism, and unsettled pluralism.

Monism is characterized by one superior value subordinating any other value across social spheres. Monism with stable levels means that the subordinate value is sovereign in certain subordinate social spheres. (Relatively) stable pluralism means that the relationship between values and their respective social spheres approximates equilibrium because the values are incommensurable and the spheres on a par with one another. Unsettled pluralism obtains in situations where two superordinate values are in direct conflict.

Robbins (2013: 112) makes it clear that "[t]hese cases in no way cover all possible configurations," and I hope to show that a variant of unsettled pluralism is one where a superior value loses its organizing vigor and relevance, giving way to its opposite, the configuration subsequently settling as monism with stable levels. One likely scenario would be when a superior value is recognized as such by a dwindling section of the population and obtains to this section only, pertaining to a circumscribed sphere of social life, while the opposite value is embraced by the population at large and pertains to social life more generally.

The value discrepancies I focus on here are two fundamentally different ideological constructs that parallel those put forward by Howell (this issue), who has also carried out fieldwork on Flores (although the situation that Howell describes differs markedly from that explored in this article). The first construct is articulated as a social organization characterized by hereditary rank. The other echoes ideas of a more democratic and egalitarian social order. The first finds its legitimacy in the cosmo-mythical past, the second in a far more recent discourse. I shall argue that the social organization premised on rank is rapidly losing ground—partly due to the influence of 'the modern', but even more so because its internal logic works against it. However, I also want to show that when the oppositional values in question are activated by a complex ritual, the intensity of their presence in people's minds produces profound and unavoidable emotional turmoil.

The rationale for the ritual can be stated very briefly, although its salient particulars require some fleshing out. In telegram style, among the Ngadha in Flores, eastern Indonesia, noble women can legitimately marry only noble men. Noble men are free to marry anyone. Noble women who marry (or engage in sexual relations with) common men lose their noble status immediately and are banished. They can only return to or visit their natal village after enduring a humiliating and costly ritual.

In the following, I draw on personal observations of two such returns and accompanying rituals and show how attitudes among the nobility toward traditional values are now changing. Today's grandparental generation adheres to the ideology of the past and judges these cross-rank unions as simply despicable. The parental generation, however, tends to see these couples' unions in a more positive, even positively liberating light. I note in passing that the commoners, who constitute at least 95 percent of the Ngadha population, view the traditionalist values of the nobles as faintly ridiculous, unnecessary, and demeaning.

Before I turn to the ritual, I should note that to describe the social organization to which it is integral triggers a theoretical concern. There are two aspects to this. The first is how this particular kind of inherited social status and the social whole within which it exists are best understood. Among the Ngadha, nobility entails neither riches nor particular social functions, political offices, or economic privilege, nor does it confer prerogatives such as the right to command commoners (see Smedal 2009a: 216–217). So while nobility is known by all Ngadha as a superior status, one that is inherited and can never be otherwise achieved, it is difficult to point to any advantages nobles might have. Indeed, nobles themselves would readily point to certain disadvantages they endure (marital restrictions on their women being one).

The second aspect emerges directly from the first. Depending on how Ngadha nobility and their ranking system are understood, Dumont's work (1980) on hierarchy in India may or may not be relevant. I shall argue here that although the Ngadha rank order superficially resembles the Indian caste order (with notions of 'purity' being a central feature), it fails to be a proper parallel because Ngadha social life does not hinge on the existence of a class of nobles. The total social order does not depend on it. The sacrificial work Brahmins do exclusively in Hindu India—without which that entire socio-cosmic order would collapse (as I understand the situation)—simply does not have any equivalent in Ngadhaland. Yet it is difficult to find an English word that better captures the Ngadha rank order than 'hierarchy'. Thus, I am in sympathy with the editors when in their introduction they propose an understanding of hierarchy that does not entail encompassment. Rather, as they put it, hierarchy "refers not to encompassment but rather to difference and asymmetry, and often also to rank" (Haynes and Hickel, this issue). There is in Ngadhaland no lack of difference, asymmetry, and rank, but however exalted nobles (at present) may be, they are not—ultimately—indispensable. And they know this.

Ethnographic Background

The Ngadha in central Flores, eastern Indonesia, are an ethnic group of some 60,000 people, most of whom are swidden agriculturalists tilling land from the seashore up to some 1,500 meters above sea level. The chief subsistence crops are rice, maize, pulses, cassava, and banana, while major cash crops include coffee, cocoa, candlenut, cloves, and—although at high risk—vanilla. Most people keep chicken and pigs, and a few raise water buffalo. These animals feature frequently in rituals as sacrificial victims.

The Ngadha are organized in kin-based groups they call Houses (*sa'o*).[1] While these may appear at first glance to be predicated on a principle of matrilineal descent, as Schröter (2005) has asserted, closer analysis reveals that a more fundamental feature of House recruitment is a rule of residence, which again is a function of variability in the size of bride wealth prestations. In short, Ngadha social organization is basically exchange driven, not descent driven.[2] In the area I am most familiar with, in the vast majority of cases the amount of bride wealth paid is small. Accordingly, upon marriage women routinely stay put, men move in, and the couple's children are affiliated with her House, not his.

The characteristic of Ngadha social organization that most concerns me here is that of inherited rank: the nobles or aristocrats (*ga'é*) and the commoners (*kisa*). There are a few individuals in scattered settlements known to be descendants of former slaves, but they play virtually no role in what is a vigorous socio-ritual life, and they never feature in House genealogies. Their slave status derives from when—in the past—their forebears were either taken as war captives, became mired in bottomless debt, or sought refuge after having been banished from their home domains, often due to witchcraft accusations.

Since the 1920s, Catholic missionaries have been extremely successful in converting the Ngadha to Christianity. This fact notwithstanding, ancestral and other spirits continue to play a vital role in the life of almost every Ngadha man and woman I know. The opinion of one's ancestors is frequently sought through a variety of divinatory techniques.[3]

Rank and Sexuality

The term in the Ngadha language that designates illegitimate sexual relationships is *la'a sala*. It means roughly 'to make a misstep' or 'to take the wrong path'. The term covers what are arguably two separate kinds of infractions: (1) sexual relations between close relatives (incest),[4] and (2) sexual relations between noble women and men of lesser rank, regardless of whether they are otherwise related. In the following, it is the second kind of infraction I shall consider.

In order to appreciate what is at stake, it is important to note that rank is transmitted to children only from their mother—never from their father. But a noble woman known to have had sex with a man of commoner or slave extraction is promptly, automatically, and irreversibly demoted to the rank of her partner. She is also immediately exiled from her natal House and village. This is so whether or not the union has resulted in a pregnancy and whether or not the union at any point becomes sanctioned as a marriage proper, for example, in church. It follows that in the event that a child is born, it will inherit its mother's new and lower rank, as shown in table 1.

The demotion of commoner women to slave status takes place without further ado. But the formal demotion of noble women is a dramatic and humiliating affair. It is dramatic partly because prior to the advent of missionaries, the woman and her 'partner in crime' were not simply demoted—they were also executed, if caught. Nowadays, the execution is symbolic and effected in ritual. It takes place before dawn at a good distance from the village. A second stage in the demotion, which takes place the following day, is public. This is the part that is humiliating.

TABLE 1 Production of rank among the Ngadha

Father	Mother	Child
noble	noble	noble
noble	commoner	commoner
noble	slave	slave
(commoner)	(noble) →	commoner
commoner	commoner	commoner
commoner	slave	slave
(slave)	(noble) →	slave
(slave)	(commoner) →	slave
slave	slave	slave

Note: Illegitimate combinations are marked by parentheses. These pairings lead to a change, invariably negative, in the woman's rank, which becomes that of her partner or 'husband' (whose rank is never affected by his sexual-marital liaisons). The demotions are marked with an arrow.

The Ritual

I shall presently recount the salient events of the two days, but I should note that crucial ritual work must be undertaken during the night prior to the couple entering the scene. This work takes place inside the locked and barred House of the errant woman. Its main purpose is to alert the ancestors to what is being planned and to ask their assistance in selecting personnel for the separate tasks to be carried out on the following days. The divinations integral to this work—sacrificing chickens and pigs and 'reading' their entrails and making bamboo sticks explode in the hearth fire—cannot be carried out in the presence of women, as the House is now 'contaminated'.[5] Properly managed, noble men can deal with this danger. However, noble women must keep away, as they are vulnerable. Scraps from the sacrificial meals throughout the night, the spent bamboo sticks, and a few other items, collectively referred to as 'the dirty stuff' (BI *kotoran*), are bundled in banana leaves only to feature later in the ritual proper.

Day One

A couple of hours before dawn, heading a small group of noble men of the woman's House, the errant couple is made to walk in almost total darkness along a path into the forest. The man carries the bundle of 'filth' prepared a few hours earlier. The woman has a section of giant bamboo filled with water strapped to her back. The container represents the woman's body and the water her blood. Without warning, one of the men behind her slashes at the bamboo container with his bush knife. The bamboo shatters, and the water gushes out.[6] The male dog that the men have brought to stand in for the woman's partner is tied to the top of a bamboo and stoned to death. While the yelping dog loses its life, the male transgressor, who is watching the proceedings, is verbally abused ("Die, you dirty dog!") for having 'taken the wrong path'.

Upon the death of the dog, the errant couple must hurry away, without looking over their shoulders, and take a bath in a nearby brook before they encounter other people. Through this ritual cleansing, their *zaki zé'é* (moral filth) is washed away.[7] Afterward, the woman is no longer referred to as a sexual transgressor (*la'a sala*) but simply as a commoner (*kisa*), into which the ritual has transformed her. The couple is bidden good riddance by the men of the House with the words *To'o si, la'a si né'é zala miu* (Get up, walk off your own way).

Daylight has now come, and the couple remains in their lodgings outside the village perimeter, still barred from entering the village plaza and its named Houses. The male transgressor plays no role in what follows; in ritual terms, he has made his exit. But the woman now faces another tribulation when she is to be reintegrated as a *persona grata* commoner in the village and her natal House.

Meanwhile, the men who have fulfilled their ritual responsibilities by ridding their noble kin group of the *la'a sala* couple return to the village. But they soon saunter back into the forest, regrouping at an agreed-upon spot to celebrate, in a grand if highly informal manner, what just took place. A buffalo calf, provided by the *la'a sala* man (now disposed of) as partial fulfillment of his punitive fee, is unceremoniously killed (i.e., not sacrificed) and butchered, its meat grilled, boiled, or smoked. While some of it is consumed on the spot, accompanied by copious amounts of palm gin, the better part is saved for later. But none of this meat can be stored or consumed within the village (*nua*) perimeter, nor can it be consumed by commoners or noble women. The heavily charged meat from this 'filthy' calf must therefore be kept in places such as field huts, where noble males will partake of it during the following weeks, their nobility and gender guaranteeing them the constitution to avoid ancestral retribution in the form of *sa'i* (a category of allopathically incurable disease).

Day Two

The second day is all about the errant woman and her reintegration into her kin group, a ritual known as *nuka nua* (to return to the village), which is also the blanket term for the entire set of events. In the early morning, in full daylight, the woman enters the village plaza. Her hair is loose and her clothing simple. She cannot go directly to her House. On signal, she must first circle the village plaza in a manner known as *ja'i laba polo* (dancing to the witch drum), escorted by a woman who was herself once demoted and accordingly underwent this ritual. On festive occasions, those who dance to drums and gongs 'follow the right foot', that is, when facing the plaza center, they circle anti-clockwise. The witch drum dance uses the reverse movement; not only that, the drums and gongs consist of coconut shells and sections of bamboo. In short, *ja'i laba polo* has everything heinous, cheap, and despicable about it, expressing the very opposite of a celebration. Yet it also signals that the time of the woman's exile, both socio-ritual and economic (a point I shall return to), is all but over.

Having publically announced her witch-like behavior in broad daylight, circling the village plaza backward, so to speak, the errant woman arrives at her natal House where she is bidden to ender the veranda, not yet being allowed into the dwelling proper—its ritual center. She is given a set of fresh traditional (BI *adat*) clothes to wear, puts up her hair, and returns to the village square where she joins the woman who accompanied her in 'dancing to the witch drum' earlier. This time, however, the dance is led by a noble, married woman of the same House as the fallen woman herself (i.e., one who has married a man of her own rank), preferably her full sister. The three of them circle the village plaza in the proper, anti-clockwise movement known as *ja'i laba kita* (dance to our drum, i.e., the drum of living people). This time the men in the orchestra have brought out their proper drums and gongs to celebrate the arrival of a village daughter who has long been absent. But importantly, before she is allowed into the terraced village plaza, the married noble woman precedes her and dances at the lowest terrace. Only when she ascends to the next level does the 'fallen' woman (accompanied by at least one other woman whose fate was once the same) begin to dance. This procedure is repeated at every terrace, making it plain to the onlookers that noble women and commoner women belong to different stations.

Upon completing the circle, the women return to the House. Here the noble woman invites her errant sister inside, but in a manner deeply humiliating to the now officially accepted commoner woman. Both are visibly distressed. The noble woman places herself on a step above the other and says, facing her,

Ja'o éta tolo turé	I am up on the stone platform
Kau zai kali ngaté	You are below on the ladder

Then, as she moves up several successive levels, she says, having reached each one,

Ja'o éta téda au	I am up on the outer veranda
Kau zai tolo turé	You are below on the stone platform
Ja'o dia téda wawo	I am here on the inner veranda
Kau zai téda au	You are below on the outer veranda
Ja'o dia éta tolo péna	I am up here on the stairs
Kau zai au péna	You are below the stairs
Ja'o dheké éta one	I have ascended into the dwelling
Kau dia tolo péna	You are there by the stairs
Ja'o éta mena dhiri	I am up here by the left corner [by the hearth]
Kau mena papa léwa	You are there by the right corner [for guests]

Prior to her demotion, the errant woman would have sat along the wall near the hearth, but under no circumstances may a commoner sit there as long as the House is considered noble (*sa'o da ga'é*). Only when there are no remaining nobles may a commoner woman place herself in this position. Thus, the final—and permanent—humiliation that the transgressing woman must endure is to sit in the 'guest corner' of her own House, being fed, for she is also forever barred from cooking at that hearth.

At this point, everyone is ready for the final stage of the *nuka nua* ritual: the buffalo sacrifice. This animal, too, has been procured by the male transgressor and his family, but since the ritual has now verified that the woman is a commoner, just as he is, there is no hint at ill feelings. The buffalo killed at the center of the village plaza in the prescribed, ritual way will now be butchered, along with a pig or two. Soon the village mood begins to swing from apprehensive grief to festive anticipation as it sinks in that the village daughter really is back and that there will be more than enough to eat and drink for the entire village population and for the transgressive man's sizable entourage as well, since his family are now received as in-laws.

The Origin of Rank

I began working among the Ngadha in the late 1980s, but it was not until 2007 that I witnessed this ritual for the first time, and a second time in 2009. The topic has always been treated with grave seriousness in conversation, and nobles have repeatedly told me how fiercely they deal with what they see as one of the greatest social evils. They perceive inter-rank *la'a sala* as a combination of assault and betrayal, the commoner (or slave) man having attacked not only the noble woman but the ennobled nature of aristocracy itself, and the noble woman not only having betrayed her own high standing—as an individual—but also having forfeited the possibility of bearing daughters who can transmit high rank to succeeding generations. If the man in such cases has taken what is not his, the woman has wasted what is not hers—that is, not hers alone.

One might ask from where this distinction between nobles and commoners derives.[8] It originates, according to a number of versions of a commonly known myth, in the incestuous relationship between a brother and a sister (unbeknownst to them, according to some versions). These siblings were both noble, although properly speaking there were no distinctions of rank then (Arndt 1954: 321–325; 1955: 273–274; 1960a: 42), nobility being, as it were, the natural state.[9] It was the brother who belatedly discovered that they were siblings and who pronounced his own and his sister's punishment: the two of them were to go separate ways and never see each other again lest, according to at least one version, the Earth perish in drought. Upon this, they became stars in the heavens, yet kept their earthly names. At one level, the myth therefore explains why the Antares, *Wawi Toro* or *Dala Wawi* (the brother) and the Pleiades, *Dala Ko* (the sister) are never seen simultaneously.[10]

A notable detail is that the name for Antares, *Dala Wawi*, means 'Boar Star', while the Pleiades are called *Dala Ko* or 'Trap Star' because the constellation resembles the kind of net trap the Ngadha use to catch wild pigs. So here is a case of 'woman the hunter' being barred—by cosmological principle if not in carnal reality—from ever catching her male prey (cf. Bloch 1992). Be that as it may, in taking it upon himself to draw the consequences, the male remained noble, while the female, irrevocably disgraced, having been caught seducing her brother, became a commoner. Indeed, a close reading of some versions of the myth (Arndt 1954: 321ff.) reveals that the sister-wife knew all along that she was her husband's sister; or else that, even more scandalously, when her brother-husband, shocked by the realization that they were siblings, asked her what to do, she replied, "Nothing." The general idea, given narrative form in these myths, appears, therefore, to be that women, rather than men, are responsible for sexual transgressions (*Ko* having disgracefully trapped *Wawi*).[11] And from this time onward, sexual relations, and by extension marriage, between noble women and commoner men have been strictly prohibited. Even today it is only women who, on account of sexual liaisons with men of lower rank, can fall from grace, be banished, become a person of lower rank, and henceforth give birth only to persons of lower rank.[12]

It is important to keep in mind that it is impossible to ascend the ladder of traditional social rank. Only women can transmit noble status to their offspring. Since it originated in the dim past, nobility should perhaps most properly be understood as one of the greatest bestowals the ancestors were able to offer. To yield it by yielding to sexual desire is therefore much at the level of defiling a gift. And whether that desire is one's own or someone else's makes, according to Ngadha jurisprudence, no difference. Thus, the 'moral filth' of which the transgressors must be cleansed takes on an added dimension. For by behaving 'like animals'—which is how Ngadha describe any kind of *la'a sala*, including incest—they subvert the human social order as it has been transmitted through the ages. In the past, the transgressors were treated much like animals, not only in the ritual but also in 'ordinary life' preceding it, sometimes by being locked up among the pigs under the House. It is therefore fitting that the substitute for the male human victim in the expiatory ritual is a dog, an animal whose access to the House is especially regulated and the birth of which, inside a House, necessitates major ritual 'cleansing', if not outright abandonment, of the House. And if in the past the transgressing noblewoman was killed by her male kin—as an act of human sacrifice in order to preserve the dignity of her natal House—she is still a sacrificial victim in the twenty-first century, only now her death is symbolic.

Rank Compared

I have noted some reasons why it is difficult to see how the Ngadha rank system and the Indian caste system can be usefully compared. But difficult is not the same as impossible. At stake here is arguably that each order depends on the relative presence or absence of a certain quality. This quality is in both cases that of purity. In a discussion of the rank order among the Bugis people in Sulawesi, Indonesia, Acciaioli (2009) shows precisely how the Bugis rank order, too, is based on gradations of purity, and I think his analysis can be applied to the Ngadha material without much modification.

Acciaioli's chief concern here is with possible parallels and overlaps between two kinds of status gradation system: (Dumontian) hierarchy and what has become known as 'order of precedence'. The latter term was introduced by E. Douglas Lewis (1988), according to James J. Fox (2009: 2ff.), and, along with its companion term 'origin structure' of Fox's own device, has been much discussed, especially among anthropologists based at the Australian National University in Canberra who study Austronesian social formations.[13] Instructive as this aspect of Acciaioli's argument is, it need not detain us here, so I proceed directly to a few Bugis particulars.

The Bugis distinguish nobles from commoners based on the color of their blood: the whiter it is, the closer one is to the deities and the greater one's potency and natural right to rule (Acciaioli 2009: 66) over those with red blood. Ngadha nobles, too, have blood with a different color than that of other people: theirs is black, while commoner blood is yellow and that of (former) slaves is white. For the Ngadha, noble blood is also 'hot' (Arndt 1954: 328, 336), as is the blood of the sun (Arndt 1960a: 49) and the water buffalo, an animal with semi-divine noble status and black blood (Smedal 2009b: 283–287). In Ngadhaland and in South Sulawesi alike, only marriage between people whose blood has the same color will yield offspring with blood of that color.[14]

As Acciaioli (2009: 55ff.) points out, the concept of purity easily lends itself to a veritable inventory of discourses and associated practices—myth, tradition, cunning, and so on—that reign free to determine pollutants and polluters (food, drink, and occupation being obvious candidates) and to inform precautionary action accordingly. Bodily contact, however, appears to be something of a cross-cultural constant. Thus, although there is little in the Ngadha or Bugis material suggesting that occupation and food play decisive roles in this regard—even if Ngadha nobles associate a certain cereal, foxtail millet or Italian millet (*Setaria italica*), with slave status and still would find it odd to be offered it in a dish—sexual relations clearly do. In fact, marriage between high-ranking women and lower-ranking men is assessed in South Sulawesi much as it is in Ngadhaland, as Acciaioli explains (ibid.: 89n17):

> In all cases marrying downward is a possibility only acknowledged for male members of a particular rank. Marriage with a status inferior on the part of a noble woman was a heinous crime among the Bugis and Makasar (Friedericy 1933: 557), resulting in the execution of the offending man (and, in most cases, the woman as well). Even among commoners, such a marriage would result at least in the exile of the couple from the local community. Friedericy states that the original ideal was status-level endogamy, but over time hypergamous marriages came to be accepted. In fact, the possibility of polygyny among the nobility required

permitting such marriages. Even in the contemporay [*sic*] context, marriages of daughters with husbands of lower status are rejected by many parents, often leading to the scenario of elopement (*silariang*) and subsequent retribution carried out by the woman's brothers, father or other near relative against the offending man and often against the offending sister/daughter/niece as well ...

As should be clear by now, practically everything said here could be said about Ngadha noble/commoner relations, too, including (in the past) polygyny and (current) elopement.

For reasons of space, I cannot follow up on Acciaioli's efforts to show how notions of precedence and origins articulate in complex ways with orders of hierarchy based on conceptions of purity. I should state for the record, however, that the Ngadha ritual calendar contains an abundance of rituals in which instances of precedence and structures of origin are displayed and celebrated.

Still, if the parallels between the Indonesian and Indian cases are obvious, one should not lose sight of the differences—that is, the absence among the Ngadha of anything resembling the *jajmani* system and the fact that ritual leadership, including sacrificial actions, even when this involves the exalted water buffalo (Smedal 2009b), is not the exclusive province of nobles. Indeed, as already hinted at, the very existence of nobility is now in question because strictly enforced hypergamy, in combination with the impossibility to ascend the ladder of rank, spells certain demographic extinction,[15] a point I shall return to shortly. So even if 'purity' is the pivot, and inauspicious bodily contact its main threat (as in India), although here restricted to the foundational procreative exercises of sex, the totality of Ngadha social formations (communities, villages) does not in any way depend on the presence of a category of 'pure' humans. No one to my knowledge has undertaken an inventory of rank in Ngadha villages in order to quantify the presence or otherwise of extant noble Houses, but everyone knows that in many villages there are none.

Testimonies and Prospects

In this section I turn to the experiences and reflections of some of the most relevant protagonists at one instance of the *nuka nua* ritual described above. The center of attention in 2009 was Linda, born in 1973. She has lived in Java since her late teens when she trained as a nurse. Now she is a fully qualified midwife employed in a hospital. In 2004, she married Albert in a Catholic church in East Java. Albert teaches religion in a private Catholic high school. They told their relatives in Flores nothing about their wedding. Originally from adjacent villages in Flores, they had attended the same elementary school, noting that they had never harbored romantic feelings for one another at the time. She was born noble; he was born a commoner. They have two children. Her last appearance in her natal village had been nine years earlier.

I asked them why they had decided to visit the village. Albert answered:

In English it is perhaps 'back to basics', yes? We wanted to return ... it wasn't simply the issue of returning to our place of origin, but the experience of 'the lost child' [BI *anak hilang*] in the Gospel according to Luke [15:22–24]—*that* was exceptionally inspirational to us in that however far we travel, and *as whatever* we travel, at one point we have to return. It is not that we return as in returning home after travels or temporary migration. But we wanted to assert that this is indeed where we come from. We want to pay our respects to everything here.

And I asked, "So, could you say that Linda *is* the lost child!?" To which Albert replied, while Linda burst out laughing:

You could say that. Perhaps you cannot *equate* them, but perhaps you can? What we wanted to return for was, firstly, to ask forgiveness. Secondly, we wanted to return to express our gratitude. And that gratitude, if each of us had come *alone*, might not be fulfilling. We wished to celebrate that feeling of gratitude *together*.

But if Albert and Linda could now talk about forgiveness and gratitude, the previous years had been upsetting. A corollary of Linda's exile from her natal village and House when her marriage became known was that any financial assistance from her to her family was precluded. Linda found this particularly troubling:

You know, I was working; I wanted to *give* something to people here. But I was not allowed to. After I married nothing of what I gave ever reached here. Because of the rules, none of my gifts could be admitted to the village, or the House, until the ritual had been carried out—even money. Money stayed in their bank account, untouched.

And reflecting upon the ritual she had just experienced, center stage, it is clear how emotionally taxing it was:

Yesterday, just as I stepped inside [the House], I began to cry. The thing is, since I was a baby I was always here, in the House, and for nine years I was away. Then I return for this ritual. I bring my husband, I bring my children ... maybe I feel ... a strong yearning, and fulfillment, and there's a feeling of relief, too. My emotions were in a muddle. I felt compassion because I saw my elder sister [Monika] weeping. She felt ... deserted. And I also felt [that] I had already sinned [BI *dosa*] against 'tradition' [BI *adat*]. But what could I do? It was my choice. I have returned now because I wanted to atone for my mistake. I want to restore relationships. So I felt that this is the first good step for ... the future. That was what I felt so compassionate about yesterday, when I was dancing. So I wept.

As to the requirement or otherwise of the ritual, Linda's full brother Sammy insisted that it is indispensable, at least for the present, but he emphasized that it is mistaken to see it as being about humiliation:

It's actually a *cleansing* process. The elders say that if a noble woman marries someone below her station without going through that ritual, it is tantamount to suicide on her descendants—slowly but surely. The economy will definitely not be good. Even if the economy is good, their health will certainly not be good.

The ritual can therefore perhaps best be understood as a protective device. For by the public acknowledgment that the woman and her partner have 'sinned', as Linda calls it, the noble ancestors are satisfied that their edicts are still heeded and hence they will not cast misfortune or ill health upon the perpetrators or their kin.

Linda, as it happens, was raised by foster parents, both noble.[16] This is how her foster father, Billy, explained the importance of the ritual:

It is because we nobles do not have leaders that we have *bought* somewhere. There is no area where we can say, "That area is noble"—as in Norway, for example. *"In Norway, everyone is noble. And because we have so much money we can buy nobles in Norway."* Not true! Because there have *always* been nobles among the Ngadha. It even says in the hymn, "From the west to the east, nobles and commoners." Meaning, who are the nobles? Who are the commoners? Nobles *as well as* commoners means that nobles are nobles, commoners are commoners. That's it.

The very timelessness of the essence of the Ngadha social fabric, as nobles see it, can hardly be stated with more clarity or conviction. It is therefore significant how Billy responded when I asked him about the future prospects of nobility as an institution:

I don't know if nobles will still be around in 2050 for example. If later generations want to dispense with high rank, then go ahead. It's up to those who come after us. It's up to the young kids ...

His wife Sally cut in, "When we are dead." So while it is unthinkable for them to discontinue the ritual or to relinquish their noble status, they do acknowledge that the ranking system is not eternal.

Importantly, compared with what Billy and Sally had to say, representatives of the parental generation have an even more realistic view. Sammy said he loathed watching his sister's ordeal but stressed that her future prospects had now improved immeasurably, as had those of her children and, by extension, her (and his own) entire kin group. He also saw economic as well as demographic benefits in this:

The ritual has a positive impact. She now feels lucky, for the future. She will have more descendants because from now on every marriage will be—for the women—free. They [her female descendants] don't have to look only among the nobility anymore. It's not right to treat her this way. But whether we like it or not we must accept it. And from a genetic perspective, in our Great House we will definitely get descendants. There will be more of them.

And this is what Sammy said about the future:

> So many things change now, social relations become increasingly free. Who says the aristocracy will last forever? You know, that's impossible. Surely, in the long run, there will be no more nobles. It will be *neutral*. All people will have *the same* rank. Nobles, commoners, all will be the same.

Sammy is probably right. It will be increasingly difficult and in the end impossible for a small social formation—actually a tiny elite minority in it—to embrace two widely different value configurations when they are both truly fundamental and at odds, as they are here. Modernity will probably prevail over tradition, given time.

Although the dominant value of this ranked social formation is still very much in force and ideologically supported—if only by the nobles, who see it as important and necessary because "there have *always* been nobles," at least since the mythical brother-husband banished his sister-wife to the far side of the firmament—the writing on the wall is plain for all to see. The bitter truth is of course that the rule that noble women can only legitimately marry noble men is a formula for demographic decline. Noble men have always been free to marry women of lesser rank, and most of them do. This is why in many noble Houses there are 'waiting maidens' or *bu'é dugé* (what was once in respectful English referred to as 'spinsters') who never had children and no longer can bear them. But this is now compounded by 'modern times'. Nowadays young women, too, want higher education, and even noble women travel to other islands to attend college. Once on campus, chances are slim indeed that they will encounter Ngadha aristocrats. In fact, the demographic realities have sunk in to such a degree that in a recent case the unmarried women of a noble House collectively demoted themselves, effectively changing the status of the entire House from noble to commoner, in order to avoid the potential fate of spinsterhood.

Pulling in the same direction, after decades of military rule, is the more recent glasnost in Indonesia, which has resulted in popular democracy, media pluralism, and a relatively free press.[17] Add to this what a middle-aged commoner woman (herself the daughter of a noble father and a commoner woman, a legitimate cross-rank union), recently told me, drawing on Christian values:

> For myself ... I wish ... one day ... that there will be no more 'noble, commoner, and slave' because I wish to see all humans having the same rights and rank, as beings created by God who value each other equally. But on this matter I do not dare speak with my father, or with ritual leaders, because they will surely be rather angry. But I do dare to help and protect people who have been treated unfairly.

Indeed, all other commoners with whom I have discussed this issue over the years concur with her. This helps explain the near-total absence of commoners in the village during the *nuka nua* ritual. As one man put it, "I take no pleasure in watching someone being humiliated for becoming like us."

Considering these diverse statements together, then, Sammy's prediction that in the long run all people will have the same rank is but a projection of currently widespread experience and sentiment—and their likely conclusion. But I want to end this section on a slightly different note because I do not think it is quite fair to transpose, as I have come dangerously close to doing, Sammy's 'modernist' outlook on rank demotion and its beneficial consequences for Linda and her descendants into one of strategic or cynical demographic/economic choice. Sammy, too—and I am certain of this—would rather that Linda had married a nobleman. That would have been best for everyone. The reason I want to tread carefully here is because there is evidence from other instances of inter-rank sexual offenses I am familiar with that their transgressive nature is fundamentally perceived in ways that elicit first and last emotional responses: shock, anger, and grief. Shock and anger are felt because a planned and hitherto likely House stewardship succession has been thwarted by what I take to be interpreted as a daughter's willfulness, Linda being a case in point. Grief is felt because the woman in question is barred from entering her natal House and village until and unless she agrees to go through with the ritual. Not only is it very costly (a cause of regret in itself that I have not dealt with here), but there is also, as I have tried to make clear, the sadness, the emotional turmoil of watching one's daughter, one's sister—even one's wife—become the center of such denigrating attention. What that spectacle actually signals is in fact the irreversible collapse of a certain—however minor—form of life.

Conclusion

One might plausibly view the *nuka nua* ritual as an occasion for the nobles to simply assert their superior value in public, authoritatively compelling the errant couple and especially the demoted woman to do their bidding and endure the demeaning ritual. But I would argue that what matters more in the twenty-first century is that the nobles have come to realize that the stamp of their embodied superior value on the social order is rapidly losing its purchase. The title of this article, "Demotion as Value," is meant to accentuate this troubling fact by highlighting the irresolvable discrepancy between two opposite values. One is that of hierarchy. Premised on conceptions of purity and legitimized by mythical accounts of a foundational case of brother-sister incest, it is safeguarded and treasured by the nobility and transmitted by their women. However, this value—sustaining the rank order itself—is of peripheral concern to the vast majority of Ngadha men and women, the commoners. If they come within its orbit, it is when their menfolk commit that heinous act known as *la'a sala*, the term designating not only the cross-rank transgression that this article deals with but also incest. From the point of view of the nobles, the two kinds of violation are equally bestial.

The other value, equality, is at odds with the ideology of purity. It draws on Christian (Catholic) teachings, especially the New Testament, but is fueled by the broad post-Suharto liberational politico-economic developments in Indonesia known as *Reformasi*, which have been in progress since the turn of the millennium. This 'modernist' outlook is gaining ground, not only among the commoners (who see no reason to occupy themselves with the tribulations of the nobles anyway), but among younger nobles as well.

Returning, finally, to Robbins's monist/pluralist schemes, I stress that what nobles do in order to defend their superior status—such as the *nuka nua* ritual, which demonstrates especially to their unmarried women the consequences they must suffer if they look beyond their own rank for a lover or husband—has no bearing on other aspects of social life. It follows that the nobles pose no threat to the more egalitarian ethos of the commoners except when one of their men defiles a noble woman: then he, in turn, is defiled by the nobles. In short, the sphere of social action in which this superior value—purity—reigns paramount (see Robbins 2013) is limited to that which affects the matrimonial affairs of the nobles. Beyond the strictures operative in this sphere, further behavioral features of nobles that can result in the loss of rank are largely irrelevant to the Ngadha population at large.

The nobles are disappearing, but as long as they are here, they live their lives, after a fashion, according to the precepts of their standing. There is a straight-backed almost defiant air among elderly nobles when they talk about the particular responsibilities they shoulder, but, as I have attempted to make clear, they realize if resignedly that their golden days have passed. Younger nobles, however, see in this very fact a glint of liberating light and increased prosperity. If hierarchy among the Ngadha will continue to have value—as in 'goodness'—in the future, it is likely to be an increasingly subordinate one.

Acknowledgments

With this article I have incurred unusually many debts. First of all and as always, I thank my Ngadha friends and acquaintances in Flores (and Indonesian Borneo) who for 25 years have endured my dogged probing into their way of life. For reasons I hope they will accept, especially with respect to a text that touches on as many sensitive issues as this does, I hesitate to name them. Secondly, I owe thanks to institutions that have assisted me: the Faculty of Social Science and the Meltzer Fund, University of Bergen, financially; Lembaga Ilmu Pengetahuan Indonesia (LIPI, Indonesian Institute of Sciences), Nusa Cendana University in Kupang, Timor, and Palang Karaya University in Central Kalimantan in terms of academic sponsorship. Thirdly, I wish to thank those who invited me to present some of this material to audiences: Steffen Dalsgaard and Ton Otto, who organized the workshop "Values of Dominance and Difference" at James Cook University, Cairns; Ingjerd Hoëm and Sidsel Roalkvam, who organized the Oslo seminar in honor of Signe Howell's service to social anthropology; and Naomi Haynes and Jason Hickel, who asked me to contribute to their AAA panel "Hierarchy, Values, and the Value of Hierarchy." Fourthly, I extend thanks to colleagues at the University of Bergen who have read versions of this article and have offered suggestions and mild criticism, principally Knut M. Rio and Bruce Kapferer. The latter discussed with me in

Cairns some of the thornier issues of my argument, as did Corinne Fortier (CNRS, Paris), whose own work on hypergamy, milk kinship, and much else I admire. I am also grateful to two anonymous reviewers for their thoughtful criticisms. I have attempted to attend to many of them, while others remain as challenges for future work. Without Naomi Haynes's gentle prodding and generous encouragement, this piece would probably still be unpublished. Lastly, I wish to dedicate this article to Signe Howell, my teacher.

Olaf H. Smedal is a Professor in the Department of Social Anthropology, University of Bergen. Some four and a half years of field research in Indonesia resulted in *Order and Difference* (1989) and a series of articles and book chapters on social organization, kinship, language, hierarchy of values, economic change, and aesthetic expressions among two ethnic groups in Indonesia. He edited the Norwegian-language textbook *Mellom himmel og jord: Tradisjoner, teorier og tendenser i sosialantropologien* (2000, with Finn Sivert Nielsen) and wrote the introductory chapter to the first anthology on kinship in Norway, *Blod—tykkere enn vann?* (2001). With Knut M. Rio, he edited *Hierarchy: Persistence and Transformation in Social Formations* (2009), and he has been the editor of the Norwegian Journal of Anthropology. At present he is pursuing research on migration processes in Indonesia and on local effects of the massive political and economic changes in the country since the fall of President Suharto in 1999.

Notes

1. Sets of Houses—between 2 and perhaps 10—constitute what I have called elsewhere 'House coalition networks' (*woé*), the nature and workings of which need not concern us here. Note that italicized non-English terms are in the Ngadha language unless marked BI (Bahasa Indonesia) for the Indonesian language.
2. See Smedal (2002, 2011) for analyses of this aspect of Ngadha social organization.
3. The differential (hierarchical) relationship between the egalitarian values of the Catholic Church and the hierarchical values of the social organization of the Lio described by Howell in this issue is largely paralleled in Ngadhaland. See also Molnar (1997), who analyzes 'inculturation' as it applies to the Hoga Sara, immediate neighbors of the Ngadha.
4. Relations considered incestuous include sexual relations between parents and children, grandparents and grandchildren, siblings and half-siblings, parents' siblings and their nephews and nieces, but not, traditionally, between cousins. First-cousin marriage, while allowed in the past, is no longer practiced; the missionaries put a stop to it. But second-cousin (and third-cousin, etc.) marriage, cross and parallel, is accepted by the Church, approved by most Ngadha men and women, approbated by Ngadha traditions (BI *adat*) as evidenced in the maxim *fai weta, haki nara* (the female cousin as wife, the male cousin as husband), and does take place (see Smedal 2002).
5. See Smedal (1996: 47–53) for an account of similar ritual practices.

6. This is referred to as *tabho toké* (*tabho* 'cut right through'; *toké* 'bamboo water container'). Due to its strength, hardness, durability, and resilience, bamboo, especially the giant bamboo (*bheto*) employed here, is often invoked in ritual speech as a model for human characteristics.

7. 'Moral filth' is a free translation. Some of the relevant glosses Arndt (1961) provides for each lexeme are *zaki* (dirt), 'muck', 'soiled' (ibid.: 631); *zé'é* (bad), 'harmful', 'sick', 'covered in sores', 'base' (as of instinct), 'morally bad in the widest sense', 'wicked' (1961: 632). The expression 'moral filth' probably owes much of its significance to the former practice of locking the perpetrators in among the pigs, often in the pen under the House, whereupon villagers would shower them with all kinds of filth of a more literal variety, as well as verbal abuse.

8. I have elaborated on this myth elsewhere (see Smedal 2009b: 280ff.).

9. This point about nobility being the natural state is crucial because it means that any comparison between Ngadha rank divisions and the Indian caste order is bound to raise problems. In the Ngadha scheme of things, there is no equivalent to the Indian *jajmani* system whereby people of inherently and inherited different 'kinds' (*jati*) have separate kinds of responsibility with regard to social reproduction (i.e., occupations, 'service'), the total of which adds up to the whole. In Ngadhaland, nobles and commoners do the same kind of work—all, in principle, are first and last tillers of the soil—and 'specializations' (e.g., midwifery, healing, weaving, wood carving, oratory, divination) are not exclusive to either rank.

10. A parallel myth can be seen from the other side of the world in the Colombian Amazon: "She attempted to seduce her own brothers, and therefore the creator banished her to the outskirts of the land of moral Real People" (Sulkin 2005: 15).

11. Indeed, Arndt makes the same point, if only more forcefully, in subsequent publications: "According to another myth the sister whom *Wawi Toro* had banished deliberately returned and married him, without *Wawi Toro* recognizing her" (Arndt 1958: 125). And yet again: "Then said the wife: 'Have you really not recognized me? Has the *polo*, the bad spirit, kept your eyes closed?' At these words the brother repined over his sister" (Arndt 1955: 273–274).

12. Noble men can lose rank, too, but not on grounds of inter-rank sexual transgression. Arndt (1954: 335–343; 1960b: 242–250) provides further details on the prescriptions and proscriptions on nobles' behavior.

13. See Reuter (1992) for an early synthesis based on an analysis of precedence in Sumatra.

14. A vital difference between the Ngadha and South Sulawesi rank distinction orders, however, is that only the latter generates gradations or intermediate ranks. For example, the South Sulawesi class of nobles consists of divisions with subdivisions, not unlike the caste (*jati*) system or the sinking status of royal lines in Bali (Acciaioli 2009: 63ff., 69ff.) or, indeed, the apartheid system in South Africa.

15. For further details on Ngadha 'hypergamy', see Smedal (2002: 499; 2009a: 218–220, 227n12), where I note that a more apposite designation might be 'hypogamy prohibition'. This tends to apply in South Asia, too (Milner 1988: 145). It is well to remember in this connection that the Ngadha recognize no status advantage in hypergamous unions. As I have stressed, only women transmit status.

16. The couple in question never had biological children in common, and Linda was but one of several children they fostered (not all of them noble, not all of them female), doubtless with a view to late-in-life assistance. This is not the place to discuss issues pertaining to kinship theory, yet I should make it clear that while Linda here refers to the House of her foster parents—where she was raised since she was six months old because it was obvious that her biological mother just

could not cope with another infant—her *formal* entry (at the end of the ritual when she followed her married, noble sister Monika up the steps) was to her *natal* House where her biological father, long widowed, still resided with Monika and her family. Biology trumps sociality.

17. A caveat may be called for. Referring to recent political developments, I do not imply that the nation, the state, local governments, or indeed global capitalism pay any attention to the kind of ritual rectification Ngadha nobles see fit to effectuate. Nor does the Church involve itself in this regard. That said, representatives of local government at the district and sub-district levels and Church leaders have repeatedly voiced complaints about the 'wasteful' extravagance of the sometimes large-scale animal sacrifice that accompanies Ngadha ritual life. But commoners are as enthusiastic (and as regretful) about such carnage as are the nobles. And so it continues.

References

Acciaioli, Greg. 2009. "Distinguishing Hierarchy and Precedence: Comparing Status Distinctions in South Asia and the Austronesian World, with Special Reference to South Sulawesi." Pp. 51–90 in Vischer 2009.

Arndt, Paul, SVD. 1954. *Gesellschaftliche Verhältnisse der Ngadha*. Wien-Mödling: Verlag der Missionsdruckerei St. Gabriel.

Arndt, Paul, SVD. 1955. "Die Rangschichten in der Gesellschaft der Ngadha." *Actes du IVe Congrès International des Sciences Anthropologiques et Ethnologiques*. Tome II, Ethnologica, 1: 272–277.

Arndt, Paul, SVD. 1958. "Hinduismus der Ngadha." *Asian Folklore Studies* 17: 99–136.

Arndt, Paul, SVD. 1960a. "Mythen der Ngadha." *Annali Lateranensi* 24: 9–137.

Arndt, Paul, SVD. 1960b. "Opfer und Opferfeiern der Ngadha." *Asian Folklore Studies* 19: 175–250.

Arndt, Paul, SVD. 1961. *Wörterbuch der Ngadhasprache*. Fribourg: Pertjetakan Arnoldus, Endeh/Posieux.

Bloch, Maurice. 1992. *Prey into Hunter: The Politics of Religious Experience*. Cambridge: Cambridge University Press.

Dumont, Louis. 1980. *Homo Hierarchicus: The Caste System and Its Implications*. Rev. ed. Chicago: University of Chicago Press.

Fox, James J. 2009. "Precedence in Perspective." Pp. 1–19 in Vischer 2009.

Friedericy, Herman J. 1933. "De standen bij de Boegineezen en Makassaren." *Bijdragen tot de Taal-, Land- en Volkenkunde van Nederlandsch Indië* 90: 447–602.

Lewis, E. Douglas. 1988. *People of the Source: The Social and Ceremonial order of Tana Wai Brama on Flores*. Dordrecht/Providence, RI: Foris Publications.

Milner, Murray, Jr. 1988. "Status Relations in South Asian Marriage Alliances: Toward a General Theory." *Contributions to Indian Sociology* (n.s.) 22, no. 2: 145–169.

Molnar, Andrea K. 1997. "Christianity and Traditional Religion among the Hoga Sara of West-Central Flores." *Anthropos* 92, no. 4–6: 393–408.

Reuter, Thomas A. 1992. "Precedence in Sumatra: An Analysis of the Construction of Status in Affinal Relations and Origin Groups." *Bijdragen tot de Taal-, Land- en Volkenkunde* 148, no. 3–4: 489–520.

Robbins, Joel. 2013. "Monism, Pluralism, and the Structure of Value Relations: A Dumontian Contribution to the Contemporary Study of Value." *HAU: Journal of Ethnographic Theory* 3, no. 1: 99–115.

Schröter, Susanne. 2005. "Red Cocks and Black Hens: Gendered Symbolism, Kinship and Social Practice in the Ngada Highlands." *Bijdragen tot de Taal-, Land- en Volkenkunde* 161, no. 2–3: 318–349.

Smedal, Olaf H. 1996. "Conquest and Comfort: The Ngadha 'Bad Death' Ritual." Pp. 43–72 in *For the Sake of Our Future: Sacrificing in Eastern Indonesia*, ed. Signe Howell. Leiden: CNWS.

Smedal, Olaf H. 2002. "Ngadha Relationship Terms in Context: Description, Analysis, and Implications." *Asian Journal of Social Science* 30, no. 3: 493–524.

Smedal, Olaf H. 2009a. "Hierarchy, Precedence and Values: Scopes for Social Action in Ngadhaland, Central Flores." Pp. 209–227 in Vischer 2009.

Smedal, Olaf H. 2009b. "On the Value of the Beast or the Limit of Money: Notes on the Meaning of Marriage Prestations among the Ngadha, Central Flores (Indonesia)." Pp. 269–297 in *Hierarchy: Persistence and Transformation in Social Formations*, ed. Knut M. Rio and Olaf H. Smedal. New York: Berghahn Books.

Smedal, Olaf H. 2011. "Unilineal Descent and the House—Again: The Ngadha, Eastern Indonesia." *Bijdragen tot de Taal-, Land- en Volkenkunde* 167, no. 2–3: 270–302.

Sulkin, Carlos D. Londoño. 2005. "Inhuman Beings: Morality and Perspectivism among Muinane People (Colombian Amazon)." *Ethnos* 70, no. 1: 7–30.

Vischer, Michael P., ed. 2009. *Precedence: Social Differentiation in the Austronesian World*. Canberra: ANU E Press.

AFTERWORD
The Rise of Hierarchy

David Graeber

> Some primal termite knocked on wood
> And tasted it, and found it good!
> And that is why your Cousin May
> Fell through the parlor floor today.
>
> — Ogden Nash

Most anthropologists consider themselves politically left of center, and to a large extent contemporary anthropological theory could be said to reflect a left-wing, or at the very least broadly populist, sensibility. So much is this true that we often act as if conservative currents within the discipline do not even exist, or, at best, are limited to marginal and vaguely comical figures like Napoleon Chagnon.

True, courses in the history of anthropology will acknowledge that this was not always so. But the usual way to deal with that is to represent all early anthropology, up until perhaps around 1965 or 1968, as inherently imperialist and racist, whereafter it appears to morph overnight into the uniformly progressive discipline it is presumed to be today. Needless to say, in reality things were never this simple. As with any other discipline, anthropology was marked

Notes for this section begin on page 148.

from the start by a number of often clashing political allegiances and perspectives, and continues so today. An honest history of the discipline, for instance, would show that conservative anthropology has taken very different forms in different national traditions. In the United States, for example, the 'anthropological right' has tended at least since the Cold War to be entangled to one degree or another in the national security state, the paradigmatic and oft-cited example being Clifford Geertz's CIA-funded research in Java and Bali in the 1950s, and the broader effort at Harvard and Yale to find anthropology a place in State Department efforts to create a Weberian social science to counterpose Marx. To be honest, though, it is not clear that it is entirely fair to call such authors 'right wing'; they might better be thought of as Cold War liberals. Here in the United Kingdom, things were very different. There was an overtly conservative movement within anthropology, such as the Catholic traditionalism of Mary Douglas or the latter-day Evans-Pritchard. Intellectual historians usually attribute this to a retreat into hierarchy as a bastion of traditional stability in the wake of the chaos and destruction of World War II and the welfare state governments that followed.[1] It is not clear how influential this current really turned out to be. Certainly, Mary Douglas's work was hugely successful inside and outside the academy, but most of her more explicitly political interventions (in favor of consumerism, against the ecological movement) were not.

France, again, is quite another story. Much though Anglophones have come to think of Paris as a continual font of radical ideas, the anthropological tradition in that country has been predominantly right of center, and far and away the most influential conservative ideas in the discipline have come from France. I speak here not primarily of Claude Lévi-Strauss, who though in no sense a man of the Left remained intentionally coy about the political implications of his own work, but above all to the work of Louis Dumont. Dumont's project, about which he was in no sense coy, was, superficially, to introduce the notion of 'hierarchy' as a central tool of anthropological analysis. In a deeper sense, however, I think it was to change the basic mythic structure of the discipline, and through it all academic disciplines, and through that, ultimately, popular common sense. While this might seem an astoundingly ambitious and quixotic intellectual project, the remarkable thing is that it was largely successful. What I would like to talk about in this essay, then, is what this project really was, as well as its long-term political and theoretical effects.

• • •

First of all, the project. Where once theorists all saw themselves, after their own fashion, as grappling with Rousseau's problem of understanding the nature and origins of social inequality, Dumont sought to substitute an entirely different problematic—one that assumed society is, by its nature, necessarily hierarchical (since, he argued, societies are structures of meaning and meaning is always organized on hierarchical terms). Therefore, the thing to be explained was how modern, egalitarian ideologies could ever have emerged to begin with. For Dumont, equality itself cannot be a value. This would be a contradiction in terms, since value is by definition the placing of one thing above another. What would appear to be an egalitarian ideology, then, cannot really be an embrace of equality, which is simply the lack of evaluation, but must be the side effect of something else—in the case of modern societies, he argued, individualism.

This is an extremely conservative argument, and Dumont made his case by staking out a series of equally extreme, and in some ways obviously absurd, positions: that all societies other than modern, individualistic ones can be considered 'holistic'; that all holistic societies are hierarchical; that all hierarchies are based on an interlocking set of binary oppositions; and that all binary oppositions take the form of marked and unmarked terms in which the superior value encompasses the lower. It is not clear whether he really believed all this to be true (it obviously is not), but such positions can easily be defended on circular grounds: any 'society' that does not conceive itself as a hierarchical totality is not really a society, any binary opposition that does not involve 'encompassment of the contrary' is not really a binary opposition, and so forth.[2] Taking this kind of maximalist position is often a very effective political stratagem, since it allows one to define the field of debate. Before long, everyone is arguing over whether hierarchy is itself a value, or whether it is really so all-encompassing, but no one is arguing about the relevance of the term itself.

This is precisely what happened in Dumont's case.

• • •

Dumont himself was known to complain that his efforts had come to nothing. "I have been trying in recent years to sell the profession the idea of hierarchy, with little success" he wrote in *Essays on Individualism* (1986: 235). In fact, the project was almost unimaginably successful. True, the word 'hierarchy', barely used at all in the early years of the discipline, was already becoming more popular at the time he was writing. But after the publication of Dumont's ([1966] 1980) *Homo Hierarchicus*, its rise became spectacular.

Below is the total number of articles in JSTOR's collection of anthropology journals in English in which the word 'hierarchy' appears, followed by the percent of the total number of all articles:

1910–1920:	9 (of 2,433)	=	0.38 percent
1921–1930:	18 (of 2,442)	=	0.74 percent
1931–1940:	39 (of 3,391)	=	1.15 percent
1941–1950:	87 (of 3,409)	=	2.55 percent
1951–1960:	281 (of 5,783)	=	4.86 percent
1961–1970:	636 (of 7,628)	=	8.33 percent
1971–1980:	1,115 (of 9,614)	=	12.01 percent
1981–1990:	1,657 (of 10,990)	=	15.08 percent
1991–2000:	2,143 (of 10,786)	=	19.87 percent
2001–2010:	1,889 (of 10,806)	=	17.48 percent

Even allowing for the slight leveling off in recent years, this is startling. Over the course of a century, the percentage of works using the word has gone up by a factor of 50.

It would appear, then, that 'hierarchy' has gradually become a term of choice for describing social arrangements that would previously have been described in other terms, for example, 'rank', 'dominance', 'social stratification', or simply 'inequality'. To give a sense of the change, here is a list of a series of terms for unequal social relations, with a breakdown of how many times each appears in two books about the same Nilotic people: Evans-Pritchard's (1940) classic study, *The Nuer*, and Sharon Hutchinson's (1996) *Nuer Dilemmas*:

	The Nuer (1940)	Nuer Dilemmas (1996)
Status	40	45
Authority	21	45
Prestige	10	4
Privilege	9	11
Rank	6	1
Domination/dominant	55	28
Seniority/senior	18	21
Superiority/superior	15	7
Stratification/stratified	8	0
Inequality/unequal	1	2
Hierarchy/hierarchies/hierarchical	0	45

In Evans-Pritchard's account, neither the word 'hierarchy' nor any of its cognates appears even once. In Hutchinson, the term appears a total of 45 times, roughly once every eight pages. No other word on this list appears more often, although some terms appear a roughly approximate number of times. At the same time, purely descriptive words like 'rank' and 'dominance' decline sharply, and the word 'stratification' disappears altogether.

This is not simply a reflection of authorial taste, nor can it be attributed to the difference between British social and American cultural anthropology. In the definitive collection of Franz Boas's (1940) essays, the word 'hierarchy' never appears, and it is either entirely or nearly absent from classics of the Boasian school, such as Benedict's (1934) *Patterns of Culture* (two appearances) or Kroeber's (1947) *Configurations of Culture Growth* (zero appearances), just as it is in the collected essays of Radcliffe-Brown (1952, zero) and Malinowski (1944, two). The change in vocabulary would appear, then, to reflect a much broader transformation in the habits of both ethnographic description and comparative analysis.

Where once anthropologists had tended to present simple, often quite cold-blooded descriptions of relations of rank and power between groups (to speak of 'dominant lineages', in the Nuer case, 'social stratification', and so on), and only then to consider how those relationships came to be ideologically legitimated, there has been a broad drift toward terms—'status', 'authority', and especially 'hierarchy'—that imply those relationships are always already legitimated, or even that they do not need to be legitimated since they are fundamentally constitutive of social reality itself. Now, obviously, all this cannot be an effect of the work of Louis Dumont. The change seems to find its roots in a much more general tendency toward the intellectualization of social life that had already begun well before he took up his pen. To adopt a somewhat ungainly metaphor, the discipline was already beginning to roll in a certain direction, and Dumont just gave it a very sharp kick—speeding things up immeasurably by insisting that we think of myths, rituals, and patterns of marriage alliance not just as mental structures, first and foremost, but as power relations as well.

• • •

Such was Dumont's success that in anthropology as it is written today, the question that this volume addresses—how is it that hierarchy has come to be seen as legitimate?—often seems close to redundant. The moment one labels power relations 'hierarchy', one is already claiming that they are considered legitimate. This is because hierarchical arrangements are themselves viewed as the criteria for legitimacy. In fact, I think one could go so far as to say that, given the way we have come to organize our theoretical terms, it is well-nigh impossible nowadays to write an anthropological work that is genuinely critical of relations of what used to be called 'social stratification', because imagining a world without them would be very close to inconceivable.

The intellectualization of social life began, of course, with Claude Lévi-Strauss. He himself largely avoided the subject of power and domination, except when it came to gender, where he argued that male power over women was definitive, universal, and (it would appear) unobjectionable. Especially after *The Elementary Structures of Kinship*, Lévi-Strauss (1969) tended to focus on societies where stratification was limited to age and gender, or else, as when he looked at ranked societies such as those of the American northwest coast (Lévi-Strauss 1966), on anything other than the inequality itself. In a way, it is all very Rousseauian. There is a sense in much of Lévi-Strauss's work that relations of power and exploitation ultimately spoiled the ecologically attuned science of what he terms 'neolithic civilization'—a science that operated by analogy and bricolage in a fundamentally non-hierarchical fashion. The paradigm for this science is totemism. Totemic relations rank neither animal species nor the human groups that are mapped on to them. In fact, Lévi-Strauss argues that when rank is introduced, totemism degrades into caste, and the whole system effectively falls apart. Similarly, sacrificial ritual, of which Lévi-Strauss strongly disapproves, seems to emerge along with gods and kingdoms, as a false form of engineering that sweeps away the more contemplative science of neolithic thought (ibid.). Rather than thinking through animals, we come to simply massacre them as a way of winning favor with non-existent gods. Once power structures appear, everything goes wrong.

Lévi-Strauss's world-weary, apolitical structuralism was conservative, to be sure. But at least one could make an honest case that it was conservative in the best sense of the term, expressing a desire to conserve social and ecological arrangements that its proponents saw as values in themselves.[3] Dumont had quite a different project in mind. By moving the date of the Fall from Grace from the end of the Paleolithic to the birth of modern individualism, he placed his argument squarely in that tradition of French conservative thought that, in the wake of the Revolution, saw the Terror as a direct consequence of the dissolution of the coherent hierarchical universe of the Middle Ages, in which everyone knew their place.[4] Even the origin of the term 'hierarchy' is theological. It originally meant 'sacred or divine rule' and was first used by Pseudo-Dionysius in the sixth century to designate the orders of celestial intelligences (angels and archangels, thrones, dominions, and powers) that governed the cosmos. It was only in the High Middle Ages that it came to be extended to the ecclesiastical hierarchy modeled after it, and in the Renaissance, to the whole of creation. Dumont's main departure from that tradition is his argument that even medieval Catholicism, in its insistence that all believers were ultimately equal owing to their possession of a unique and incommensurable soul, bore within it seeds of the very individualism that would ultimately destroy it.

According to Dumont, as I have noted, equality cannot be a value because value *is* hierarchy. Egalitarianism is not and cannot be a value in itself, in Dumontian terms; it can only be a side effect of individualism. However, other traditions—not just the Indian caste system that was his particular area of specialty, but all 'normal' societies, as Dumont put it, from Lévi-Strauss's beloved Amazonians to African sultanates—are intrinsically hierarchical in exactly the way that the old reactionary thinkers had imagined the Medieval Church to be. They were each founded on a total ('holistic') view of the cosmos continuous with human society, in which everyone did indeed know his/her place.

If you think about it, this was quite an ingenious inversion of the tradition of Rousseau. For Dumontians, hierarchy, not equality, plays the same role as Rousseau's primordial innocence—one might even say that it *is* a kind of primordial innocence. The formulation was also a rather clever inversion of contemporary Marxist theories of ideology, as Dumont was occasionally willing to admit. Dumontians agreed with, say, Roland Barthes that ideology was a matter of taking arbitrary power relations and making them seem as if they were inscribed in the very order of the natural universe. But Dumontians saw this as a good thing, since they insisted it was the only way to create a moral order based on stable values of any sort at all. Finally, liberating the conservative tradition from any possible charge of ethnocentrism saved it from the disrepute into which it had largely fallen in the years after World War II. As Nicolas Verdier (2005: 34) has noted, the word 'hierarchy' itself had largely disappeared from the social sciences in the 1950s and 1960s, when Dumont was writing his principal work, tainted by its association with Nazism.[5] Dumont had an answer to that, too. He argued that once modernity is born, and the genie of individualism has been released from its bottle, there is simply no putting it back. Any political project aimed at restoring holism will inevitably lead to totalitarianism, whether of the fascist or communist variety. Stalin and Hitler alike were the products of the impossibility of any return to genuine conservatism.

The Marxist anthropology of the 1970s and 1980s made a brief splash and then largely disappeared. Lévi-Straussian structuralism peaked around the same time and is now considered slightly ridiculous. Yet, for some reason, Dumontianism lives on. In fact, the stripped-down, almost cartoonish version of structuralism that Dumont promulgated is really the only sort of structuralism that most anthropologists nowadays take at all seriously. Meanwhile, its key term, hierarchy, has become so utterly pervasive that anthropologists—and I must include myself among them—find it difficult to even think about how one might write about unequal social relations without employing it.

• • •

What I would like to suggest, then, is that we might do well to start considering how to think outside the hierarchical box because the effects of the term's ubiquity have in many ways become quite insidious. This is true, I would say, for two reasons above all. The first is ideological. The adoption of the word 'hierarchy' has been essentially to naturalize inequality—not just to treat human systems of domination as forms of meaning (even, in the extreme Dumontian formulation, the only possible form of meaning), but to see them as always already justified. The second is subtler. It is not just that Dumontians claim that holistic societies tend to ground systems of social stratification in the very order of nature; they are doing the same thing themselves when they present their ideas of hierarchy as somehow inherent in the very nature of human language and thought. In other words, they are not just presenting us with a sloppy and ill-thought-out version of structuralism: the sloppiness is inherent in the nature of the program. In order to naturalize hierarchy, they *have* to persist in logical errors that would otherwise be readily apparent.

This, too, I have written about before (Graeber 1997: 703–709). Here I can offer only a brief summary. Essentially, the concept of hierarchy, as currently employed, is based on a kind of conceptual sleight of hand involving the conflation of two different forms of logical operation—ranking and the creation of taxonomies–which, while sometimes overlapping in practice, are in fact entirely distinct.

Ranking involves arranging elements along a single, unilinear chain where any one element is either superior or inferior to any other. The result might be considered a linear hierarchy, since it exists in a single dimension. A classic example of such a linear hierarchy is the notion of 'the chain of being', first proposed (as far as we know) in Plato's *Timaeus*, developed by Augustine, and popular in Renaissance times. As described by Arthur Lovejoy (1936), this 'Great Chain of Being' ranked every aspect of creation—from angels to animals, plants, and geological formations—on a single scale of proximity to God. Ranking, of course, is key to any system of value, since it enables one to say that one element in the system is superior (more valuable in some way) than another.[6] As Lovejoy was quick to point out, such systems can work only if there is a single criterion of ranking. The Great Chain measured the value, and hence position, of every creature according to the degree to which it was endowed with the faculty of reason (and hence to which it partook of divinity, which was identified with reason). But the moment that any other criteria were introduced, the whole system tended to fall apart.

The birth of modern biology, of course, corresponds to the point where the Great Chain of Being was replaced by Carl Linnaeus's system of taxonomic hierarchy. Taxonomic hierarchies are organized on a completely different principle. They are not linear but operate by creating ranked levels of inclusion: sparrows are included in the larger category of birds, birds are included in the larger class of vertebrates, and so on. While in both cases we can speak of rank orders of a sort, taxonomies involve a very different sort of ranking, since they rank not the elements being classified, but a series of increasingly higher levels of abstraction: sparrow, bird, vertebrate, and so forth. There is no sense in which one sparrow is superior (more sparrow-like, more bird-like, more vertebrate-like) than any other; rather, it is the categories that are ranked, by degree of inclusiveness, not the individuals that make them up.[7] Obviously, this is entirely different from a linear hierarchy, where by definition certain species of bird *are* superior to others, any given mammal *is* superior to any given bird, and so on.

Dumont's trick is to treat these two meanings of hierarchy as if they were ultimately the same. He is effectively arguing (I say 'effectively' because he does not make an explicit case for why this should be true, but just writes as if it is self-evident that it is true) that in social hierarchies, one from every category is always selected to represent the more inclusive category. This makes sense if you go back to the first application of the term 'hierarchy' to social relations, where it referred to the ranked organization of prelates in the Catholic Church. Here believers were indeed organized into parishes, each with its priest (one member of the parish who represented the whole parish before God), just as parishes were organized into bishoprics, in which one cleric represented everyone, including subordinate priests, and so forth. So there is both a rank hierarchy of offices—priest, bishop, archbishop, cardinal, Pope—and each is one of a collective meant to represent the whole on a more inclusive level of organization. The paradox here is that the higher up in the hierarchy one is, the more exclusive a group one belongs to, and therefore the more 'sacred' or 'set apart' from ordinary mortals one is taken to be. Yet at the same time, the more inclusive is one's purview, since one represents a larger and more inclusive group. Priests represent their parishioners, who are in a sense 'included' in them, but *as a class of people*, priests are also an exclusive group of sacred people set apart from the laity. Bishops represent a more inclusive group of parishioners and parish priests, and as a class, they form an even more exclusive and more sacred group set apart from all others. In such systems, rank order and taxonomic hierarchy form a perfect, integrated order.

• • •

Nowadays this is indeed a common form of organization. Examples of similar structures, balancing (taxonomic) hierarchies of inclusion with (linear) hierarchies of exclusion, can be found in many contexts in many parts of the world.

Armies, for instance, almost always tend to be organized this way. There is a rank order of officers (corporal, sergeant, lieutenant, captain, etc.), and the higher one's rank, the larger and more inclusive a unit of soldiers one commands. Still, it is clearly absurd to argue that all social arrangements, or even all hierarchical ones, are organized by synthesizing linear and taxonomic principles. To take one familiar anthropological example, while ranked Polynesian-style conical clan systems could be said to synthesize the two, most African segmentary forms of organization do not. The Nuer segmentary lineage system is marked by an elaborate taxonomic hierarchy of evermore inclusive sub-lineages, lineages, clans, and tribes, but units on the same level (whether clans, lineages, or for that matter individual lineage members) are not ranked against one another, so no linear hierarchy of exclusions results. On the contrary, Nuer are notoriously egalitarian.

At the same time, within each Nuer tribe, all males are organized into a series of age sets. These age sets are indeed ranked against each other in the linear sense: any individual is either 'senior' or 'junior' to any other. One addresses all people of a higher age set as 'fathers' and of a lower one as 'sons'. But this has nothing to do with lineage or clan affiliation. Nor is there any principle of marked and unmarked terms. Members of senior age sets do not 'include' or 'encompass' their juniors. The two principles—taxonomic and linear—co-exist, but they remain separate, or as separate as anyone can possibly allow them to be.

Since ranking and taxonomizing are both very basic logical operations, there is every reason to believe that they will be present, in some form or another, in any human group. People will always be ranking things on scales, saying that this is better or higher or purer or faster or more beautiful than that. They will also always be classifying things into more and more inclusive kinds. It is probably inevitable that they will apply both of these logics to people as well—at least in certain ways in certain contexts. But there is simply no reason to believe that when they do one, they are always necessarily doing the other. Humans are not more mammalian than any other mammal. Five-star restaurants do not 'include' or 'encompass' four-star ones. An 'A' paper does not necessarily incorporate all the good points made in a 'B' paper. True, the two principles can and often do overlap and occasionally fuse together to produce hierarchies of the ecclesiastical, military, or conical clan variety. But there is absolutely no reason to believe that most hierarchies will take this sort of hybrid form, and it is self-evidently absurd to insist that all of them do.

How does Dumont get around this problem? Basically, he begs the question, insisting that since all holistic societies are hierarchical, and all hierarchies are hierarchies of inclusion, then there must be *some* sense in which the two really are, necessarily, aspects of the same thing. In order to demonstrate this, he often stretches logic to what can only be called a conceptual breaking point. Take, for example, his formal analysis of the Indian varna system (Dumont [1966] 1980: 67). This system looks to all the world like a simple linear hierarchy, a series of groups ranked by ascending order of purity, and this is how he initially describes it. Brahmans (priests) are purer than Kshatriyas (warriors),

Kshatriyas are purer than Vaishyas (farmers), and Vaishyas are purer than Shudras (servants).[8] But he then goes on to argue that although this looks like a
linear order, it really is not (ibid.):

> Thanks to Hocart and, more precisely, to Dumézil, the hierarchy of the varnas
> can be seen not as a linear order, but as a series of successive dichotomies or
> inclusions. The set of the four varnas divides into two: the last category, that
> of the Shudras, is opposed to the block of the first three, whose members are
> 'twice-born' in the sense that they participate in initiation, second birth, and
> in the religious life in general. These twice-born in turn divide into two: the
> Vaishyas are opposed to the block formed by the Kshatriyas and the Brahmans,
> which in turn divides into two.

So at any point along the ladder, members of a given varna can see themselves
as united with those above them in representing humanity as a whole before
the gods, and opposed to those below them, who are lumped together as part
of the generic, undifferentiated humanity they are representing.

There are two obvious objections to be raised here. One is that what is
being described as a series of inclusions is, logically speaking, much easier to
describe as a series of *exclusions*. The Brahmans, who are at the top, see themselves as set off from all others, as particularly pure and holy. From their perspective, everyone else can be seen as a kind of undifferentiated mass, shading
into each other and even into non-human creatures, insofar as they all lack the
purity of Brahmans. However, from the point of view of the next highest group,
the Kshatriyas, the more relevant opposition is that which sets both them and
the Brahmans apart from another residual category, which is again relatively
impure. Then comes the opposition between the twice-born and the others,
which would include both Shudras and presumably whoever else falls in this
residual category—Dalits, Adivasis, and so on. This would certainly seem to be
how the ritual logic plays itself out in everyday practice.

Now, one can still argue, as a Dumontian no doubt would, that the entire
arrangement is 'really' a variation of the logic of a segmentary system, where
the more inclusive ranks are also set off as purer, higher, or otherwise superior
to those that they encompass. But to make the case that Hinduism is a structure
of inclusions requires something very close to special pleading—emphasizing
the way things look from the perspective of certain obscure ancient texts, and
ignoring almost everything we know about how these categories play themselves out in ordinary life. To go on to argue that *all* systems of rank order must
always necessarily work by such a logic of encompassment is, as I have already
pointed out, simply untrue.[9] And to argue that even those that do contain an
element of encompassment are not, therefore, 'really' structures of exclusion
is not just absurd, but about as politically reactionary as it is possible to be.

Insofar as there is something of lasting importance in all of this—and I
would not want to leave the reader with the impression that there is not—it
surely turns on the question of value. When Dumontians talk about linear hierarchies as being hierarchies of encompassment, what they mainly seem to be

saying is that these hierarchies often involve a kind of ranking of value spheres. This is what Dumont (1982: 230) is getting at when he speaks of "value reversals" on different levels of a hierarchy: in dealings between merchants, wealth is the paramount value, since even power and purity might best be considered valuable as ways of obtaining wealth; between warriors, wealth and purity are subordinated to the interests of power; for priests, wealth and power are only really important as ways of maintaining the ritual purity of people like themselves. Dumont's point is that the varna system ranks not only people but also those value spheres themselves, and that the sphere in which purity is the consummate value is the highest sphere. This in itself is a useful concept, not unlike Weber's notion of status groups (*stand*) or even Bourdieu's social fields. But the key difference is that for Weber or Bourdieu, the ranking is not fixed— it is always under contestation. In fact, one might even say that the ultimate stakes of politics for either is the ability to assert what one's own group holds dearest as the crowning value of the system. What Dumont refers to as holistic societies, then, are those in which he believes such matters to be definitively, and permanently, settled. Hence, his famous remark that the structure of the Indian caste system, for instance, cannot, by definition, be changed. It must either stay in place, unaffected by history, or collapse and be replaced entirely:

> A form of organization does not change, it is replaced by another; a structure is either present or absent, *it does not change*. If we are entitled to say that *so far* the changes that have occurred have not *visibly* altered what we have taken to be the heart, the living nucleus of the society, who can say but that these changes have not built up their corrosive action in the dark, and that the caste order will not one day collapse like a piece of furniture gnawed from within by termites? (Dumont [1966] 1980: 219; emphasis in original)

While this makes sense according to a certain classic conception of structuralism, it is obviously not the case for contemporary societies. So are we to conclude that structuralism applies to non-Western societies and that only the contemporary West is post-structuralist? It is hard to avoid the impression that this is exactly what Dumont thinks is going on here. But surely, to insist that pre-modern societies simply do not have politics in this sense, since their overall structure is by definition fixed, and that only in modern societies is value up for grabs is clearly just another variation on the old romantic trope that contrasts timeless societies innocent of history (whether Lévi-Strauss's 'cold' societies or Eliade's primordial ones trapped in circular history) with modern ones condemned to live in cumulative, historical time. That this is the one aspect of classical structuralism that is still taken seriously in contemporary anthropology would be very strange indeed.

• • •

How does all this bear on the essays assembled in this collection? The unifying premise is that a focus on power, domination, and resistance has made it difficult for anthropologists to talk about the fact that hierarchy (which, the editors note, can in no sense be reduced to power or inequality) is often considered a good thing, even a value in itself, by those we study. Some resist power structures not in the name of opposition to power itself, but in order to restore more familiar forms of hierarchy or utopian hierarchical visions (whether set in the future or in the past).

I would not contest that this is often the case. In fact, the language of 'resistance' took on its present popularity around the same time as the increased appearance of the word 'hierarchy'. This is an interesting phenomenon in itself because one almost never sees an ethnographer speak of resistance to hierarchy, but always instead of resistance to power and domination. This is true despite the fact that the word 'hierarchy' has come to be applied to more and more forms of unequal social relations over time: one now has age hierarchies, gender hierarchies, patronage hierarchies, and so on.

The great political advantage of the term 'resistance', of course, is that it defines political action purely in terms of what it is against, and not what it is for. To draw an analogy from more obvious propaganda, anyone reading mainstream US newspapers in the 1980s would learn that there were basically two types of guerrillas in the world: 'communist' and 'anti-communist'. It was obvious which they were being asked to favor. Any way the anti-communist guerrillas could have been described in terms of what they were actually for would surely have made them sound decidedly less appealing. In a similar way, anthropological discourse that identified popular forces as resisting power, hegemony, global capitalism, and neo-liberal governmentality, or some similar, largely abstract force, managed to avoid grappling with what those engaged in such resistance actually considered a good life worth defending, or what they ultimately aspired to achieve. In other words, this approach allows the analyst to sidestep the question of the values that ultimately motivate such resistance. The self-consciously political framing rather implies that resistance is in the name of some sort of egalitarian ideal or instinct, or at least some principle of justice with egalitarian implications, but this is never stated outright, and often the Foucauldian language used makes it unlikely that this could really be the case. The widespread adoption of the word 'hierarchy' for those forms of inequality that are not being challenged makes a certain complementary sense.

In fact, one might go even further. All this makes perfect sense to describe a world where global power structures—whether NATO or Credit Suisse—increasingly dress themselves up as the voice of human freedom, and the most overtly political forms of opposition to those power structures are increasingly likely to take traditionalist, nationalist, fundamentalist, or authoritarian forms. A Dumontian framework is perfectly tailored to theorize such a world. Dumont himself was no friend of capitalism. Much of his theoretical work (see, e.g., Dumont 1977, 1986, 1994) was dedicated to developing the critique of 'possessive individualism', economism, and utilitarian rationality proposed by left-wing thinkers such as Karl Polanyi (1944), C. B. Macpherson (1962), and Marshall Sahlins (1972; see also Sahlins et al. 1996)—if only to turn it against the Left as well. In this sense, Louis Dumont might almost be seen as a kind of prophet of conservative anti-capitalist movements to come—movements that barely existed in his lifetime. By 'conservative anti-capitalist movements', I mean those that reject the values of bourgeois modernity, not in the name of egalitarian universalism or of some fantasy of lost European social harmony, but instead in the name of what are taken to be more genuinely holistic (but equally authoritarian) forms of social order preserved on Europe's fringes or within its former imperial dominions. In a world where opposition to the American empire is now being spearheaded above all by Putin's patriarchal authoritarianism, a Chinese government increasingly shedding Marxism for Confucianism, and a ragtag collection of would-be Islamist theocracies, all this seems genuinely prescient.

• • •

I have described Dumont's formulations as fundamentally incoherent, based on a false conflation of two kinds of logical operation: linear ranking and the arrangement of taxonomies. I have further argued that adopting the resulting language, and thereby reducing relations of what used to be called power, domination, stratification, or inequality to a single uniform category of hierarchy (as anthropologists of all political stripes have increasingly come to do under Dumont's influence), means presenting those relations never as the contingent result of a play of forces (like Evans-Pritchard's 'dominant lineages'), but always as inherently meaningful arrangements that should be treated as already fully justified in the minds of those we study—indeed, as the very foundation of their sense of what is good and right and beautiful. But surely this is not the case. While some relations of power or inequality might be like this, others are most decidedly not. None go unchallenged. There are tensions within even the most deeply internalized systems—tensions that could, under the right circumstances, allow them to be transformed into something else. Finally, people argue about such matters all the time. It might well be that the only time people are strongly unified around the legitimacy of such arrangements in the way Dumont implies is precisely when they come to seem values in themselves opposed to those of the larger capitalist world-system.

Clearly, we need to rethink our terms. It would be impossible at this juncture to simply jettison the term 'hierarchy' entirely, nor am I suggesting it would be wise to do so. But we definitely would do well to seriously rethink the way we are deploying such terms, and to think more deeply about the tacit assumptions that lie behind their use. This volume, it seems to me, might be considered a first step in such a project. Almost every author sets out to speak of hierarchy in a broadly Dumontian sense and ends up discovering some way that this standard approach is inadequate. Dumont's distinction between hierarchical and individualistic/egalitarian societies is incoherent (Feuchtwang). Rank is not necessarily about inclusion (Smedal, Khan). The structure of values is not necessarily holistic (Haynes and Hickel). Equality can indeed be a value (Howell). The relation of power and legitimacy is not a given (Malara and Boylston). Hierarchical relations are not prior but continually created through acts of destruction (Damon). Combine all these insights together and very little of the Dumontian edifice remains. Perhaps it, too, should collapse like a piece of furniture gnawed by termites. And on its ruins, we can begin, like the authors in this volume, to think more seriously about what the wellsprings of the deeply felt appeal of unequal forms of social relations actually are.

David Graeber is currently a Professor of Anthropology at the London School of Economics. He has done ethnographic work on magic and slavery in Madagascar and direct action in the United States, as well as theoretical monographs on a variety of subjects, ranging from value theory (*Toward an Anthropological Theory of Value*, 2001), debt (*Debt: The First 5,000 Years*, 2011), bureaucracy (*The Utopia of Rules*, 2015), kingship (*On Kings*, 2017, with Marshall Sahlins), and work (*Bullshit Jobs: A Theory*, 2018).

Notes

1. I speak here of outright conservatism: Tories in England, Gaullists in France. There has also been a strain of what I would consider neo-liberal anthropology since the 1980s, of which authors like Arjun Appadurai and Daniel Miller are probably the best-known avatars, but this might be considered a separate phenomenon.
2. I have critiqued Dumont's formal definition of hierarchy quite sharply in two different places (Graeber 1997, 2001). I have never seen any of these arguments taken up by anyone else or even cited in lists of critiques of Dumont, and I have never understood precisely why.
3. A case could also be made that Lévi-Strauss's structuralism was not conservative. He appears to have been a dogged anti-feminist, and he expelled Pierre Clastres from his *laboratoire* when Clastres tried to make a case that the anti-authoritarianism of the neolithic societies Lévi-Strauss favored might be relevant to the politics of his day.
4. I would not wish to discount the intellectual power of this tradition, first exemplified by authors like Louis de Bonald, Joseph de Maistre, and of course Auguste Comte. As Nisbett (1966) has pointed out, almost all of the basic problems of the sociological tradition—not just hierarchy, but community, solidarity, authority, alienation—emerge from it.
5. Verdier (2005: 34) makes this point as follows: "Finally the most recent forms of usage of the word *hierarchy* can be mentioned. In this respect, one of the most noteworthy aspects is its spread at the end of the 1930s, first in relation to questions of society, in some cases resulting in deviations such as those already noted in the work by Franz Joseph Gall, whose successors are to be found in Germany in the ruins of the Prussian military state and elsewhere, whether among geographers like Christaller ... or among Nazi theoreticians. This probably also explains the disgrace of the word in the years directly after the 1939–45 war."
6. But not quite any element. There are three ways a value system can operate. It can (1) operate in a binary system, value versus not-value, as with Dumont's individuals who are each unique, incomparable values; (2) form a simple ordinal rank

series; or (3) form a more complex cardinal rank system where each item can be seen as a proportion of any other, as with money.

7. I suppose I should dutifully point out here that cognitive science would qualify this statement somewhat in practice. Whereas in formal terms, taxonomies do operate in this way, in fact we usually have a paradigmatic example of 'bird' in our heads—with English-speakers, often a robin—around which others are measured. However, I am speaking here in terms of the formal logic of the system.

8. In later times, Vaishyas were more likely to be merchants and Shudras to be farmers. But Dumont is here speaking of the earliest period.

9. Indeed, such a claim can be maintained only by purely circular arguments, that is, insisting that any way a ruling elite represents its concerns as universal proves that its members see themselves as 'including' those over whom they rule, and any way that the same ruling elite does the opposite, representing its concerns as peculiar to itself, is not an example of exclusiveness, but of the making-sacred of the more inclusive category. By this kind of reasoning, one can obviously prove anything at all. There is absolutely no reason one could not make the exact opposite argument and say that wherever there are structures of exclusion, they have the effect of allowing those in the superior, exclusive group to think of themselves as generic humans simply because they do not have to think very much about those they have excluded.

References

Benedict, Ruth. 1934. *Patterns of Culture*. New York: Mentor Books.

Boas, Franz. 1940. *Race, Language, and Culture*. New York: Macmillan.

Dumont, Louis. (1966) 1980. *Homo Hierarchicus: The Caste System and Its Implications*. Chicago: University of Chicago Press.

Dumont, Louis. 1977. *From Mandeville to Marx: The Genesis and Triumph of Economic Ideology*. Chicago: University of Chicago Press.

Dumont, Louis. 1982. "On Value." *Proceedings of the British Academy* 66: 207–241.

Dumont, Louis. 1986. *Essays on Individualism*. Chicago: University of Chicago Press.

Dumont, Louis. 1994. *German Ideology: From France to Germany and Back*. Chicago: University of Chicago Press.

Evans-Pritchard, E. E. 1940. *The Nuer: A Description of the Modes of Livelihood and Political Institutions of a Nilotic People*. Oxford: Clarendon Press.

Graeber, David. 1997. "Manners, Deference, and Private Property in Early Modern Europe." *Comparative Studies in Society and History* 39 (4): 694–728.

Graeber, David. 2001. *Toward an Anthropological Theory of Value: The False Coin of Our Own Dreams*. New York: Palgrave Macmillan.

Hutchinson, Sharon E. 1996. *Nuer Dilemmas: Coping with Money, War, and the State*. Berkeley: University of California Press.

Kroeber, Alfred L. 1947. *Configurations of Culture Growth*. Berkeley: University of California Press.

Lévi-Strauss, Claude. 1966. *The Savage Mind*. Chicago: University of Chicago Press.

Lévi-Strauss, Claude. 1969. *The Elementary Structures of Kinship*. Boston: Beacon Press.

Lovejoy, Arthur O. 1936. *The Great Chain of Being: A Study of the History of an Idea*. Cambridge, MA: Harvard University Press.

Macpherson, C. B. 1962. *The Political Theory of Possessive Individualism: Hobbes to Locke*. Oxford: Clarendon Press.

Malinowski, Bronislaw. 1944. *A Scientific Theory of Culture and Other Essays*. Chapel Hill: University of North Carolina Press.

Nisbet, Robert A. 1966. *The Sociological Tradition*. London: Heinemann.

Polanyi, Karl. 1944. *The Great Transformation: The Political and Economic Origins of Our Time*. New York: Farrar & Rinehart.

Radcliffe-Brown, A. R. 1952. *Structure and Function in Primitive Society: Essays and Addresses*. London: Cohen & West.

Sahlins, Marshall. 1972. *Stone Age Economics*. Chicago: Aldine-Atherton.

Sahlins, Marshall, Thomas Bargatzky, Nurit Bird-David, et al. 1996. "The Sadness of Sweetness: The Native Anthropology of Western Cosmology (and Comments and Reply)." *Current Anthropology* 37 (3): 395–428.

Verdier, Nicolas. 2006. "Hierarchy: A Short History of a Word in Western Thought." In *Hierarchy in Natural and Social Sciences*, ed. Denise Pumain, 13–37. Dordrecht: Springer.

INDEX

Central Asia, 87
Chagnon, Napoleon, 135
chain of being, the, 141
children, role of fathers (Ethiopia), 50–54
China: Buddhism in, 89; civilization in, 78, 86–89, 93; emperors, 92; hierarchy in, 86–89
Christianity, 3, 7, 68, 129; introduction of, 22; Ngadha, 118; in South Africa, 9; spread of, 32, 34. *See also* Ethiopian Orthodox Christians
Christian love, 45
church: *adat* and, 25–28; *adat* versus, 31–35. *See also* Catholic Church; Christianity
civilization: in China, 78, 86–89, 93; hierarchy and axial, 84–86; long-term change of, 89–92; Mauss, Marcel, 78–80; and political-economic equality, 77–94
Civilizing Process, The (Elias), 81
Civil War (1861–1865), 63, 64, 67
Clapham, Christopher S., 52
class structures, 81
cleansing processes, 126
clientelism, 46, 48
Cold War, 136
Cole, Jennifer, 45
collective self, 81
companion (*sahaabi*), 105
Confucianism, x, 90, 147
constants, identifying, 82
conversions, Catholic Church, 33
Copperbelt Pentecostalism hierarchy, 10
cross-rank unions (Ngadha), 116

da Cunha, Carneiro, 13
Dala Ko (the sister), 122, 123
Dala Wawi (the brother), 122
Damon, Frederick, 13, 14, 148
Daoists, 90
darja (spiritual rank), 103
Dar-ul-Uloom seminary, 99
dawat (face-to-face preaching), 97, 98, 99–102; definition of, 101; ethics, 102; ideology, 105; pious sociality, 102–106; against *politiks*, 106–110; tours, 104; transformative power of, 100
debt, pig, 66
democracy, 3, 7
demons, 50

demotion as value, 115–131
Dening, Greg, 60, 61, 62
destruction: formal integuments of sacrifice, 61–65; killing, 67–71; lies, 65–67; in the organization of social life, 59–72
Detroit Free Press, 65
development, 7
diffusion, 79
dini amal (practice), 98
Discourses of the State (Guoyu), 88
domains in public life (Indonesia), 26
domesticity, ix
Douglas, Mary, 136
Dower, John, 65
Dumont, Louis, ix, x, 3–5, 11, 14, 16, 23, 42, 60, 63, 68, 93, 115, 136, 137, 139, 140, 141, 142, 143, 145, 146, 147; categories of holism/hierarchy, 54; classic formulation of hierarchy, 106; concept of civilization, 78; concept of hierarchy, 77, 80–84; hierarchy, 67, 82; ideologies, 81; power and value, 44; religion, 69; social stratification, 24
dunya (world), 98
dynastic rule, 91

eastern Indonesia, 28, 116, 117
Easter services, 32, 33
egalitarian individualism, 98
egalitarianism, 2, 3, 80, 111, 140; hierarchy, 5; in South Africa, 9
Eickelman, Dale F., 110
Eisenstadt, S. N., 84
Elders, the (*buzurg*), 102, 104
Elementary Structures of Kinship, The (Lévi-Strauss), 139
Elias, Norbert, 81
elopement, 125
emperors (China), 92
encompassment, 77, 78, 81, 82, 83, 86, 93, 117
enlightenment, 5
Erdoğan, Tayyip, viii
Essays on Individualism (Dumont), 137
ethics: *dawat* (face-to-face preaching), 102–106; of hierarchy in Tablighi Jamaat (Pakistan), 97–112
Ethiopia, 41–58; Addis Ababa, 49; hierarchy and love, 43–46; hierarchy and submission, 50–54; mediation and hierarchy, 48–50

www.ingramcontent.com/pod-product-compliance
Lightning Source LLC
Chambersburg PA
CBHW070933030426
42336CB00014BA/2658